ROBERT'S STORY

A TEXAS COWBOY'S TROUBLED LIFE AND HORRIFYING DEATH

STEPHEN G. MICHAUD

COYOTE
PUBLISHING

This is a true story. The events in this book all took place, and the conversations are based on deposition transcripts, recordings, public statements, and interviews. Some names and other identifying details have been changed to protect the individuals' privacy. Any resemblance between these characters and a real person is strictly coincidental. Stuttered speech, vocal tics, and repeated words have been edited in quoted dialogue for readability.

Published by Coyote Publishing
Lutherville, MD

Distributed by Greenleaf Book Group

For ordering information or special discounts for bulk purchases, please contact Greenleaf Book Group at PO Box 91869, Austin, TX 78709, 512.891.6100.

Design and composition by Greenleaf Book Group and Mimi Bark
Cover design by Greenleaf Book Group and Mimi Bark
Cover photograph courtesy of the East family from their private collection.
Cover images used under license from ©Shutterstock.com/pingebat

Publisher's Cataloging-in-Publication data is available.

Print ISBN: 979-8-9852650-0-2

eBook ISBN: 979-8-9852650-1-9

Part of the Tree Neutral® program, which offsets the number of trees consumed in the production and printing of this book by taking proactive steps, such as planting trees in direct proportion to the number of trees used: www.treeneutral.com

Printed in the United States of America on acid-free paper

24 25 26 27 28 29 30 31 32   11 10 9 8 7 6 5 4 3

First Edition

For Tom and Alice

PROLOG

In May of 2007, Helen Kleberg Groves, of Kleberg County, Texas, received the dire news that her 87-year-old cousin, Robert Claude East, was failing rapidly. Robert's nephew, Mike East, informed Groves by telephone that he had not been allowed to see Uncle Robert, the aged *patrón* of the San Antonio Viejo cattle ranch, deep in the South Texas brush country, for weeks. But he'd learned from reliable ranch employees that Robert was not receiving adequate medical treatment and was next to death.

Helenita, as Mrs. Groves is known, had also been trying to reach her cousin without success. Mike told her that, on his last visit to the ranch, Robert had seemed to be in steep decline. He appeared to have suffered a stroke, had been diagnosed with pneumonia, and developed atrial fibrillation, or AFib, a potentially fatal irregular heartbeat. The ranch hands said he was sleeping poorly, had lost considerable weight, and was depressed and often disoriented.

Distracted as they were by the old man's serious medical and mental issues, Robert's family and close friends did not know that, as his health failed, he'd also signed away control of his estate, lately swollen to hundreds of millions of dollars by a vast natural gas strike on East lands.

When someone at the ranch finally answered Helenita's calls, she was told that Robert wasn't taking visitors. Mrs. Groves was not to be deterred. At the suggestion of her friend and lawyer, Dick DeGuerin, she at once turned to Ed Hennessy, a civil attorney in Houston, with instructions to get her into the ranch house at once, by whatever means necessary.

Her driver, Héctor Muñoz, also took the matter to his brother-in-law, Richard Kirkpatrick, then an investigator with the South Texas Specialized Crimes and Narcotics Task Force. The two lived next door to one another in Kleberg County.

"Can you talk to Mrs. Groves?" Muñoz asked the lawman. "Just listen to her, and see what she says? Maybe you guys can help them out."

Kirkpatrick called Helenita, a great-granddaughter of Captain Richard King, founder of the King Ranch. She put him in touch with Mike East. "We don't know whether Robert's alive and well or whether he has been dead for some time," East told the investigator. "No one has been allowed to go out there, to the ranch."

Kirkpatrick saw the East family's predicament as essentially a civil matter in a remote setting, probably outside the task force's jurisdiction. But when Mike added that he believed either one of Robert's lawyers or Oscar Ozuna, the San Antonio Viejo ranch *caporal*, or foreman, was behind the old man's isolation, the drug detective took note.

"It had long been rumored that Ozuna was involved in drug trafficking," says Kirkpatrick, who later became sheriff of Kleberg County. "That's kind of why we had interest in the case. Several intelligence-based cases that we developed during that time suggested he was involved in it."

Kirkpatrick repeated what he'd heard from Mrs. Groves and Mike East to Jaime Garza, his boss on the drug task force. Commander Garza says he tried, with no luck, to interest local authorities in what was transpiring at the East ranch, a possible kidnap or unlawful confinement—or worse. So he improvised an alternative strategy for getting law enforcement involved.

Garza contacted Ray Ramón, an old friend and law enforcement colleague, since deceased. Ramón was then employed as a Texas Ranger, based in Alice, the seat of Jim Wells County, about 30 miles northwest of Kingsville. After Garza explained the situation, Ramón reached out for assistance from

Ranger Sergeant Robert Hunter, stationed in Laredo, approximately 80 miles northwest of the San Antonio Viejo ranch.

Mike East soon heard from Sergeant Hunter, who offered to visit the ranch to conduct a wellness check on Uncle Robert. Unaware of the Garza–Ramón–Hunter connection, East was surprised by the Ranger's offer, but glad to accept it. Hunter indicated that he would leave at once for the ranch.

As Mike recalls, about an hour later, he received a second call from Ranger Hunter, who said he had driven as far as Hebbronville, about 40 miles from the San Antonio Viejo's main gate, where he had stopped to confer with Christopher H. Huff, a state game warden and a friend of his. East also was familiar with Huff, whose territory included his uncle's ranch, where Warden Huff had spent considerable time chasing would-be poachers out gunning for Robert East's huge white-tailed deer.

Hunter told Mike that all was well at the ranch; he said Chris Huff had assured him that the old man was in good health and that there was no need for a welfare check. He was returning to Laredo. The contradiction between Hunter's account and what Mike had seen for himself, as well as what he had heard from ranch employees, disturbed East.

At one point, he says, Hunter told him, "Those people have guns out there." He wondered how Hunter knew and why that mattered to a Texas Ranger.

Hunter also somehow knew of Robert being taken by ambulance that day to see Dr. Michael D. Evans, a Weslaco cardiologist, presumably on account of his AFib. Dr. Evans would also discover two aneurysms on Robert's visit, one a huge lesion on his aorta, measuring almost three inches by three inches, just below the renal artery. Aneurysms generally do not develop quickly. This one's size suggested that Robert, who had a history of cardiovascular issues, had not received a thorough cardiovascular exam in quite some time.

Although Ranger Hunter failed to personally check on Robert, Helenita Groves would not. On the fair and hot Saturday morning of May 26, she climbed into her silver Suburban, carrying a court order secured by Ed Hennessy. With Héctor Muñoz at the wheel, she traveled about a hundred dusty miles from her residence in Kleberg County across an ancient seabed to her cousin's ranch, approximately 40 miles north of the Rio Grande. They reached the San Antonio Viejo's main gate at about eleven o'clock that morning.

Helenita had worked her will, as usual, but what Mrs. Groves now discovered would turn her day hellishly surreal.

"There was a guard who looked like an N. C. Wyeth pirate," she remembers. This was Celestino, known as Tino, Canales. Despite his appearance and station in life, Tino Canales had recently become one of three trustees of Robert East's management trust, as well as a director of his estate. On paper, the gate guard stood to soon become a rich and powerful man.

"Instead of having a bandana on his head, he had a baseball cap on backwards," says Mrs. Groves. "He had a patch over one eye, and he looked pretty unsavory. We had to show him the court order, then we went through."

They were met at the house by the foreman, Oscar Ozuna, who was polite but quiet and watchful, she recalls. Like the gateman, Ozuna had lately become a trustee and a director of East's estate, worth hundreds of millions of dollars.

Absent from the ranch that day was Carilu Cantú Leal, 37, the third recently appointed manager of Robert's estate. Carilu had worked as Robert's driver and ranch provisioner since 1990. Together with Canales and Ozuna, she also held East's power of attorney.

The visitors encountered five or six people gathered outside the main house and a similar number within. "They were all townspeople," Muñoz recalls. "You could tell by the way they were dressed."

One of them was Dr. Jesús "Chuy" Ochoa, Robert East's dentist, for whom Carilu once worked as a receptionist. "The first thing I thought," says Muñoz, was, "'*What is his dentist doing out at the ranch? What happened to his doctor?*'"

Once they were inside the ranch house, says Mrs. Groves, "there was some greasy soup we could smell cooking on the stove." It was uncomfortably warm in the residence that day, except for Robert East's bedroom, which was cooled by a single window air conditioner.

"Somebody said Robert wouldn't talk to anybody if there was more than one person in the room," Mrs. Groves recalls. "Of course, they all went in the room with us. He was in bed. He took my arm, and he held on to it very tight."

Muñoz describes East that day as "very, very fragile. He could mumble a little bit, but he was very frail. Lack of nutrition. You could tell that. His bones weren't fleshed out. He needed water."

Helenita stayed with her emaciated cousin, his face curiously lopsided, for an hour or more.

Her driver stepped outside, where Ozuna took him on a brief walking tour. Héctor was surprised to see a number of new trucks parked around the house. He knew by reputation that Robert was tight with his dollars, unlikely to own any new work vehicles—and certainly not air-conditioned models, which he disdained as a costly frill, likely to promote a taste for ease among his employees.

"Robert East was not a man of new trucks," Muñoz says. "He never was. The pickup trucks were brand new. I asked Oscar if the new vehicles were work trucks. He said, 'No. They're for the town people to come back and forth.'"

Before departing, Mrs. Groves handed her driver a disposable camera and asked him to take a picture of her with Robert. She later showed the photo to her family doctor's wife, a nurse. According to Mrs. Groves, "When she saw it, she said, 'He's had a terrible stroke!' She did not know Robert, had never seen him. She said, 'Look how his face is twisted! He can't swallow!'"

Héctor Muñoz believes Robert recognized his cousin that day. Helenita isn't sure. "It was very disconcerting to see him in that state," she says. "He *did not* want me to leave."

She did so, reluctantly, departing Robert's bedroom with one indelible impression: "I was *horrified*," she says. "He didn't deserve to die that way. No. If I was a judge, I would say, at the least, it was manslaughter. At the least.

"I think it was more premeditated than that. But you know, how am I going to prove something like that? I've had some lessons in life. Knowing is one thing. Proving is another."

CHAPTER 1

Robert East was born into two prominent Texas cattle-ranching clans. On his mother's side, he descended from the legendary Captain King. His paternal grandfather was Edward Hudson East, known as Ed, a farm boy from Clinton, Illinois, who helped build the huge Bar X and OX ranches in Archer County, near Wichita Falls, Texas. With an estimated combined area of a million acres or more, they were then among the largest—if not *the* largest—cattle ranches in the state and thus the country.

Ed met 21-year-old Hattie Baxter from Trenton, Missouri, at Archer. They married in 1880. On that year's federal census form, he modestly described himself as a "laborer." But not for long.

Ed flourished as a cattleman. As an East family genealogist once put it, he "pretty much controlled the county with his payroll."

Lillian Hart Kerr, a visitor to the area, described East as a "rich cattleman" and Mrs. East as the community's "great lady." They lived in a log house, where Hattie bore six of their seven children, all boys.

When farms and fences began to overtake open-range ranching as Archer County's main economic engine, Ed and Hattie moved their family deeper into Texas, where they settled for a time in the new town of Alice, already a major cattle-shipping center, about 50 miles west of Corpus Christi. The community was named for one of Captain King's two daughters, Alice

Gertrudis King, whose own daughter, Alice King Kleberg, would marry Tom Timmons East, Ed and Hattie's fifth son.

Tom was as a horse trader and breeder, known especially for his top-quality line back dun quarter horses. Texas line back duns are distinctive for a dark line along their spines from mane to hock, as well as vivid zebra markings from their knees to their pasterns. Many Texas cattle ranchers prize line back duns for their durability and toughness, even though they can be ornery. The breed is also resistant to a type of photosensitivity called *sand burn*, caused or exacerbated by consumption of certain range plants.

Tom was tall and handsome, with grey eyes and red hair. Alice King Kleberg might have met him while shopping for a horse. Slender and athletic, she bore a strong resemblance to her younger brother, Robert Justus Kleberg Jr., later famous for transforming the King Ranch into a mid-twentieth century agribusiness colossus.

Alice loved animals. She loved to raise them and loved to hunt them. She merged the two passions in what her niece, Helenita Groves, remembers was "a whole huge kennel of bird dogs" at the ranch headquarters.

She apparently didn't much care for the classroom but did graduate in 1911 from Gunston Hall, an exclusive girls' boarding and day school in northwest Washington, DC, where Alice was a member of the tennis club and captain of the school's basketball team.

Although the details of how Tom and Alice met are lost, the upshot was courtship and engagement.

Tom—unusual for wearing business clothes, including fedoras and silk neckties whether at his desk or atop a horse, even when out in his pastures—was then moving from the horse trade into ranching like his father. Central to his ambitions was the San Antonio Viejo ranch, then about 24,000 acres, located in Starr County, about 50 miles north of the Rio Grande.

The ranch was originally part of a Spanish land grant. In 1805, when Texas still belonged to Spain, the property was surveyed under the authority of the province of Nuevo Santander (to become the Mexican state of Tamaulipas in 1824), which assigned ownership to the heirs of a Francisco

Xavier Vela. The ranch changed hands a number of times until 1913, when East struck a deal for it with Don Manuel Guerra of Roma, Texas, a small settlement on the Rio Grande's left bank.

The purchase price for the future center of East family ranching operations was $124,992.97. Tom made an initial payment of $10,000 and would remit the balance, according to the contract, in four more installments at six percent interest spread over six years.

As soon as the deal was sealed, the young rancher registered his brand, an upright diamond, the rough shape of the ranch's perimeter as shown on maps.

Alice King Kleberg and Tom Timmons East were married in an 8:30 a.m. ceremony on January 30, 1915, in the King Ranch's newly completed, two-story, 37,000-square-foot prairie Xanadu on Santa Gertrudis Creek. She was 22, and he was 25.

The big house was roofed with terra-cotta tiles above exterior walls of "dazzling whiteness," as author Tom Lea described them in his two-volume chronicle, *The King Ranch*.

The mansion's grand interior featured custom furniture from Tiffany & Co., as well as dramatic architectural touches, including three 18-foot stained-glass windows soaring together above a stone-paved courtyard.

Alice's older sister, Henrietta Kleberg, was her maid of honor for the Presbyterian rite. Caesar Kleberg, Alice's cousin, was Tom's best man. Another cousin, Minerva King, entertained the wedding guests at the piano, and Dick Kleberg, the bride's brother and a future congressman, sang a popular tune of the day, "Till the Sands of the Desert Grow Cold."

The newlyweds reportedly skipped the honeymoon and saddled up for the San Antonio Viejo to begin their life together.

Don Manuel Guerra died in 1915. His widow, Virginia Cox-Barrera de Guerra, completed the ranch transaction with Tom and Alice. In 1916, they remitted $50,000 to retire a lien on the property. Another $10,000 came due on July 1 of that year, followed in 1917 by a $20,000 installment, and then a final payment of $34,992.97 in 1919.

In an untitled biographical fragment, Hart Mussey, the Easts' onetime bookkeeper and ranch hand, wrote that Alice used some of the money her grandmother, Henrietta King, gave her as a wedding gift to buy a small herd of registered Hereford cows and a bull, which she had branded with her mark—a sideways, or lazy, diamond.

According to Texas historian Dora Villarreal, the bride and groom's first residence at the San Antonio Viejo was *La Perla*—the pearl—a two-story stone structure that dated to the late 1880s. The massive building, which stood in a pasture of the same name, was erected as a fortress against marauding bandits and Comanches. Long since abandoned, it has been allowed to collapse into ruins.

There is a story—possibly apocryphal but familiar nonetheless among former San Antonio Viejo employees—of how Tom and Alice, in search of more practical housing, found a structure built from locally scarce hardwood in the nearby village of Agua Nueva. They are said to have dismantled the building and hauled it to the ranch where it was reassembled to serve as the San Antonio Viejo headquarters.

Such a house did exist and sheltered the East family, and then their employees, for several decades. It was replaced in the early 1950s with a single-story, V-shaped brick residence. The old house has since been demolished.

Hart Mussey wrote that Tom East enjoyed early success as a cattleman, with 2,500 breeding cows of his own and a one-quarter interest in a partnership that included his older brother, Arthur, who, in 1910, had married into another Texas cattle dynasty, the Kenedys, descended from Captain Mifflin Kenedy, Captain Richard King's old partner in their Rio Grande steamboating days, and his Mexican wife, Petra Vela.

Arthur's bride was Sarah, known as Sarita, Kenedy, Mifflin's granddaughter. The ceremony took place at the old Corpus Christi cathedral. It was said locally and in good humor that those East boys certainly knew how to marry.

CHAPTER 2

Tom and Alice were a formidable pair. Married under favorable portents, they brought to their new life together considerable knowledge and skills and the determination to succeed in a demanding business on a raw frontier. Adversity would test them time and again.

A severe drought fell over the region in 1916, devastating Texas cattle raisers. Hart Mussey wrote that, following a big sale to a Mr. Zimmerman in Pennsylvania, Tom "started buying cattle for himself to restock. He bought a good many cows and heifers and some steers. He would have been a lot better off and would have avoided a big financial loss if he had not bought any cattle, and if he had also sold all he had. But, of course, neither he nor anyone else knew the year 1916 would experience the worst drought many of us had ever seen."

There also was trouble on the border. Pancho Villa, the Mexican bandit turned revolutionary, had crossed the Rio Grande to assault a detachment of US cavalry at Columbus, New Mexico. US General John Joseph "Black Jack" Pershing led 10,000 American troops, the so-called Mexican Punitive Expedition, across northern Mexico in a failed attempt to capture Villa, who was assassinated six years later.

The violence spilled north into Texas, reaching the San Antonio Viejo on

March 3, 1917. Dora Villarreal writes of a group of Mexican bandits who rode onto the ranch that day, headed for Hebbronville, where they intended to rob a bank.

The outlaws found Alice East in a barn. She was wearing her favorite silver- and gold-plated spurs, which the raiders surely would have stolen had Alice not sheltered them from sight under her skirts.

The gang appropriated a ranch truck and instructed Rosendo Garza, who was both the Easts' driver and the ranch cook, to take them to town. On the way, Garza warned them that detachments of Texas Rangers frequented Hebbronville, which therefore was a poor choice for attempting robbery. After some thought, the outlaws directed their chauffeur to steer them back to the ranch.

They demanded food. Helenita Groves remembers being told that, rather than take them to the ranch house, where they might discover a bottle of champagne that Alice had hoped to share that night with Tom, she directed the outlaws to the house of Steve Franklin, a ranch foreman, where they were fed.

It happened that a posse of Texas Rangers under a Captain Will L. Wright was in the neighborhood that day, en route by truck from Laredo to Hebbronville. Early the next morning, a rider caught up with the Rangers at their camp with news of the raid at the ranch. Captain Wright led his men at once to the headquarters, where they found, to their relief, that Mrs. East was untouched and unharmed.

The bandits had ransacked the San Antonio Viejo commissary and stole some money and several horses, including a speedy pinto their leader took for himself. But they hadn't hurt anyone yet. Then they galloped off toward the border.

Captain Wright and his Rangers also saddled some ranch mounts and headed out in pursuit. They tracked the outlaw band south to the old San Antonio Viejo ranch headquarters, located near present-day Guerra. They were told by townspeople that the bandits had already come and gone, after some more pillaging.

Their tracks indicated that they were still headed for the river and probably had a long enough head start to make it safely across, back into Mexico. Just then, however, the Rangers met up with the Ramos brothers, Gabriel, Maximino, and El Güero, who knew a shortcut that would enable the posse to set an ambush up ahead, where the episode would turn bloody.

Wright and his men surprised the Mexican raiders at El Javalín Ranch, killing eight of them. Their leader, aboard the purloined pinto, was the only outlaw to escape back across the Rio Grande. It is not known how many, if any, casualties the Rangers sustained. Among the stolen property the lawmen recovered were mules, saddles, pistols, and bridles.

In a grim postscript, the badly decomposed corpse of a Mexican man was later discovered by Guerra residents, hanged by a rope from a tree. The dead man's identity was never established.

It was assumed that he was a drifter whom the outlaws had picked up, perhaps as a hostage, and then murdered. His remains were in such an advanced state of decay that it was necessary to bury him where he was discovered. A small headstone was placed at his grave and is still to be found on a lot on Roosevelt Street, property of Alfredo Villarreal Jr.

The drought eased. World War I ended, and the border violence abated by 1919. Then the beef market contracted, placing a further squeeze on East family finances. Their creditors, notably the Alice State Bank & Trust and the Union National Bank of Houston, grew nervous and began dispatching representatives to personally count Tom and Alice's cattle, which the lenders had accepted as loan collateral.

It was occasionally a problem for Tom to gather a sufficient number of animals from his pastures to satisfy the bankers, so he innovated a subterfuge to create the impression, if not the fact, of bountiful steers and heifers, calves, cows, and bulls on hand. Loan officers were brought to East's pens, where the stock was paraded before them in a closed rotation that easily persuaded the unsuspecting money guys that they'd seen many more cattle than in fact were on hand.

The cavalry arrived at last in 1922 in the person of Henrietta King, Captain Richard's widow, who intervened mightily by assuming all of the Easts' debt in exchange for the title to the San Antonio Viejo, by then grown to nearly 77,000 acres. The King Ranch's 90-year-old *patrona* then leased the ranch back to her granddaughter and her husband.

CHAPTER 3

The Easts' first child, Tom Timmons East Jr., was born January 2, 1917. He was a healthy infant. Years later, Alice would tell how she managed her brown-eyed baby boy when working cattle with Tom Sr. She said she'd fashion a lightweight mobile crib and carefully suspend Tom Jr. in it from a sturdy tree limb. The little fellow could sway away in safety above the herd while his parents kept watch as they worked.

Young Tom and both his siblings were born in Corpus Christi. Robert arrived October 5, 1919. Then came Alice Hattie, who would be known as Lica, pronounced Lisa, on November 27, 1920. The three spent much of their childhoods at the King Ranch in the company of their many cousins.

"Tom and Robert had a so-called tutor," recalls Helenita Groves, who was about 10 years younger than the East children. "I don't know if he could even read, but his job was to make sure that they went to school.

"They did get through high school somehow. They had horses and ponies and goats. They roped goats every afternoon. And they had hounds, and they would go hunting at the creek at night together."

When the children stayed with their mother at the King Ranch during the school year, they occupied two rooms in the big house. Each day, Robert and Tom and Lica would be driven along with their cousins to and from school in Kingsville.

One morning, as Robert later told the story, he and Tom brought their ropes along. When they arrived at the school, they chased one of their female cousins across the schoolyard, roped her, and tied her to the flagpole.

Tom's daughter Lica Elena, says this was the sort of antic for which Alice would punish her two boys by dressing them as girls and marching them around the ranch's cowboy commissary.

The rowdy brothers were undeterred. When visitors came to the big house, Alice often stashed her sons upstairs. It was no use. Robert and Tom employed their ever-handy ropes to escape through the windows, down to the mansion grounds, and over to the creek, where, with the help of their father's fox terriers, they'd catch raccoons and carry them into the house to scamper among the guests.

Alice once hired a man to scare her sons out of their shenanigans. He waited until he saw young Tom up on a ladder, poking with a stick at a raccoon hidden in a niche on the big house's outer wall. When he sneaked up behind the boy with a sheet over his head, hoping to scare him, Tom instead turned suddenly and whacked him with his stick.

Tom sometimes ditched his little brother to go play with his slightly older cousin, Richard Mifflin Kleberg Jr., which would send Robert into tears and anger. According to Lica Elena, Robert would run to his sister Lica to be comforted.

As the boys grew older, their mother treated them to more dignified diversions, such as trips to Corpus Christi to visit her cousin, Richard King, a banker, and his family. Uncle Richard would always dispatch the country roughnecks to a barber shop before admitting them to his temple of finance.

Tom Jr. grew tall like his father, square-jawed and muscular, a casting director's image of a Texas cowboy. There seems never to have been a doubt that he'd one day be a rancher. He was indifferent to schooling. Tom earned a degree in 1934 from Kingsville's Henrietta M. King High School only because his mother bribed him with the promise of a mare he coveted if he successfully completed his studies, which he accomplished via correspondence school.

Rescued from penury in 1922, his parents spent the rest of the decade aggressively expanding their landholdings and cattle operations. But they still found time to pursue their varied side interests, as well. Alice was a demon amateur photographer, who shot stills and movie footage all over their ranches. Both she and Tom also dabbled in the motion picture world.

If an article in the September 7, 1924, editions of the *Houston Chronicle* is accurate, they joined his cousin James "Monty" East in scouting Texas locations for *North of 36*, a silent western movie produced by Adolph Zukor's Famous Players–Lasky Corporation, a forerunner of Paramount Pictures. The film, starring Jack Holt, told the story of a 1,000-mile cattle drive in 1867 from Texas to Abilene, Kansas. Among Tom, Alice, and Monty's various assignments, they had to round up a respectable-size herd of longhorns for the picture. *North of 36* was filmed at Houston and California locations.

Tom installed an alligator in a pond near the main ranch house and kept a herd of exotic deer. He also introduced black syndactyl, or mulefoot, hogs to Texas. A rare breed celebrated for its flavorsome hams, a mulefoot's uncloven hooves resemble those of mules.

CHAPTER 4

Alice East's brother Robert Kleberg Jr., by then in charge of the King Ranch, so admired her son Tom's ranching prowess that, in 1935, he made him foreman of the San Antonio Viejo, as well as the King Ranch's Encino Division, about 40 miles east of the big ranch.

Tom came to work on January 1, sporting a handgun in a red sash around his waist. The young man had flair. To lead such a sprawling operation would have been a challenge for a seasoned trail hand, much less a teenager, among the youngest members of his outfit. He was boss over about 20 cowboys, including two *remuderos*, or horse wranglers, plus a cook and his helper. Rounding up the cattle was known as a *corrida* in Texas. Elsewhere, corrida is the term for a bullfight.

Working cattle would keep all of them in nearly constant daily motion across hundreds of thousands of acres: driving the animals from pasture to pasture, herding them, culling them, branding and castrating them, chasing strays, weaning the yearlings, clipping horns, vaccinating the animals, and dipping them for ticks. There would be very little rest.

According to the terse daily diary Tom kept that year, his outfit rounded up a *remuda*, or herd, of cow horses the first morning. The next day, his 18th birthday, they worked cattle in the Muralla pasture, a short distance north-west of the ranch headquarters.

He developed a foot infection, which required professional medical care in Kingsville. "I hurt myself running a wild steer," he scribbled in pencil two weeks later, probably on horseback. "By morning, had lots of fever."

January 16, he wrote, "I have lots of fever and feel sick. Got most of the wild stuff [cattle] and cleaned up pasture good. Cattle very wild. Lots of mavericks roped."

He felt no better on the 17th. "I am very sick and have lots of fever and a bad cold. Cut the herd. Got a load of fat calves and a load of wild cows and mavericks. Cut and weaned 49 yearlings."

Alice East drove her son to a doctor in Kingsville as his vaqueros traveled on to the Agua Verde pasture, where Tom rejoined them on the 21st. "I am still sick," he noted, "but getting better."

The outfit sent off 112 calves that day, as well as 36 cows and 9 bulls to the Norias pens on the San Antonio Viejo. According to East's penciled notes, they left behind 897 cows, 57 bulls, and 226 calves to be worked at a later time.

In the ensuing years, he'd regularly lead the long cattle drives to the Tex-Mex Railroad shipping pens at Hebbronville himself. There were several beer joints along the way. Tom often would halt the herd at these establishments, buy up their entire beer inventory, and enjoy a few cold ones with his vaqueros before pushing on.

On February 2, East noted in his diary that Macario Mallorga, a famous King Ranch vaquero, was "kicked bad by a grey mare." The next day, Leonardo Pérez, the remuda man, "was sent to Kingsville without three fingers caused by roping a wild cow."

February 7, East reported "lots of fog. Did not start work until after dinner. Weaned yearlings. Cut out white face heifers for Mr. Caesar [Kleberg]. Yearlings stampeded and tore San Tomas pens down last night."

February 11: "Awful cold. Roped wild boar."

February 12: "Rounded up steers. 470 total. Steers weighed out at 703 lbs., not taking off 3% shrinkage. Sold at 5¢ a lb. Cattle shipped after dinner at the King Ranch Norias pens. Outfit slept at Chaparosa tonight. Lots of rain, mud, and cold weather."

February 18: "Outfit moves to the San Antonio Viejo," where part of the crew was given the first time off since the year began. The next day, Macario Mallorga gave notice for unexplained reasons. Beginning in late February, Tom stepped up the corrida's operations considerably.

The camp cook and his helper traveled apart from the corrida in two mule-drawn wagons, carrying provisions, utensils, and the vaqueros' gear, principally bed rolls. The wagons, eventually retired from roundup work, would be among Robert East's proudest possessions, embodiments of the old days and old ways.

At the Moritas pasture, the outfit branded 352 two-year-old steers for the Atwoods, another branch of the King family, and held them in the Norias trap before turning them in to the Old Ranch pasture on the San Antonio Viejo. They next headed for the Martimiano pasture, also on the San Antonio Viejo, where they cut out 401 more steers for the Atwoods, dipped and branded them, then transferred the entire herd, 779 head, into the Santa Fe and Middle pastures. The whole complex series of interconnected operations necessary to efficiently gather, sort, and deliver cattle in optimum condition for their trip to the packing house required more than a month to complete.

In April, the outfit gathered a herd of 1,649 steers at La Parra—the Kenedy Ranch—and drove them to the railroad pens in Hebbronville. They rested along the route at the tiny, 640-acre Gauchapín Ranch, about half-way between the San Antonio Viejo and Hebbronville, and at the 5,200-acre Ranchito—where the senior Tom T. East kept his herd of exotic deer—before loading the animals onto the cattle cars.

In the middle of April, Tom shipped 1,649 three-year-old steers from the Hebbronville pens to J. L. Borrum, a rancher in Blackland, Oklahoma.

A storm surprised them on April 28 as they were gathering the remuda at the Martimiano pasture. "Lots of trees torn up," East wrote. "Manuel Vira and I were hurt by horses falling on us."

The pace did not let up for the balance of the year. East reported only one other brush with harm in his diary. On September 24, he wrote, he lost control of his car on a sandy stretch of pasture. The vehicle rolled over twice, but neither the driver nor any of his four passengers were hurt, or so he claimed.

An unexpected health issue arose on November 19, when three cowboys came down with malaria.

CHAPTER 5

Robert East, who turned 16 in October of 1935, would soon become another working hand on the ranch. He was as skilled as any vaquero and worked cattle with natural ease. His friend, James King, Captain Richard King's great, great, great grandson, remembers, "Robert had a gentle philosophy with cattle. He taught me to settle down and work with them, not against them."

But Robert had a contrary streak. He seemed to struggle all his life with what has been called second child syndrome. He loved his big brother but believed that Tom was unfairly favored in the family and given a disproportionate share of meaningful responsibilities. Confused and resentful, Robert was prone to act out his frustrations.

When working cattle, for example, at times, he paid more attention to his horses than his work, which could lead to trouble. Accordingly, big brother Tom regularly assigned Robert to ride with the oxen that often were brought along to steady a herd.

"My father wasn't trying to be mean to Robert," says Tom Jr.'s son, Mike. "But he knew if Robert had to run too much, he'd let cattle go by because he wanted to protect his horse. Of course, Robert wanted to be where there was more action, so he'd get mad."

Robert enjoyed the danger and excitement of roping half-ton feral strays deep in the South Texas brush. But even then, any perceived slight could set him off. On one occasion, Mike recalls, his uncle decided that the vaqueros were pointing out more strays for Tom to work than they were for Robert, and he grew furious.

"I mean, he threw a fit," Mike says. "He told off the whole crew, every one of them. 'All you care about is Tom! You're just telling *him* where everything is.'"

However, as difficult as Robert could be, Tom was always quick to remind the cowhands that his brother was one of the bosses. Once at the San Antonio Viejo, Rosendo Garza, the cook and driver, brusquely refused to carry out an order from Robert. Tom immediately intervened, reminding Garza in front of Robert that he was to take orders from all the Easts, not just him and his father.

CHAPTER 6

"Alice K. and Tom East made valiant and successful efforts, both jointly and individually, to enlarge their holdings," reads an unsigned court document composed decades later, "and to consolidate the land around the San Antonio Viejo ranch by buying up property contiguous with and near to the ranch. They also leased considerable acreage on which to ranch their cattle.

"At his peak, Tom T. East was ranching on quite a large scale, in the neighborhood of 350,000–400,000 acres. In addition to increasing and improving their land holdings, the Easts were always looking to increase the size of and quality of their cattle stock by continuous purchasing and cross-breeding programs."

Yet for all their hard work and innovation, Tom and Alice once more faced significant head winds with the onset of the Great Depression. According to Mike East, his grandparents might not have survived the economically ruinous 1930s were it not for income from the sale of oil-drilling rights at multiple locations around San Antonio Viejo.

In 1940, the family formed an East Brothers partnership to jointly manage its numerous ranch properties. There was a total of five shares: one each for Tom Jr., Robert, and Lica and two shares jointly held by Tom and Alice.

In May of that year, Lica graduated from Gunston Hall, as her mother had in 1911. She also played basketball and sang with the Glee Club. "Here's to surprising Lica," wrote an editor at *Echoes*, the Gunston Hall yearbook, "an irresistible Texan who won't allow you to forget her home state for a second. Next to her siestas, she shows unexpected enthusiasm for food at any time.

"Her luminous long hair, aristocratic profile, and the music of her fluent Spanish distinguish her. Alert but not talkative, Lica's languid grace usually hides the energy with which she rides her ranch and shoots deer, as well as basketball goals."

A month before graduation, Lica wrote her brother, Tom, to thank him for a box of candy he'd mailed her. "I surely was surprised," she told him. "The picture on top of the box is so pretty, and already, we have it hanging on the wall. Everybody on this floor has commented on how good Hebbronville candy is."

Their parents, she reported, were driving from the ranch to attend her graduation on May 24. "I wish you could come," she wrote. "Really, I don't see how I can wait. It will make me so happy not to have to go to school anymore." She'd return that spring to the San Antonio Viejo and live there with Robert and her mother for the rest of her life. Lica never married.

By autumn of 1940, there loomed the threat of another world war. The year before, Hitler and Stalin had overrun Poland. France fell in June. The Battle of Britain was underway.

On October 16, the first day that American males could register for the draft, Robert submitted his paperwork, claiming that he was six feet tall and weighed 155 pounds. On April 1 of 1941, when he reported for duty at Fort Sam Houston, in San Antonio, the Army found him five pounds lighter and three inches shorter.

Robert was dispatched to a facility near Laredo where he was assigned to breaking mules, unpleasant work that he did not relish. He complained to his parents, who brought him home to spend World War II on the ranch.

Tom Jr. had flat feet, it was discovered, so he was excluded from the fighting as well.

In January of 1943, Tom, then 26, married 19-year-old Evelyn Kuenstler, of Encinal, whom he'd met through rodeo friends. Evelyn was the youngest of nine children in a farming family. Their first child, Mike, named for a great uncle, reputedly the ablest of all East cowboys, was born October 31st.

CHAPTER 7

Less than a month after Tom and Evelyn's marriage, Tom Sr. died of a coronary occlusion 10 days short of his 54th birthday. Three of his brothers (Ed Jr., 45; Roy, 54; and Arthur, 60) also died of heart disease within two years of Tom Sr.'s demise, leaving Allen B. East, the seventh of Ed and Hattie East's sons, the last survivor among them.

Tom and Alice East's net worth at his death was $55,273.37. He left an undivided estate to Alice and the children, who formed a new East Brothers Cattle Company. Although Tom Jr. had been in charge of the San Antonio Viejo since 1935, when their father died, Robert asked to be put in charge of the big ranch. He also wanted to run the East Brothers office at 318 East Galbraith Street in Hebbronville, between the New York Store, where the ranch hands bought their work clothing, and Dr. Manuel Guerra's medical office.

Robert knew little and cared less about the world beyond the San Antonio Viejo, where, like his sister Lica, he would live his entire life. He also had no head for business, and the consequences were quickly apparent. He soon stopped arriving regularly at the office and then failed to appear altogether. He abandoned the business side on his own accord and returned to the only role that he cared to play: a cowboy among cowboys. Recognizing that cow pastures were Robert's natural element, Alice let Tom pick up the executive reins, ensuring that East Brothers would have stable leadership as long as he was around.

Except for rare visits to San Antonio and Corpus Christi, Robert is not known to have ever traveled far outside the lower Rio Grande Valley. He and Tom were taken once or twice as boys as far away as West Texas to shoot prairie dogs. That was all of the world Robert cared to see.

He was lean like most cowboys, with sandy blond hair and hazel eyes. In later life, he'd develop extremely bowed legs. Walking became an agony.

His lifelong routine was to awaken each morning by five thirty, eat breakfast, and then stride out onto the porch to deliver the day's orders to his vaqueros. He'd be dressed as usual, in a threadbare and a heavily patched pair of blue jeans; a well-worn cowboy shirt, also patched; plus boots, a hat, and a bandana. Few people remember ever seeing Robert otherwise attired.

He enjoyed paperback westerns. In his later years, he liked to watch television after dinner. A regular Fox News viewer, according to Carilu Cantú Leal, Robert especially enjoyed the evenings when Paula Jones, the Arkansas state employee who sued former president Bill Clinton for sexual harassment, appeared on Fox. He watched *Lonesome Dove*, the miniseries, whenever it aired.

Robert's favorite meal was *carne seca*, or beef jerky. His favorite restaurant was any Whataburger. He was seldom seen in Hebbronville or anywhere else even a few miles away from his ranches. On the rare days Robert did travel to town, he'd bring his own food to save money. The noon meal typically consisted of an American cheese sandwich on white bread, Fritos, a Snickers bar, and a little box of pineapple juice. His cowboys recall that, on days they went into town, each was issued an orange and a piece of jerky for lunch on the road. *El Patrón* consumed very little alcohol, only an occasional beer or two.

Robert was disorganized, with a short attention span, and changed his mind frequently, traits associated with second child syndrome. Most of his ranch hands nonetheless treated *him* with a warm deference. They appreciated that he preferentially communicated with them in border Spanish, albeit with a Texas accent. But he also heedlessly antagonized the men, often for some trivial or miserly purpose.

For example, the time-honored practice at the San Antonio Viejo was for the hired hands to receive two weeks' paid vacation each year at Christmastime. When Robert succeeded his father, he canceled the paid part and, in some cases, their annual bonuses as well. It was not a popular decision. Some of the ablest and most loyal ranch employees began to leave. The exodus included men who'd been through the Depression with Tom East Sr., when their checks were sometimes late, but their trust in Robert's father was never betrayed.

Paydays were the 15th and the end of the month. Employees who were in the US legally were issued checks from which Lica deducted income tax and FICA payments. Mexican nationals, about half his workers, were given cash in envelopes from which Robert often extracted a $100 bill or more before handing them out.

When Lica learned of this, she quietly replaced the money. She also paid for all the ranch hands' work clothes purchased on credit at the New York Store, next to the ranch office in Hebbronville. Each month, she'd pull each hand's New York Store credit receipts for jeans, hats, boots, shirts, and the like and would pay the balance herself.

One payday during roundup, when the men put on their best clothes to head for town, Robert asked them to wash down the cattle trucks before they left. Enemorio Serna balked. Teco, as he was known, refused to get himself dirty, even when Robert offered him a new pair of boots if he would do so.

So Robert turned to his mother, as he often did, to settle disputes with his vaqueros. By then, Alice was known in the family as Old Mama. To the ranch hands, she was *La Madama*. Teco was one of her favorites. She called him Ennie. After a few minutes of discussion, Serna was on his way to town, his shirt and jeans and boots unsoiled. He agreed to remain at the ranch for the rest of the roundup, then left for a year in Montana before returning to work for Robert's older brother, Tom.

Another time, when Robert wanted one of his workers to trap cattle at a water lot, he offered the cowboy a pair of jeans for the job. Hour after hour, the vaquero carefully kept downwind of the animals as they warily passed through the fence toward the water. When he finally closed the gate on the cattle, Robert rewarded him with an old pair of his own jeans.

He thought he was being clever when he instructed a hay truck driver to unload his cargo at several different stops all over the ranch. Once the hay man was finished, Robert informed him that the price he'd agreed to pay was too high and that he was going to give the man less money.

As Mike East tells it, "The driver said, 'Robert, that's not what we agreed to.'

"'If you don't like it,' Robert replied, 'then load it up, and take it back to town.'

"Of course, the man wasn't going to do that. For my Uncle Robert, that was a victory."

CHAPTER 8

Besides overseeing the East Brothers business, Tom also managed three comparatively modest ranches that his father had leased. They were the 26,000-acre La Mota Ranch, in Zapata County; the 40,000-acre Los Muertos Ranch in Bruni, about 15 miles northwest of Hebbronville; and the 14,000-acre Buena Vista, about 10 miles east of the main ranch. The Buena Vista would later be added to the East Brothers' holdings.

Mike lived with his parents, Tom and Evelyn, at the Zapata ranch. By the time their daughters, Alice and Lica Elena, came along, the family had moved to a house Tom built for them at Los Muertos. Neither ranch residence had electricity. At La Mota, both heat and light were provided by a half-inch natural gas pipe that ran along the ceiling through the rooms. The pipe was fitted at intervals with mesh globes, called mantles, that could be individually ignited and extinguished, like a gas camp lantern. The pipe also fed the kitchen's gas stove. Water for any purpose was collected from the roof and stored in an underground cistern. Los Muertos was warmed by gas heaters. A windmill provided the house's water.

Mike remembers a day when he was about seven that his father drove him and Uncle Robert in the family coupe to their house at the Bruni ranch. When they arrived, the boy climbed out of the back seat and went inside, leaving Tom and Robert together in the front seat.

A few minutes later, the coupe's horn could be heard inside the house, honking rhythmically from the driveway. Mike ran out the door to find his dad in the driver's seat, shaking Uncle Robert by his elbows on the passenger side, shouting, "You're my brother, and you know it!" Each time he shook Robert, Tom's left elbow bumped the steering wheel, honking the horn.

Then he was pummeling Robert on the ground. Tom looked up to see his son gaping at the scene and calmly announced that Uncle Robert, on his back in the dust, would be coming inside for a kiss from everyone, which he did.

Besides La Mota and Los Muertos, Tom and Evelyn and the children also lived in a number of rental houses. The last of these was a small place behind the East Brothers office in Hebbronville. Dr. Guerra's wife, Berta, collected the rent each month.

Although their parents were practicing Protestants, the three East children received Catholic educations. They all attended grades one through eight at Hebbronville's Little Flower parochial school that Sarita Kenedy East founded in 1931. They left home for high school. Mike boarded at St. Edward's Academy, in Austin. Alice and Lica Elena went to St. Mary's Hall, in San Antonio.

The children spent much of their summers at the San Antonio Viejo, where their aunt, uncle, and grandmother doted on them. A major attraction was Aunt Lica's menagerie, her extensive collection of just about any wild or tame Texas animal suitable as a pet, with the general exceptions of fish, serpents, and reptiles.

Old Mama ruled over them all, often by whim, an artifact of her own upbringing, according to Helenita Groves. Alice was indulged as a child, says Groves, and behaved however she pleased for the rest of her life.

Once, when Tom and Evelyn had left La Mota ranch for a weeklong trip, Alice showed up with Lica "and painted all the furniture green," Mike says. "Everything. Chairs. Beds. Everything was painted green. I guess they thought they were doing something good.

"Of course, when my mother got back, she wasn't too happy with that. I'm sure my dad got an earful. I remember she always used to bring it up. This was one of her gripes."

Years later, when Mike built a chapel on his ranch, he installed a green door to visually commemorate Old Mama's green paint caper, as he explains, "because it was quite an event in my life." He also keeps a souvenir of the occasion in a corner of his kitchen, a green rifle cabinet from La Mota.

Like many Texas ranchers of her day, men and women, Alice enjoyed hard liquor. Her preference was tequila. Tom tried in vain to curtail his mother's drinking habit and even recruited Mike in the effort.

Mike recalls an occasion when Rosendo Garza drove him, Old Mama, and his Aunt Lica to a wedding in Amarillo. "Dad told me, 'When you get up there, don't let your grandmother drink. Whatever you do, don't let her drink.'

"So we get up there, and the first thing my grandmother does is have too much to drink.

"We're coming back from Amarillo, and time and time again, my grandmother tells me, 'No matter what you do, don't spill the beans.'

"I said, 'Okay.'

"We get home, and my dad gets me and asks, 'Well, did Old Mama drink?' He kept asking me, and finally, I said, 'Yeah.'

"'Did she get drunk?'

"'Yeah. She got drunk.'

"So I go out to my grandmother's, and she interrogates me. She asked me two or three times, 'Did you spill the beans?'

"I told her, 'Yeah, I spilled the beans.'

"Well, that was one of the biggest scoldings I ever got from her. She said I was 'just a damn snitch.'

"There was another kid at the ranch about my age, named Oscar Ozuna, and *he* was just a snitch. Nobody liked *him* because he just went around spilling the beans."

CHAPTER 9

The East family began taking their legal business to Judge W. R. Perkins in Alice nearly as soon as Perkins opened his law office there in the early 1900s. In 1919, the judge added 25-year-old Jacob S. "Jake" Floyd, a World War I veteran, as an associate. Floyd was made a name partner on Judge Perkins's death in 1943 and remained with the firm for the rest of his life. He also became a director of the Alice National Bank, the successor to the Alice State Bank & Trust Co., one of Tom East Sr.'s lenders, which folded at the start of the Great Depression. The Alice National Bank was among the Perkins firm's most important clients.

Tom Jr. and Jake Floyd became political allies in the 1940s, united in their opposition to the epic criminality of Archer Parr and his son, George. The Parrs were known as the "Dukes of Duval," and were widely accused of carrying on, as a common phrase went, a "brush-country saga of graft, shootouts, unsolved murders, [and] arson."

George Parr, who eventually committed suicide, gave Floyd a nickname, *La Viboro Seca*, The Dry Snake. It was a salute of sorts from a deadly foe. Parr was behind the September 9, 1952, gunshot murder of Jake's son, 22-year-old Jake "Buddy" Floyd Jr., a law student. Parr's hired killer mistook Buddy for his father.

Both Tom and Old Mama entrusted Jake Floyd with their most important and sensitive legal work, of which there was much. At the top of both their lists was escape from under Bob Kleberg's long shadow.

Robert J. Kleberg Jr. was just 21 when his father's sudden incapacity forced the young man into the unenviable role of the King Ranch's acting manager. But Alice's younger brother was more than equal to the challenge, eventually becoming the most successful and famous American cattleman of his or any other time.

Mr. Bob, as he was known, would be feted in a December 1947 *Time* magazine cover story as "the liege lord of all the King ranches," about 825,000 acres in all, a colorful way to describe Mr. Bob's absolutism under which his sister and her family chafed and eventually rebelled.

Old Mama owned approximately one-fifth of the King Ranch. That earned her a seat on the corporation's board of directors but not much of a say in corporate management. She objected to what she regarded as her brother's lavish hand in a whole range of new King Ranch initiatives, from acquiring overseas ranches to diversification into new ventures, such as breeding and racing Thoroughbred horses and acquiring a turf farm in Florida.

There were stark differences between the ways the Easts and the Klebergs managed their businesses.

"I'm familiar with the style in which the East family operated their ranches," says James A. Mayo Jr., a former president of the Alice National Bank, who was close to Tom East Jr., "and it was light years different than how King Ranch operated their ranches.

"There was much less overhead involved in the East family's approach to running ranchlands. I don't think that there was great involvement by professionals—meaning attorneys, accountants, the corporate aspect. I don't think that was a part of the East family operations at all."

Old Mama also shared her son Tom's resentment at Uncle Bob's refusal to delegate authority, even to a fellow rancher he respected as much as he'd respected his nephew since the long-ago time when Tom, as a teenager, operated both the San Antonio Viejo and Encino Division for him.

Tom was ambitious; he aimed to someday surpass his uncle as the most successful and powerful cattleman in Texas. As matters stood, however, Tom, like his mother, was afforded almost no say in King Ranch business. Neither side of the issue would give an inch; a breach was inevitable.

On the dining room wall of her grandson Mike's ranch house is a framed handwritten letter from Alice, addressed to Jake Floyd, composed sometime in the 1950s. The message is in her voice, but the handwriting looks like Tom's.

"Mr. Floyd," it reads, "I do want to get out of the King Ranch and the quicker the better—sell or get what is mine or trade or lose it if necessary. The thing is that I'm sick and tired of it all. I am just used so they can spend my money and I don't want to be in there anymore with them. I hate to go to the meetings and hear the fool things that are thought of how to spend money on a sewer project from Corpus to Laureles—just anything to keep from coming to the point. Please make it clear to [Leroy] Denman, [Jr.]— the lead King Ranch attorney—when you see him as he tries to act like he never heard of some of the things we told him before. I think, if he was a good lawyer or man, he couldn't help but see why I want out. Certainly, we can get out if we *all* want to as much as I do. Please put your thinking cap on and think of something. With best regards, A. K. East."

Alice may have been a King and a Kleberg, but she sounded a whole lot more like an East.

A flashpoint came in 1957, at a King Ranch board meeting, when Mr. Bob once more refused to consider sharing some power and authority with Tom and made disparaging remarks about him and his brother that left Old Mama in tears.

Later that day, when she told her son of the episode, Tom drove to Kingsville to have it out with his uncle. Adán Muñoz, Hector's father and Kleberg's driver and bodyguard at the time, intercepted East in front of the house.

"I want to see my Uncle Bob," Tom said.

Muñoz replied that was not possible at the moment. Mr. Bob was hosting a dinner party.

Tom told him to go bring Kleberg out or he'd do it himself.

Mr. Bob emerged from the house to confront his nephew. There were words. Tom lost his temper and slugged his uncle in the jaw, dropping him into the swimming pool.

According to Mike East, his dad regretted the incident as an overreaction. He respected Mr. Bob; their differences, in the main, were a matter of dueling egos. "My dad was a whole lot like his Uncle Bob Kleberg, in that they were both tyrants," says Mike. "They ran everything themselves."

Jake Floyd and Tom East, working together with banker Richard King's nephew, Alfred King, cobbled together an agreeable exit deal for Alice, and solved a couple other issues in the process. "My great uncle, Alfred King, was a very smart man," says James King, Robert's old friend, who, today, is a prominent dealer in Texas ranchland. "He orchestrated a three-way swap among the Easts, Kings, and Klebergs so there was no tax event."

In the final agreement, Alice traded her share in all King Ranch land and minerals in exchange for the unencumbered title to the San Antonio Viejo, including surface rights and remaining mineral rights. Old Mama also was to receive the Santa Fe Ranch, southeast of the San Antonio Viejo, in Hidalgo and Brooks Counties. The deal included both surface and mineral rights.

But, first, Bob Kleberg needed to acquire the Santa Fe himself. The land was originally part of the King Ranch, known then as Norias West. Henrietta King bequeathed it to her grandson, Richard King, and his two sisters, Mary and Minerva, who had played piano at Tom and Alice East's 1915 wedding. By the 1950s, all three Kings were ready to get out of the ranching business and agreed to swap the Santa Fe to Kleberg for 10 percent of the King Ranch's minerals.

Once that was accomplished, Kleberg signed the Santa Fe over to Alice, leaving everyone satisfied—almost. Mr. Bob, however, did not leave the Santa Fe cattle for his sister. Tom would have to stock the ranch with 2,000 East Brothers cattle from Los Muertos Ranch in Bruni and a couple hundred from the Buena Vista. Robert contributed some cattle from the San Antonio Viejo as well.

CHAPTER 10

Experience taught Tom East Jr. that the safest way to avoid what Robert called "friction" between them was to give his younger brother plenty of leeway in running the San Antonio Viejo's livestock operations. If Robert asked Tom to help him work cattle, he'd do so. If not, he kept his distance. He also knew better than to loan Robert machinery or tools, because his younger brother likely would never return what he borrowed.

Sometimes, "friction" seemed to develop out of nowhere. Once, when the two of them with their separate crews were loading cattle onto railcars at the Hebbronville pens, Tom showed his appreciation for Robert's hands' hard work by giving each of them a tip. Robert wanted to know why he didn't receive a tip too.

There was an occasional comedic side to their confrontations. When, for example, one of his ranch hands told Robert that banks only keep a fraction of their depositors' balances in the form of cash, he began nagging Tom about it, demanding to see hard proof of how much money they had in the Alice National Bank.

Tom, then a director of the bank, finally went to Bruno Goldapp, its president at the time, and asked how much currency the bank usually kept on hand.

About $200,000 or so, Goldapp told him.

East asked if Goldapp could put together a million dollars in cash. The answer was yes; it could be done through the Federal Reserve in Dallas but would take a few days.

When the money arrived, Tom asked that the bills be stacked on the wall shelves of the bank's walk-in vault. Then Robert was brought in.

"See that?" Goldapp said to him. "That's your money."

"*¡Está bueno!*" Robert exclaimed.

Unsophisticated as he was about money, especially large sums, Robert was far from indifferent to the topic. Jim Mayo remembers a call he received one morning from Robert back in the mid-1980s, when Texas savings and loans and banks were dying all over the state.

"He said, 'Mayo, I've been reading in them newspapers that a lot of these S&Ls are having big problems.'

"I said, 'That's right. They are.'

"'And I also read that some of them banks are having big problems.'

"I said, 'That's right.'"

At that time, Robert and Lica and Old Mama had tens of millions of dollars on deposit at the Alice bank.

"He said, 'What kind of shape are we in there?'

"I said, 'We're in good shape.'

"He said, 'Are you sure?'

"I thought, *What can I say to him that he can relate to, that is truthful, and [that] emphasizes the point that he is safe?*

"So I said to him, 'Robert, my mother has every dime to her name in this bank. Do you think I would let her keep her money in this bank if we weren't safe?'

"He said, 'No, I don't reckon you would.'

"Well, I wouldn't.

"He said, 'Okay. But if you get to having trouble, be sure to draw out my money, and we'll split it later.'"

"Friction" between her sons was one of Old Mama's common cares.

"Tom Dear," she wrote her older boy from the San Antonio Viejo amid one such set-to. Tom had packed his gear and headed home to the Santa Fe ranch. "Last night, when you talked to me, I just couldn't say much over the phone, as there are always so many people listening. When you said you would need a few days to move your things out of the house, I just don't think that is <u>right.</u> There must be some other way.

"Do you think you could go on with all the work at the Santa Fe and then just let Robert know when Mike was ready to work the Julián pasture?

"I am very old now and do hate for this to happen. I wish you both could see it <u>my way.</u> Let's talk about how you all can settle it as soon as I am gone. Robert is not too well himself, and [I] am sure he gets upset very easily, and I know all this is hard for you and you have so much to see about.

"Tom, you must know how very close you are to me, and I just would <u>never want </u>to hurt you in any way. I do believe if you ask Robert to come and work the Julián with Mike, it will work out better than for East Bros to separate. All my love. Will see you Sunday about 3:00 PM. Love, Mama."

Robert took the family by surprise in early 1958 with the announcement of his intention to marry 28-year-old Evelyn Reagan, known as Gussie. She was the pretty, sweet-tempered daughter of Rocky Reagan, a stockman, writer, and regionally well-known rodeo impresario from Beeville, about 60 miles northwest of Corpus Christi.

Evelyn, who graduated from high school in 1947, was the youngest of Reagan's seven children. According to the Beeville *Bee-Picayune*, she attended Southern Methodist University, in Dallas, where Gussie was a Tri Delta sorority sister. She then moved home to take up school teaching.

Robert might have met her at a rodeo; Gussie was skilled aboard a cutting horse—which would have impressed him—and she is said to have competed against his sister Lica in the arena.

Their wedded life quickly came to grief.

"The story I heard," says Helenita Groves, "is that when she asked him, 'Where are we going to live?' he said, 'You can stay in my room.'" Robert's room at the San Antonio Viejo was in the east or family wing of the headquarters house. He shared a bathroom with Old Mama.

As Helenita Groves recollects the story, when Robert telephoned his mother that he intended to marry Gussie Reagan, "She said, 'Don't be silly! What are you talking about? You need to get back here. You've got a lot of work to do. I didn't know where you were, and you get back here and go to work!'"

But she did not block the marriage, which was celebrated on Tuesday, June 17, 1958.

Fausto Salinas Jr., a Rio Grande City hay merchant, remembers once asking Robert if he'd ever been married.

"He said, 'Yes.'

"I asked, 'For how long?'

"'Three days.'"

Robert told Salinas that there had been a misunderstanding. "She asked me, 'Where are we going on our honeymoon?' I said, 'San Antonio.' We got to the ranch, and three days later, she asked me, 'When are we going on our honeymoon?' And I told her, 'We are on our honeymoon.'"

Old Mama and Lica prepared a spacious residence on the ranch for Robert and Evelyn, but he insisted instead that he and his bride share his room. Robert seems not to have thought deeply about his new role as a husband.

When he went to work cattle, he took his mother and sister with him, as usual, and left Evelyn back at the ranch to fend for herself. She soon realized what a monumental mistake she had made and headed home to Beeville, never to return.

Robert filed for divorce in the district court of Jim Hogg County, represented by Jake Floyd. The marriage was terminated by a divorce decree entered in Cause 963, on March 2, 1959. Evelyn's one request, that her maiden name be restored, was granted.

Thirty-one years later, on July 28, 1990, Evelyn Reagan married Jack Seals, curriculum coordinator for the Beeville school system.

Robert persisted in his search for a suitable mate who might produce an heir or heiress. In the spring of 1974, Frank Yturria, a rancher, oilman, and noted conservationist from Brownsville, as well as a good friend of Tom East Jr., brought his wife, Mary, and their attractive daughter, Dorothy, then a

20-year-old junior at UT Austin, to the San Antonio Viejo for lunch with Robert and Lica and Old Mama.

The next week, Dorothy received a marriage proposal from Robert. "I ran away from that as fast as I could," she laughs. "I did not acknowledge the proposal, and the subject was never raised again."

A few years later, as Sarita Armstrong recalls, she and her parents, Tobin and Ann Armstrong, encountered Robert at a King Ranch production sale. Sure enough, the Armstrongs soon received a formal letter from East, seeking their permission for him to date their daughter, then in law school. "My father thought it would be funny," Sarita remembers, "and encouraged me to go out with Robert."

She declined.

CHAPTER 11

The 1950s brought a new and exotic presence to South Texas cattle country. Roderick Norton Gregory, known as Brother Leo to his fellow Trappist monks at St. Joseph's Abbey in Spencer, Massachusetts, was dispatched to Texas by his abbot, Dom Edmund Futterer, to scout sites for new Trappist houses, as well as wealthy Texas Catholics to finance them.

Futterer made a canny choice. A humble shoemaker within the abbey walls, once the 30-ish lay brother was temporarily released from his vows, he blossomed into a first-rate fundraiser, pulling in torrents of cash from donors for the Trappist expansion program. It seemed that no one was immune to the glib and charismatic monk's intense piety and persuasive pitch, certainly not Robert, Lica, and Tom East Jr.'s aunt, Sarita Kenedy East.

Sarita was without pretense, warmhearted, and "strictly the cowgirl type," as a relative, Jack Turcotte, once described her. She was down-to-earth in the way Old Mama was, and the two were good friends.

She lived in an imposing, white, multistory mansion, built by her father, John Gregory Kenedy, on Baffin Bay, an inlet of the Laguna Madre. Everywhere Sarita looked from the old Gatling gun turret atop her estate, she saw nothing but her boundless pastures stretching to the horizon.

But Sarita was a forlorn and sad figure by her late 50s. Her parents had both suffered painful, lingering deaths. Her one sibling, Johnny, drank himself into a premature grave. Her marriage to Arthur East had been barren. Like other East males, Arthur died young of a heart attack, leaving his widow bereft and lonely, seeking solace in her deep Catholic faith and finding forgetfulness in her evening tumblers of scotch.

Brother Leo was an accomplished fraud, believed by one of his donors to have bedded the man's mother. He brought an enveloping passion to his work and spoke of doing God's will with a fervor that reliably stirred rich older women. When he was with Sarita, according to a number of witnesses, Leo was an ardent, attentive, and adamant soulmate—"your beadsman" as he sometimes signed his many handwritten letters to her.

La Parra's devout *patrona* at first wanted to support a monastery in Texas, possibly at La Parra, but Leo had other ideas. He told her the local climate and terrain were not suitable for self-supporting communities of religious ascetics but that areas of Argentina and Uruguay definitely were. He persuaded the widow to set sail with him for Latin America to see what he meant.

Sarita soon thereafter agreed to finance the construction of two new Trappist abbeys well below the equator. Then the monk's message from God began to change, lifting the widow to consider extending her charity well beyond an order of robed and reclusive monks. Leo brought her to appreciate the desperate plight of the world's neediest.

She had previously toyed with the idea of establishing a secular foundation as part of her estate planning, then a new concept among Texas ranchers. She directed Jake Floyd to look into it. But Floyd temporized, no doubt in consultation with another client and fellow bank director, Tom East Jr.

Under Leo's tutelage, Sarita began to entertain loftier visions. When she returned to the United States, Leo's major ally, New York industrialist J. Peter Grace, presented her with a rewritten will and foundation documents courtesy of his corporate lawyers. Jake Floyd was given no role in drafting the new will or the papers establishing an international charity to be named The John G. and Marie Stella Kenedy Memorial Foundation, after her parents.

Then, just as Leo was set to help Sarita act on "God's plan" for her fortune, as he liked to call it, she was diagnosed with advanced, incurable cancer and died at St. Vincent's Hospital in New York City on February 11, 1961.

Given a little more time, Brother Leo might have successfully made off with Sarita's many millions. But with her sudden demise, all that the wayward monk and J. Peter Grace had achieved was to touch off a 20-year global struggle for her estate that reached all the way to the Vatican, with perhaps a half billion dollars or more at stake.

His next step was a stumble. At a luncheon on the day of Sarita's funeral, the monk approached Bob Kleberg with a proposal that the King Ranch, perhaps in association with the nearby Armstrong Ranch, consider assuming operational control of La Parra. Leo told Kleberg and the Armstrongs that he and Sarita had discussed just such an arrangement, and she had endorsed the idea.

Tom East was customarily tight-lipped about both his business affairs and his private life, and this policy extended to any discussion of his relationship with his Uncle Bob. But some years later, he did take one question by telephone in his room at San Antonio's St. Anthony Hotel from journalist Hugh Aynesworth, who asked East what he thought of Leo and the new foundation.

"I can't say what Aunt Sarita may have wanted done with her money," he answered. "But I know for a damn sure that she meant for La Parra to stay in the family. And you gotta understand Jake Floyd. He was for Texas. Brother Leo and them raised a boil on ol' Jake's butt."

The Easts were no different from most Texas ranch families in their strong attachment to their land, especially after a century or so and several generations of sweat equity invested in making their pastures productive.

Floyd, with Tom East at his elbow, stitched together a Texas coalition to confront Leo and J. Peter Grace in court. Tom would secretly finance the suit, styled Cause 12074 in the 79th District Court of Jim Wells County.

Once the action was filed, Bob Kleberg lost interest in operating La Parra.

The executors of Sarita Kenedy East's will were her cousin Edgar Turcotte, Jake Floyd, and the Alice National Bank. The lawsuit was barely underway when Turcotte and then Floyd died, leaving the bank as sole executor. Tom

East immediately resigned as a director of the bank and, soon enough, was ranching all of La Parra as a bank employee.

Frank Nesbitt, a Corpus Christi lawyer who represented members of the Turcotte family, was one of the several attorneys muscled aside in the maneuvering. Although, after years of work, Nesbitt was only able to cover his expenses in the long battle, he openly admired how deftly Tom East and Jake Floyd engineered the situation. "He and Jake were three-fourths of the brains behind the whole thing," Nesbitt said later, "and East was also the money and the strength."

CHAPTER 12

Tom East operated the 400,000-acre combined Kenedy ranches as an Alice National Bank employee until 1982, when the legal warfare over Sarita Kenedy East's estate finally came to a close. Sarita's foundation, now headed by the combative Bishop Rene Gracida of the Corpus Christi diocese, was the big winner.

When it came time for Gracida to consider bids for grazing and hunting rights on Sarita's half of La Parra, Tom announced that, if the King Ranch's bid was the highest, he'd match it. Plus, he would cover out of his own pocket basic expenses for both the town of Sarita, the county seat on Highway 77 at the entrance to the ranch, and its residents, mostly La Parra employees. The civic expenses included water, sewers, streets, and garbage collection.

For the residents, says Jim Mayo, "you're talking about paying these people's medical expenses, funeral expenses, and marriage expenses as well as providing them with housing, with food, and on and on and on."

Although the lease included game hunting rights—then as now much more remunerative in South Texas than cattle grazing rights—Sarita had, on many occasions, insisted that she did not want hunters on her cattle ranch. Tom would respect his aunt's wishes, although it meant a serious loss of potential revenue for his family's already strained exchequer.

Mayo made Tom two loans. "One," he says, "was a revolving line of credit for roughly $2 million, which he could draw down and pay back annually. He asked for it to cover lease costs and operating expenses.

"The second loan was $6 million to cover the livestock purchase, to be amortized over five years."

The two deals generated a small mountain of documentation. "I knew Tom was not going to read those documents," Mayo remembers. "So my secretary placed two stacks of documents on my desk. Tom looked up at her and asked, 'Have you read all these documents?'

"She said, 'Well, Mr. East, I work with those documents every day.'

"He asked her, 'Are they okay?'

"'Yes, sir,' she replied. 'They're that.'

"So he reached for his pen and started signing."

When East finished signing all the papers and rose to leave Mayo's office, he started digging with two big fingers into his shirt pocket, trying to pull out a piece of paper. It was a check for $1 million, which he handed to his banker, asking Mayo to put the sum "on account."

Tom already held a lease on the half of the ranch that belonged to his aunt, Elena Suess de Kenedy, the widow of Sarita's brother, John G. Kenedy Jr., minus the 20,000 acres which she reserved to herself. The contract permitted grazing only—hunting would be strictly banned—which brought the lease price down to $2 per acre. When Elena died in the spring of 1984 after suffering a series of strokes, her estate went into a trust. She specified that she wished Tom and Mike to have first priority to lease grazing rights. Ranching profits were to be distributed among five Catholic charities.

Tom did not put the Kenedy ranch leases under the East Brothers umbrella. "He was going to have to borrow a lot of money, and he didn't need interference," Mike explains. "You get my uncle involved in something, and that's all there was going to be—interference."

Many Texas ranchers at the time were turning to helicopters to help manage their herds. Not Tom, who continued to do it the old way, on horseback. It was a daunting personal challenge; East was risking everything, including his health. Now in his mid-60s, having already outlived his father and six of his seven paternal uncles—four of them succumbed to cardiovascular disease—Tom was too intelligent not to realize the threats he faced.

Dr. James W. Nixon Jr., a prominent San Antonio surgeon and the East family physician as his father had been, shared his concerns about Tom's health in a 1967 letter to Old Mama, advising that her son ought to "take it a little more easy," because he was "certainly doing more than he should with his present condition."

But East ignored all the warnings. Mike remembers his father's exhausting daily schedule that began at three o'clock each morning when Mike would hear him climb into his Jeep Bronco and rumble away from the Santa Fe on a cross-country route to the Kenedy Ranch. Each morning, East would stop to pick up one of his cowhands, who later reported how Tom was sometimes stricken with sudden, agonizing chest pains as they drove along. East warned the man that if he said a word about the episodes, he'd be fired.

One practical reason for hiding his heart condition was to protect those big loans. But Tom East wouldn't readily give in to what he probably saw as a weakness. So he soldiered on, conceding nothing, even his own mortality, until disaster inevitably struck.

It was nearly 80 degrees on Saturday afternoon, December 8, 1984, dry and humid, with a light breeze, as East carefully steered his Ford Bronco toward the Fernández windmill at La Parra. Just ahead of Tom and his passenger, 22-year-old Ramiro Pérez, were four or five head of cattle that Tom was expertly coaxing toward a water trap gate near the windmill in advance of a roundup.

Slowly weaving the vehicle back and forth behind the little herd, Tom was careful not to rush or disturb them. He knew from long experience that if the animals thought it was their idea to pass through the gate, they'd cooperate, although at their own unhurried pace.

Pérez remembers Tom was enjoying himself that afternoon, conducting a sort of master class in working cattle for the young cowboy. Once the animals passed through the gate and were securely inside the 300-acre trap, East lifted his right arm as if to throw an imaginary lasso, smiled, and said, "That's the way you do it, kid."

When Pérez thinks back on the afternoon, he always fixes on an unusual moment, maybe five minutes before Tom escorted the cattle into the trap, when the older man stopped the Bronco, pulled out his wallet, and handed him $30.

"What's that for?" Pérez asked.

"Take 'em," Tom replied. "You're going to need 'em—money for something." The vaquero has ever since wondered if don Tomás, at that moment, somehow knew something he didn't.

They made a U-turn in the trap and headed back through the gate and out onto a caliche road, where the vehicle lost traction in the soft ground. East stopped once more. Ramiro, looking out his passenger-side window, heard Tom moan and turned to see him bent at the waist over the gear shift.

There had been a couple such moments before. Once, at the Piedra Camp on Sarita Kenedy's side of the ranch, they were drinking water together at a trough when Tom stopped and walked over to the truck, where he bent over, grabbed his stomach, and started gasping for air. After a time, he stood up, looked straight at Pérez in a way that suggested the young man better listen up, and said, "Okay. Don't tell anybody." Pérez understood this was an order, not a request.

Something similar had also happened at the Marana pasture. Tom bent over and then fell to his knees before he recovered. Again there was the stern look and the explicit command that Pérez say nothing.

Beto Salazar, also a vaquero, witnessed similar episodes as well and was warned to keep what he had witnessed to himself.

Pérez, at first, had thought that East was reaching for the four-wheel drive lever, but he soon realized that Tom was motionless and unmistakably moaning in pain.

"Are you okay?" Pérez asked him. "Are you okay?"

No answer.

The cowboy tapped Tom on his shoulder. "Are you okay?" Again no reply. He then grabbed East by his shirt and pushed him back into the driver's seat. Tom's face was purple.

"Are you okay?" Pérez asked once more as he pushed the gear shift into park, jumped out of the vehicle, and ran around to the driver's side, where he opened Tom's door. "Are you okay? Are you all right?" he asked.

The only reply was a moan. Tom's face had turned from purple to red.

"I got scared," says Pérez. "I didn't know what to do."

Then his gaze fell on East's car phone. The device served the sole purpose of saving time when communicating with B. Goodwyn, who provided trucking service during roundups. If more or fewer trucks were required as the roundup proceeded, Tom could quickly contact Goodwyn from his Bronco rather than have to drive all the way back to the ranch office phone. Pérez didn't know how to operate the cell phone, so he punched REDIAL, hoping for the best. The last person Tom had called on the car phone was B. Goodwyn himself, who answered Pérez's call.

"My name's Ramiro," he told the trucker. "I'm just a kid. I've got Tom East here with me. We're in a pasture with nobody around."

Goodwyn thought it was a prank and admonished the young man that Tom East's car phone was for business only.

Pérez persisted. "I HAVE TOM EAST WITH ME!" he yelled. "I THINK HE'S HAVING A HEART ATTACK. SOMETHING'S WRONG WITH HIM!"

That got Goodwyn's attention. The cowboy again explained that he did not know how to use the car phone and asked the trucker to call 911 for him. "Tell them I have Tom with me," he said. "I need help!"

Goodwyn advised Pérez that he'd find help and instructed the young vaquero to try to get Tom out of the pasture to Highway 77. The trucker called the sheriff's office and Mike East as well.

Just then, Ramiro's father, Avelino Pérez, appeared in the distance, putting out hay for the cattle. Ramiro ran to him.

"I told him, 'Tom is dead!'

"'What!?'

"'Tom is dead!'

"'Nah!'

"'He's dead!'"

Avelino ran to the Bronco, grabbed Tom's wrist to search for a heartbeat, and found none.

Another young vaquero, Rubén Bueno, was with Avelino that day. Together, Bueno and Pérez were able to move Tom across the center console into the vehicle's passenger seat and then headed for the highway.

Soon after they got to the main road, Kenedy County sheriff Rafael Cuéllar Jr., known as Junior, and his deputy, Buddy Naranjo, intercepted them. The sheriff ordered Pérez to drive to the Buckhorn, a small convenience store near the entrance to La Parra. There, they carried Tom inside and laid him on the floor.

Sheriff Cuéllar attempted CPR. "But it was too late," says Pérez, who was overcome by what he'd just been through and drove away in Tom's Jeep to be alone with his feelings.

CHAPTER 13

Tom's death shattered the East family. They lost their center of gravity that day; their narrative permanently fractured. The strong ones—the two Toms—were now gone, leaving Robert with only his sister Lica and his aging mother to protect him from himself and to help guide him through the hazards ahead. Robert, however, didn't see matters that way. He viewed his brother's death as his overdue moment of emancipation.

His nephew Mike received his first glimpse of what was in store that Sunday, December 9, on the steps of the Turcotte Mortuary in Kingsville, where his uncle made it clear that, after decades of taking orders, he was ready to issue a few of his own.

"Well," said Robert, dispensing with any words of comfort, "it looks like you're working for me now." What he meant was that with Tom's death, he and Lica now controlled the East Brothers partnership, and since Lica routinely deferred to her brother, Robert was now effectively in charge.

Mike says he responded that he'd be glad to work with Robert, "but I felt I needed to make my own decisions in operating the Santa Fe."

His uncle pounced. "If it's going to be that way," he said, "you all keep your third, and my sister and I, we'll take our thirds out, and we'll operate separately."

Keeping East Brothers intact had been one of Tom and Old Mama's first priorities for more than 40 years. Robert waited less than 24 hours following his older brother's death to declare the partnership defunct. He further informed Mike that, although he and Lica together would have 30,000 acres of the Santa Fe coming to them in a partition, he felt entitled to more.

"He was going to take 40,000," Mike later testified in a bitter intrafamily estate dispute, "and he was going to take 40,000 of the best, 40,000 out of the middle, the Julián pasture. This was before my father was even buried.

"He said it could be friendly, and we could do it one-to-one, and if it couldn't be done that way, then we'd get the lawyers involved."

Robert would also soon persuade Old Mama to write a new will, cutting out Tom's family from his one-third share of her estate. At the same time, he persuaded Lica to leave her one-third share to him in her will, as he would his to her. The rupture was complete.

Tom East's funeral was held on Monday, December 10. He disdained any sort of ostentation, including showy funerals, so it was no surprise that he'd made no provisions for his own. Tom East, Jr.'s closing message to the world was a no-nonsense, double-spaced, five-page will and last testament witnessed by Bruno Goldapp at the bank and Carmel Davis of the Perkins law firm. Tom left everything to Evelyn and the children.

"As far as burying my father was concerned, we could have just dragged him off some place," Mike says. The family compromised by putting Tom in a plain pine casket.

Lica Elena wanted her father interred on the Santa Fe Ranch at some appropriate site with shade and no threat of floods or standing water. She selected a low rise, shaded by a large mesquite tree, in a cattle pasture a couple hundred yards from the main house. To gain access to Tom's grave, Mike had the ranch fence team build entrance and exit gates. Jack Walton, an Exxon executive, saw to it that caliche roadways leading to and from the new cemetery, as well as around it, were constructed in one day.

Six hundred and eighty-nine mourners signed the Santa Fe Ranch guest books that Monday afternoon. "It was like something out of *Giant*," the attorney Tom Wheat recalls.

Six vaqueros served as pallbearers, all dressed alike in new, tan brush jackets, white shirts, and jeans. A lariat was placed atop Tom's casket. His favorite horse, a line back dun gelding named Shanghai, stood near the grave, an empty saddle on his back. At the suggestion of Lica Elena and her sister Alice, the horse was attended by Ramiro Pérez.

Monsignor Paul Fee, a friend of the family, delivered the eulogy, which he titled, "Farewell, Dear Friend. We Love You."

"What can I say about him?" the priest asked the gathering. "He was a devoted husband and father, son and brother and grandfather. He loved his family with a passionate love, and with a tender heart.

"He loved his vaqueros. He not only knew them on a first-name basis, but he also knew and was interested in their families. He was always interested in what would do good, what would help. He was constructive, not destructive.

"Tom was not a church-going man, but he believed in God. He believed in an all-just God who would reward the good and punish the wicked. He had his own code of ethics. If he believed a thing was right, he did it and was willing for God to be his judge."

Jim Mayo remembers that, as the brief ceremony came to a close, Shanghai began to nicker and call, as a horse sometimes will when in search of a lost companion.

CHAPTER 14

The Perkins law firm was too closely associated with the East family's legal affairs to represent either side in the partition discussions. Mike and his family therefore selected Atlas & Hall, in McAllen, which had represented his father in the past.

At an Alice meeting of the principals in late December of 1984, Robert still wasn't giving an inch. When Morris Atlas, the managing partner at Atlas & Hall, suggested nothing be done until the holidays were past, he reluctantly agreed but only on the condition that Mike was not to work any East Brothers cattle in the interim, including the Santa Fe ranch, where Mike lived with his wife, the former Kathryn Hatmaker of Corpus Christi, and their two young sons, Thomas and Johnny.

Old Mama attended the meeting but did not take part. "I'm sorry about all this trouble," Mike told her.

"What trouble?" she asked with a blank look. It was as if Tom's death had stricken his mother into a withdrawal that would gradually deepen, stilling what had been a decisive voice in family affairs.

Mike, his mother, and his sisters next turned their attention to Jeannette Holloway, the family accountant.

The Texas-born Holloway came to Corpus Christi in the early 1950s and received her CPA degree there in 1955. In 1966, she formed a business partnership with fellow CPA Bill Dryden. Among their first clients were the Easts, both Tom and his family and Old Mama, together with Robert and Lica.

Just as the Perkins firm could not ethically represent both sides in the partition, Mike objected to the idea of having Jeannette Holloway in essence negotiating with herself. "I didn't want one person working for both entities in the partition and seeing who got what," he explains.

There were also specific issues with Holloway's approach to her work. A former client described her as disorganized and too eager to take charge. "To her credit," he says, "she won the trust and confidence of a lot of ranchers. But dealing with her was a very frustrating experience, because she liked to be in control. She wanted to manage your affairs for you to the point where she was actually more in control than you were."

Jim Mayo saw a lot of Jeannette Holloway's work product as president of the bank. He consequently counseled Mike East not to trust her with yet another important job, filing the family estate taxes in the wake of Tom's death.

"Mayo said she'd bankrupt us," Mike remembers.

In the end, Mike, Evelyn, Lica Elena, and Alice agreed to engage Alfonso J. Garza, a San Antonio CPA, as their accountant. Garza would also work with the Atlas & Hall tax lawyers on the family's estate tax filing. But even though Jeannette Holloway was no longer in their employ, she would forcefully insinuate herself into the intra-family legal struggles ahead.

Robert was very quick to engage—and then disengage—with his professional advisers, although rarely over questions of their competency. Often, he simply thought they were charging him too much.

He had already hired, fired, and rehired Jeannette Holloway, most recently in 1983. He kept her on through the partition negotiations and followed her advice to hire Hayden Wilson Head, Sr. of the Head & Kendrick firm in Corpus Christi, as his lawyer. Hayden Head was one of the most influential lawyers in Texas. He would also represent Robert, Lica, and Old Mama in the partition.

With the partition of the family lands now a fact, Morris Atlas delivered more unwelcome news to his clients.

"You know we're going to have a lot of problems with Robert," he told Mike.

"What do you mean, Morris?"

"Well," the lawyer explained, "only the two surviving East Brothers partners' names are on the bank signature card—Robert's and Lica's."

Tom's widow, Evelyn, and his family therefore had no access to his East Brothers partnership equity or to a share of the cattle business profits. So with the first Santa Fe payroll following Tom's death coming due at Christmas, Mike faced the unpleasant job of gathering the employees' unsigned checks from the ranch office in Hebbronville, then driving them out to the San Antonio Viejo for Robert's signature.

His uncle savored the situation.

"It was a stack of checks," Mike recalls. "Robert peeled one off and looked at and set it aside. Then he got another one and looked at it for a *long* time." Since it was Christmas, Santa Fe ranch bonus money had been added to the employee checks.

"'My God!' he said, 'I don't pay my people this much money!'"

"My check's in there too," Mike told him. "If you don't want to sign mine, don't. But with these other people, it's Christmas!

"Eventually, he signed them. But the larger problem was that the Santa Fe ranch's operating funds were depleted. There wasn't any way to pay the light bill or for gasoline or anything. We didn't have any personal money because my dad had spent it all setting up the two Kenedy ranches. He didn't leave us any. All the money was in the partnership."

There was also the matter of servicing Tom's loans. "The interest on them was in excess of $3,000 a day," he says. "The bank was annoyed at me."

Robert, who, like his sister, was worth about $10 million, offered to help with a loan to pay his late brother's estate taxes. Strapped as the family was, Mike declined. "You never could depend on Robert," he explains. "And even if he did follow through with it, there'd be strings attached for the rest of your life."

The fastest and surest way to raise money, then, was to sell cattle, so Mike headed for La Parra—which his father had deliberately kept outside

East Brothers control—with a cowboy crew. He spent about a month there, rounding up about a $1 million worth of stock, which he shipped to market, and wired the proceeds to Jim Mayo at the bank.

Next, he turned to the Santa Fe, which had not been worked for four or five years. The ranch was overgrazed and also low on water due to another punishing drought. The herds had to be culled before the animals started dying.

There was another complication, however. The Santa Fe was East Brothers property, which meant that Robert had a decisive say in anything Mike did there. He had already warned his nephew not to work cattle at the Santa Fe without notifying him. But if Mike asked his uncle's permission to work the cattle, Robert would take it as an invitation to come over and work alongside him, which guaranteed headaches of the sort only Robert could generate.

For example, in the days before helicopter herding, experienced cowhands usually required no more than two or three horses apiece from the remuda for a full day of working cattle. "Robert brought as many as he could, maybe 30," Mike recalls. "He spent most of his time switching horses, because he was training them. He'd cut some calves, then let them all back into the herd."

The young animals learned at once there was safety in the herd.

"Once you let the calves back in, they get really hard to cut. It turns into a real job. When I'm working cattle, I take it real easy, because if they ever get to fighting me, it takes forever. It's like trying to herd fish."

In Lica Elena's opinion, Robert didn't care if the calves stayed cut or not. "Really and truly, he was probably a better horseman than Daddy," she says. "His passion was for horses. Cattle working really was not his passion. He just did it because he had to."

"With Robert," says Mike, "if you'd get over a hundred head of cattle in the pen for him to work, it would just blow his mind, overwhelm him. It'd take him all day, working them this way and that way. Then he'd restart them.

"You'd just get frustrated. You could see what needed to be done. Then you'd see him fixin' to do something, and you'd think, *Hold on, Robert. Don't do that! We're going* to *be here until midnight!*"

Mike called A. J. Lindsey, the East Brothers livestock broker in San

Antonio. "I said, 'A. J., I need to work some cattle at the Santa Fe, but can you not tell Robert, because I'm not supposed to be working any cattle there?'"

Lindsey agreed to keep quiet as Mike generated another $600,000 or so in cattle sales, which he deposited in the East Brothers account at the Alice bank. However, Robert learned about it anyway because Jim Mayo telephoned him to ask if he wanted the money put into an interest-bearing account.

"When that happened," Mike remembers, "Robert complained to Hayden Head that I wasn't following the rules. He threw a fit. So Hayden told him, 'Don't sign the checks anymore.'"

Mike had temporized, hoping to find some way of derailing the partition process or at least deferring it long enough to get his father's estate settled. Once Robert shut off the cash flow, however, he had no choice but to come to the table. "But it also triggered something," he says, a strategy to deny his uncle the Julián pasture.

Robert had clearly prodded Hayden Head to push for a larger piece of the Santa Fe ranch than had been provided for under the East Brothers partnership agreement. In response, Head sent a letter to Morris Atlas, asserting that, since the Santa Fe was much better land than the San Antonio Viejo—it was worth twice as much, in his opinion—Robert and Lica deserved a larger share of it.

With this generous evaluation in mind, Mike departed by car from the Santa Fe for a meeting in Corpus Christi with the two of them, along with Morris Atlas and Gary Gurwitz, chief trial lawyer at the Atlas firm.

He made one stop along the way at the Exxon office in Kingsville to double check the area of the Santa Fe ranch's Mula pasture, which was brushier than the Julián, not as flat, and had fewer improvements. Mike had an old map that indicated that La Mula encompassed about 35,000 acres, which would more than satisfy the acreage due Robert and his sister in the partition, Robert's designs on the Julián notwithstanding.

Just to be certain, however, he consulted Pat Ketchum, the Exxon office head, who confirmed that La Mula did indeed encompass approximately 35,000 acres. That was the land he would offer Uncle Robert in the partition negotiations.

Mike's strategy pivoted on a provision in Tom's will. "I think my dad could see all of this coming," he says. "He put in his will that, if we couldn't work things out with Robert and we had to partition, we could sell, but if we did, we first had to offer the land and minerals, undivided, to Robert and Lica."

Mike was first into the meeting room. Then came Hayden Head. The attorney, a World War II fighter pilot, was rich and powerful, the father of a federal judge, and prominent enough in Corpus Christi civic circles to have a terminal at the international airport later named for him.

Mike found Head "intimidating."

"Hayden Head was a gnarly, hard-bitten guy who would tell you like it is," recalls Jimmy Nixon, Dr. Nixon's son and an oil and gas investor who was close to Robert in the 1980s and '90s. "But Hayden Head was honest. I had respect for Mr. Head, and he did for me too. Ultimately, when I made an oil and gas deal with Robert, I had to negotiate it with Hayden Head. He was looking after Robert's best interests, always."

Robert, Morris Atlas, and Gary Gurwitz followed Head into the conference room. Once they were seated, Mike opened the discussion with a question. "Look, why don't I just sell the whole ranch?" he asked.

Robert rose at once, grinning. "How much do you want for it?" he said.

Hayden Head scowled at his client. "Robert," he said, "if you're going to negotiate, I'm out of it. You're gonna have to get yourself another lawyer."

Robert sat down.

Then Head asked the same question. "How much do you want for it?"

"I want $80 million," Mike replied.

Head gaped in mock disbelief. "That's way, way too much money!" he said.

"You priced it already," Mike answered, and reminded the lawyer of his letter to Morris Atlas.

Robert and Head stepped out of the room to confer.

"Morris kind of snickered," Mike recalls. "'Well, they're thinking about it,' he said."

When the meeting reconvened, Mike gave the screw another turn. "I have the option to sell the ranch to somebody else," he said. "Clinton Manges."

Clinton Manges was a rogue operator who would eventually go to prison and die broke. But in 1985, he was at the zenith of his wealth and influence, so Robert and Hayden Head had to take what Mike told them seriously. Mike further informed his uncle and Head that if he sold to someone else, it would also be the whole ranch, undivided.

"Why don't you divide it and then sell?" the lawyer wondered.

"I don't want to do it that way," East replied. "That's why."

"It's easier if you divide."

"Well, I don't want to do it that way."

Robert and his lawyer rose and left the room once again.

Morris Atlas believed his client was serious. He asked if Mike really was willing to give up his home. Mike replied that he had to keep telling himself that he was ready to give it all up in order to be believable. For that purpose, the answer was yes.

Atlas asked, "Why don't you offer him something on the south end?"

"I might consider that," Mike answered.

When Robert and Head returned to the table, apparently convinced Mike was ready to sell all 90,000 acres of the Santa Fe that he and his family controlled to Clinton Manges, Mike casually offered Robert La Mula instead.

The bluff worked. "He jumped at it," Mike recollects. With La Mula, Robert received 5,000 acres more than he had coming, but the superior pasture, the 40,000-acre Julián, remained an intact part of the Santa Fe.

The final deal also included a provision that each party owned the cattle then on their respective ranches. That meant Mike could keep the $600,000 he'd raised from the sale of Santa Fe cattle.

He was reminded by the episode of something his father had told him. "He said it was normal and also okay for a family to fight, but once the fight was over, they had to remember they were family and all get back together and be family again.

"So two weeks after our fight, I took a gate key over to the Mula, where they were working, and gave it to them. I also said we were changing the locks, and when we did, I'd give them a new key."

Besides Robert, both Old Mama and Lica were working cattle too. Since La Mula lacked most improvements, Robert had built a large, box-shaped frame, covered with chicken wire, near the cowboy camp, where the three of them slept in separate compartments. The primitive structure looked like a poultry coop, which it later became and still is. The accommodation's single amenity was an outhouse Robert built for Old Mama.

"They all were glad to see me, and we talked as if nothing had ever happened," Mike recalls. "We were family again, and we had a good working relationship during that time."

One old practice that survived the partition unchanged was the use of the family's lazy diamond brand. Mike would continue to apply it to his animals' left hips as his father had, and Robert continued with the right side.

CHAPTER 15

I t's uncertain how Robert first came to consider establishing a foundation, although he often spoke admiringly of Elena Kenedy's estate trust,
established at her death in 1984. His aunt's trust supported Catholic
charities and gave Tom Jr. and Mike the preference for grazing rights on the
200,000 acres she inherited from her husband, Johnny. There was nothing
in her trust documents about wildlife, except that killing deer was prohibited
unless the herds required culling.

Jeannette Holloway took credit for first suggesting to Robert that he set
up a foundation as a wealth management or estate-planning strategy, con-
cepts with which he was unfamiliar. As Holloway later understated in Cause
732, *East v. East*, the vexed family legal quarrel that ensued, "He didn't understand all of the ramifications that have to happen with a private foundation."

The accountant said she first approached Robert, Lica, and Old Mama
with the idea in the mid-1980s when Robert was a client at the Head &
Kendrick law firm. They spoke of the foundation several times.

Hayden Head was part of the discussions. He addressed the subject in a
June 26, 1985, letter to Robert and Lica. "This is written to set out in writing
some of the ideas that we have discussed and that I have discussed with Mrs.
Holloway relative to a foundation that would be the ultimate beneficiary of
your respective wills.

"Upon the death of the last of the two of you to die, the property would vest in a foundation, which, from that time forward, would use the income for wildlife research and preservation and for medical research and health care in South Texas."

He closed, "As I told each of you together and separately, I consider my place to be to advise and recommend to you desirable courses to be followed in the management of your affairs. What you actually do is your decision, not mine, and I will be guided entirely by your wishes."

Holloway testified in *East v. East* that, when Robert resisted the foundation idea, she persisted too vigorously in urging it upon him. "He put it to Mr. Head strong enough that Hayden called me and told me that if I didn't leave Robert alone about the foundation, he was going to fire me," she said.

"Robert liked Jeannette Holloway because he liked her legs," Tom Wheat recalls. "He used to tell me, 'Mr. Wheat, you know, that Jeannette Holloway was a handsome woman in her day. . . . You ever see her legs? Handsome woman. Smart too.'"

The accountant faulted herself for not properly explaining to Robert how foundations work. "At one point, I think Robert and Lica would have liked to have had the foundation," she testified. "They wanted Mike to run it, but also [for him] to graze cattle and stuff on it, and Mike couldn't do both. The law wouldn't allow it, regardless of what Robert's desires might be."

Another of Robert's conditions for considering a foundation, said Holloway, was that it not go into operation in his lifetime.

"Because he did not want to lose control over that property?" Robert's attorney asked her.

"I don't know," Holloway answered. "He just didn't like it."

"As far as ranching is concerned, he doesn't want to take orders from somebody else. And there's no doubt about that . . . is there?"

"Well, he took orders for years."

"From whom?"

"His mother."

In July of 1987, the Head & Kendrick law firm imploded as Head's partner, Mike Kendrick Jr. succumbed to cancer on the 13th, and Head himself was killed 11 days later when he crashed his twin-engine Cessna 421 into a hangar at his ranch near Crystal City, in Zavala County.

Hayden Head, with his gruff, take-charge demeanor, had become an authority figure to Robert, a sort of surrogate father, someone he trusted. His death deprived East of yet another anchor. "When Head died, Robert started calling immediately," says Tom Wheat. "He was kind of a lost child. He didn't know what to do."

With the law firm now leaderless, much of the Head & Kendrick professional staff removed themselves across town to the Kleberg, Dyer, Redford, & Weil law firm, which restyled itself Kleberg & Head.

One of those refugees was Paul Cooper Pearson III, then 40. Pearson held a bachelor's degree in history and political science from Duke University. He earned his law degree at the University of Texas at Austin in 1972. A Corpus Christi native, he first joined the law firm of Wood, Boykin, & Walter in his hometown, then came to Head & Kendrick in 1979.

Pearson did legal work for Robert from as early as 1987 and brought East's business along with him to Kleberg & Head, where he'd rise to become managing director and chairman of the board.

"Pearson picked up the mantle," Wheat explains. "It got to where Robert called Paul Pearson every morning at seven o'clock. Paul would help him on whatever issues he was facing. Many times, he'd go down to that little ranch office in Hebbronville and meet with him."

Pearson's relationship with Robert was in some measure pastoral, as was true with all the lawyer's clients, says Wheat. He treated investors like members of his flock.

"One of Paul's strengths was that he could sit down one-on-one and just talk to you," he explains. "He was engaging. You *liked* to talk to Paul. He'd look you straight in the eye and listen intently. He would just say the right things to bring out whatever your issue was and make you feel good that there was an answer to it."

Just as important, according to Wheat, Pearson delivered. "He'd advise his clients, set up their vehicles under estate plans and stuff, and then help them place their investments. He always made money, so nobody was ever mad at him or fussed at him. If they'd ever lost money, that all would have turned and broken the deal up, but it never happened. He *always* made great investments."

Charlie Hury, formerly of the Atlas law firm, describes Paul Pearson in an unpublished manuscript as "a bespectacled little man that was the physical epitome of the business and tax lawyer he was." Hury remembers Pearson once telling him that "he felt his mission was to protect Robert from himself," in part because of "Robert's well-known proclivity for changing his mind."

Hury, who takes a jaundiced view of his profession and most of its practitioners, believes the lawyer had more in his heart than charity. "Pearson," he writes, "had long since recognized a golden opportunity to 'guide' this poor rich man.

"At least, it was to Pearson's advantage to see it that way. After all, this essentially rudderless old man was sitting on top of somewhere probably between $500 and $750 million in assets."

Lance Brunn, one of Pearson's colleagues at the Kleberg law firm, once offered his own recollection to a roomful of attorneys, "Pearson," Brunn remembered, "always said Robert's case was going to be his retirement."

CHAPTER 16

All told, Robert East ran about 9,000 head of cattle on close to a quarter-million acres of ranchland.

He operated according to long-established custom, as his brother Tom had, eschewing most modern innovations, including the use of helicopters for roundups. But as Texas cattle ranches and herds grew, spreading ever more widely, the old ways did not serve as they once did. It was much more difficult to round up the animals. More of them escaped into the brush and grew wilder and wilder as time went on.

"My recollection was that his vision, so to speak, was that he wanted the ranch to stay like it was," says Richard "Tres" Kleberg III, Robert's cousin. "In other words, if you knew what his ranch was like, it was a throwback. That's who Robert was. He did things the old way, the East way.

"Back in those days, if you had a lot of money, you moneyed up. I mean, you built, you know, kind of a monument to yourself.

"They didn't throw money at anything. They just used money to do what they had to do. Those guys operated kind of on a bare-bones type of thing, Robert more especially.

"The point being was that he wanted it to stay like it was. It's almost like creating a conservation easement or conservation type of environment."

One of Robert's fellow ranchers, willing to speak on condition of anonymity, says, "On multiple occasions, I went to his ranches, and I realized he had such a vast amount of land that he was probably not capable of ranching it with responsible range stewardship. I saw wild cows that were barren and should have been shipped, but they were too wild for them to catch. On occasion, I saw cattle that were very weak due to drought and no grass due to overgrazing, and I saw herds of nilgai at El Sauz pasture that were so heavy that they were greatly reducing the cattle stocking capacity. But it did not appear that any stocking rate adjustment had ever been made."

Helenita Groves remembers, "Robert once took me to a sort of clearing in the mesquite brush that was full of prickly pear cactus. It must have been eight feet tall. And he had these *huge* steers out there. They must have weighed 2,500 pounds or more."

Appearances meant little to Robert. Many of his ranch improvements, including buildings and fences, gates, roadways, water lots, traps, and other installations, were poorly maintained, if at all, with whatever materials were at hand or cheaply acquired. His ranches were littered with snarls of rusted wire and pipe and miscellaneous debris, each marking yet another project in which Robert had lost interest before it was finished.

His ranch vehicles were mostly old and battered from years of hard use. When tires wore out, he shopped the used-tire racks or bought recaps. He wouldn't buy trucks with air-conditioning or electric windows, believing them expensive and frivolous luxuries that softened the vaqueros and undercut their willingness to work.

By contrast, Old Mama and Lica diligently kept several of the main barns and workers' residences in good repair, repainting many of the structures annually. Lica also worked to keep up La Perla, her parents' first house.

Robert and Lica both cared deeply about their ranches' wild inhabitants and visitors, particularly their white-tailed deer, regionally famous for their prodigious bulk, as well as other game animals such as quail, wild turkeys, and javelinas, which Robert claimed were better tasting than pork. Brother and sister also doted on their dogs and horses and the many domestic and wild creatures Lica fed and cared for around the main house.

Jimmy Nixon remembers that, unlike most South Texas ranchers, Robert and Lica did not welcome oil and gas exploration on their land. "They loved that ranch," he says, "and they loved the game animals, not to hunt, but just for their beauty. Robert loved to see giant deer, huge bucks that were more like pets. So they didn't like hunters, and they didn't like oil field people driving all over their ranch. They were private, and they liked it that way."

About the only wild animals Robert disdained were coyotes, which he'd shoot at any opportunity, and nilgai antelopes, originally imported by the King Ranch from India. The nilgai competed with his stock for grass and, he claimed, were a menace to his fences. Like all Texas ranchers and farmers, he'd shoot any feral hog on sight.

Lica owned two huge macaws she kept caged near the backyard pens where she fed her deer. Alice East recalls that one of them, a vibrant blue, was given to her by a game warden. The other was multicolored and spoke a little Spanish.

According to Jimmy Nixon, this bird had escaped from fellow rancher Rafael de la Garza's place and relocated to the San Antonio Viejo, where de la Garza permitted it to remain. The animal was known to bite and could break a finger with its powerful beak.

Geese and ducks and chickens wandered where they liked. A herd of noisy peacocks, reportedly descended from an original pair that Tom Sr. and Alice had received as a wedding present, strutted around. The beautiful birds also served a practical purpose; peacocks will attack snakes, even poisonous ones, and peck them to death.

Robert raised sheep, as well as goats, just as his father had; they were a ranch tradition for decades. The goats were often given away as presents to friends, employees, and business acquaintances.

Goat herders came and went at the San Antonio Viejo. One who lives in memory was the strange and dissolute Jesús Sifuentes, called *Sereno* or *Nieblo,* Spanish for fog, who took up his post in the mid-1990s.

Sifuentes resided with 200 or more goats at Casa Verde, an old ranch structure about 20 miles from the headquarters compound, for which the pasture was named. The two-story house once served as a school and also accommodations for Holy Cross fathers who came down from St. Edward's Academy in Austin each year to hunt deer. By Sifuentes's time, Casa Verde was barely habitable, devoid of amenities save for gaslight fueled by a propane tank. To contentedly live alone with a herd of goats and a few chickens on a remote prairie takes a special mindset. Sereno was no exception.

He kept a rooster in the house as a companion. He rode shank's mare everywhere with the exception of a roadside cantina, to which he regularly pedaled an old bicycle and rarely, if ever, returned sober. The earth around his camp was torn up with telltale peyote excavations. After Sifuentes's death, syringes were discovered scattered around his attic. The goat herder subsisted in the main on regular deliveries of beans, eggs, and Vienna sausage, as well as Budweiser or Corona beer he consumed from quart bottles known as *caguamas*.

According to Ramiro Palacios, whose father, Martín, was the ranch's chief mechanic, when the goat herder overserved himself, he'd sometimes pull out his .22 rifle to play Russian roulette with the goats. Palacios says Sifuentes's favorite partner in the game was a large goat he called Pancho Villa. He remembers one time discovering Sereno passed out drunk in his yard. A comatose Pancho Villa lay nearby on his back, also sleeping it off.

Eventually, cowhands Ignacio Rocha and Miguel Rodriguez discovered Sifuentes lying in a pool of blood on his kitchen floor. He was two days dead from a .22 rifle shot to his face from close range. His rifle lay close by. According to the police report, investigators found bloody rooster tracks on the floor surrounding his body.

The goat herder hadn't finally lost at Russian roulette, but the exact circumstances of Sereno's death are unclear. The police called it a suicide. It has been pointed out, however, that Casa Verde stood—or leaned—adjacent to a smuggling route where it crossed into the ranch from a highway. Sereno may have had knowledge of the traffic in illicit drugs that cost him his life.

The herder had two sisters who lived locally. He helped in their support. After his death, they came to Casa Verde to collect his meager possessions. Robert paid for their transportation back to the family's village in Mexico.

There no longer is a goat herder on the San Antonio Viejo, nor any sheep, exotic birdlife, or any of the diverse pets that made the ranch feel as much like a game park as it did a cattle operation. But the huge deer have so far persevered.

"Deer 10 or 12 miles deep on the Sant Antonio Viejo have never been shot at," says Nixon. "Those deer had no fear of man. You could almost drive right up to them, and they wouldn't run off."

They were Robert's pride, and likely grew so large because of his strict control over who got to hunt the giant bucks and how often. Robert bragged at times that he charged hunters thousands of dollars *per shot* for the privilege of pursuing trophy kills on the San Antonio Viejo. It was too bad if they missed. He'd laugh that most of his customers were too trigger-happy to wait for a chance at a really big animal, contenting themselves instead with something less impressive for the den wall.

Aída Garza, who was hired in 1987 to help Lica manage the ranch's business records, recalls that Robert operated his hunting business out of his back pocket. All payments were in cash, she says, and the money was stashed away in a locked safe he kept in the main house.

It was characteristic of Robert to treat his white-tails and other ranch game animals, such as quail or wild turkeys, this way. Grazing rights at the time ran about $3 an acre. The same acreage leased for about 10 times as much for deer hunting. But Robert could never treat his deer as just another asset, like oil and gas or even cattle. When he talked to Mike about how he wanted the ranch operated after he was gone, Robert told his nephew to let hunters take a white-tail every now and again but only to cover the cost of corn for the deer and other wild creatures.

Among those who envied Robert his giant deer and hoped to nurture even bigger ones themselves was oral surgeon Gary Schwarz. A Texas native, Dr. Schwarz was not much enamored of dentistry. He saw the profession as a way to help finance his real ambition, producing giant deer by feeding them a proprietary growth-enhancing diet he had developed.

Dr. Schwarz needed land to pursue his dream. It happened that the Guerra family, relatives of Don Manuel Guerra, who had sold the San Antonio Viejo to Robert's father, Tom East, Sr., 70 years earlier, owned the San Ramón Ranch, adjacent to the modern San Antonio Viejo. Serendipitously, the Guerras had just then put a 1,000-acre parcel of the ranch on the market at $700 an acre.

Dr. Schwarz was inspired. He formed a seven-member partnership to acquire the land, which he would call Tecomate South, and went to work experimenting with deer diets.

But his program showed scant early success toward bigger and better bucks. One of his disappointed partners was led to agitate for opening Tecomate South to hunters anyway. Schwarz counseled patience.

To illustrate his point, he recalls, he ill-advisedly took his partner on a bicycle ride deep into the San Antonio Viejo, bringing along a video camera to capture examples of the plus-sized specimens Schwarz believed they'd be raising as soon as he had the nutrition angle worked out. "I wanted to show my guy what we could have if we stayed disciplined," he explains.

Deer hunters bang antlers together to attract bucks in a technique called "rattling." Dr. Schwarz says that he and his partner rattled up "a bunch of big deer" on the ranch and captured them on video. But they also drew the attention of two game wardens and their tracker, who arrested them, disarmed and handcuffed them, and then drove the two to the San Antonio Viejo cow camp, where Robert awaited.

Remarkably calm, even hospitable, as Schwarz remembers him, Robert invited the intruders to take some lunch while he conferred with the wardens. Then East sat down across the table from the arrestees with his own meal.

"You're from Tecomate?" he asked Schwarz.

"Yessir."

"I heard you were good people."

"We are," said Schwarz.

"Then why are you on my ranch?"

Dr. Schwarz told Robert all about his plans for raising big deer and how he'd sneaked onto the ranch to show his partner what a really big deer looked like. The camera was necessary to confirm what they saw.

"Why didn't you just ask me?" Robert wondered.

"Because I was stupid," Schwarz answered. "I was just stupid, Robert. I'm so sorry."

The two suspects were also carrying rifles that day, strongly suggesting to the wardens that they might have had poaching in mind, as well. But when Schwarz and his partner were interrogated separately, their stories matched, persuading Robert, the game wardens, and a justice of the peace in Hebbronville that they were telling the truth. So the two were allowed to plead no contest and were put on probation.

The blot on Dr. Schwarz's good name was eventually erased. "If you're good," he says, "the thing goes away."

Lica East raised orphan fawns that she fed milk from nippled bottles. The animals grew so tame that they dawdled around the ranch house with no fear of humans. From time to time, she'd foster young raccoons and, on at least one occasion, a pronghorn. Lica even nursed a coyote pup until it bit her.

Brother and sister both kept lots of dogs. She was known for the dozen or so French fox terriers she kenneled near the house, just as her mother and father had once kept hunting dogs at the King Ranch. Robert's tastes were less refined. Jimmy Nixon remembers a very friendly, light-colored, short-haired mutt named Crisco who had some cow dog in him. There was also Rock, a huge, ill-tempered canine, who once approached Nixon from behind as he was talking to Robert and bit him hard in the buttocks.

Rock died about a week later, probably from eating a highly poisonous *Bufo marinus*, or cane toad, common in the Rio Grande Valley and the largest toad in the world. Some grow as wide as dinner plates. Still another of Robert's dogs, a German shepherd named Baron, likely died in the same way, says Nixon.

Lica was the least self-assertive of any East, but her love for her fox terriers emboldened her one day to call Jim Mayo at the Alice bank.

"I need to ask you something," she told him.

"Sure Lica," Mayo answered.

"You know them cards you can use where if you buy something you can pay for it later, and they send you a bill?"

"You're talking about credit cards."

"Yeah. I suppose that's what it is. Do you think you could get me one? I don't want Robert to know about it."

Robert and Lica had no credit, because they never borrowed any money. However, Mayo told her that he was quite sure he could get her a card.

"I don't want Robert to find out about this," she told him, "because he'll *really* get upset with me. I've found a really nice dog, but it's *very* expensive. And if Robert finds out how much I'm going to pay for the dog, he *really* will blow up."

"That's fine, Lica," Mayo replied. "I can get the card, and you tell me where you want me to mail it, and you can pay for the dog with the card."

Relief was evident in her voice. "I'm going to tell you what I'm paying for this dog," she said, "but don't you *ever* tell anybody. I'm paying $450."

CHAPTER 17

Harvey Weil, a titan of Texas law who spent his entire career at the Kleberg law firm, was still practicing there at the time Paul Pearson arrived with his new client, Robert East. In the early 1950s, Weil had created a foundation for Texans Bessie and Rob Welder, who owned a 7,800-acre cattle ranch northwest of Corpus Christi on the Aransas River, not far from Sinton. Weil's foundation was considered a model for what, in Texas, was then a novel approach to estate planning.

As Tom Wheat, Weil's onetime junior colleague at Kleberg & Head puts it, the lawyer's innovations enabled the Welders "to keep the ranch together and to keep the ideals that they put in place as to the purpose and mission of the foundation. It's done every bit of that and more. Harvey was an incredible lawyer."

A concern for anyone who would establish a family foundation is to ensure that control of it will remain within the family and would not be passed on to strangers with their own—possibly incompatible—agendas. Helenita Groves urged her cousin to beware of this common issue.

"I said, 'Robert, you may have all confidence in the people you choose to be on the board of that thing. But you know, we're not going to be here forever. And if you don't have family on it, it can be changed and turned to something that you really don't want.'

"I said, 'It's happened to the Rockefellers, and it's happened to the

Carnegies, and [the] Fords, and all these big foundations. If you don't have family on there—and *insist* there'll always be family members on that foundation—then you don't know who the people are who are going to be chosen to be on there. They're going to do whatever they want.'"

Harvey Weil's legal structure fostered active Welder family participation in the foundation's management. Seventy years later, Bessie and Rob's descendants still remain among their foundation's directors.

"I think Pearson was clearly following their example," says Wheat, who worked closely with Paul Pearson at the Kleberg firm during this period. Wheat has no doubt that, although Jeannette Holloway may have first suggested a foundation to Robert, it was Paul Pearson who, in fact, persuaded him to move ahead and unknowingly dismantle the only world he'd ever known.

In the near term, however, the lawyer would sometimes get too far over his skis, as he did on an uninvited visit to the ranch in 1990.

Pearson brought with him two documents for Robert and Lica to approve and sign.

One was a draft letter to the IRS, dated March 30, 1990, outlining a pair of prospective estate-planning measures. The first was to leave the 35,000-acre La Mula pasture at the Santa Fe Ranch to Mike East and his sisters, Alice and Lica Elena. The second was a cash bequest in an unspecified amount to Mike, Alice, and Lica Elena. The letter requested the IRS provide an advance estate tax ruling on these proposals. It included a signature line for Pearson, which was blank. Lica signed both of the document's last two pages, but a line had subsequently been drawn through her signatures.

The second document Pearson brought with him was a draft will for Robert, which provided for the establishment of a wildlife foundation at Robert's demise.

In a separate letter, Pearson discussed the plan to leave La Mula pasture to Mike, Lica Elena, and Alice. "This should provide Tom's children with a significant benefit from your estate," he wrote, "and should enable them to lease the balance of the land from the foundation from the trustees if they deem that to be appropriate."

Five years later, during the *East v. East* litigation, Robert would discuss Pearson's visit under oath with lawyer Charlie Hury, who was taking his deposition. Hury showed Robert the two documents.

"It's an estate plan, right?" the lawyer asked. "And in the plan, there is a foundation set up, a wildlife foundation. [It also] basically says they get the Mula after you die. It gives you an interest in it until you die. I don't know if it ever was sent in. It's not signed."

"Well," Robert asked, "was I getting one of these letters?" He seemed unclear about the transaction.

"I don't know," Hury replied. "Did you?"

"Huh?"

"I don't know if you did or did not. I'm just trying to find out what you know about it."

"They sent these papers," Robert answered. "I believe we were in the pasture, and [they asked] for me to sign. And I told Lica—I think they maybe had seen Lica first, and I think the way it was that Lica signed those papers, and she told me, 'Are you going to sign these papers?' and I said, 'No.' She says, 'Well, I'm not going to sign them either,' and she drew a line through it."

Hury marked the two documents into evidence.

"Your proposed draft will is what you did not want to sign. Is that right?" he asked East.

"I don't know, just exactly," said Robert. "But I didn't sign it."

"Then when you told Lica that you were not going to sign it, she scratched out her name on the thing that she had signed?"

"That's right."

"Okay. Did you and Lica discuss why you were not going to sign it?"

"Well, I was gathering cattle, working, and she was there too, and I didn't want to sign any papers too quickly."

Hury asked if Robert ever read the papers that Pearson brought.

"No. I sent it back."

Why?

"Well, I wanted to put more thought in it, I guess."

"Okay. And you did put more thought into it?"

"I didn't think it had to be done that quick. We had already made up our minds what we were going to do."

"And what was that?"

"We were going to make a foundation in wildlife."

If so, Hury asked, why did Robert send back the paper unsigned?

"I didn't sign the papers because I was upset because somebody was chasing me out there in the pasture. And I wanted complete control of everything while I was alive and Lica was alive."

Hury asked if Robert ever determined whether or not Pearson's documents conferred that authority.

"I don't know if they give me complete control or didn't give me complete control. But I was upset because the man was looking for me in the car, and I was busy working."

"Okay. That then was the main reason you didn't sign?"

"That's right."

Aída Garza, then the ranch bookkeeper, remembers receiving a telephone call from Lica, asking if she had received and paid an invoice from Kleberg & Head for the work Paul Pearson had done on the rejected documents. Garza replied that the bill had arrived but that she hadn't paid it as yet. Lica told her to ignore it, and she did.

Soon thereafter, Robert fired Paul Pearson. Aída Garza, in a sworn statement, said she believed Pearson was rehired and refired again at least three or four times, according to Robert's usual pattern.

CHAPTER 18

With Tom's death and Old Mama's mental decline, Robert was more dependent than ever on his sister Lica, by all accounts his single trusted confidant. "She was both his anchor and his moral compass," writes Charlie Hury. "When either of the siblings spoke, it was with one voice."

Then came the appalling news that Lica would soon be lost as well. Even before Tom's death eight years earlier, she had been diagnosed with breast cancer. Lica underwent a mastectomy, received radiation treatments under an oncologist's care, and recovered. But it was anyone's guess if and how or when the cancer would return.

In the autumn of 1992, she developed severe headaches after helping fight a grassfire on the ranch. Lica blamed the pain on smoke inhalation. But the MRI (magnetic resonance imaging) Dr. Nixon ordered revealed that her cancer had returned and metastasized to her brain and lungs. Her prognosis was very poor. Lica would fight the disease, but her mind was on Robert, who was about to face challenges for which his sister knew he was ill prepared.

Robert and Lica now revisited their 1985 decision to leave their estates to one another. According to what Lica told a family gathering, she and Robert had reached an informal agreement on a tentative solution.

On January 9, 1993, Old Mama's 100th birthday, Lica hosted a modest family celebration. She called her sister-in-law, Evelyn East, and Evelyn's two daughters, Alice and Lica Elena, as well as other members of the family, to come speak with her privately in her bedroom. Business kept Mike away that day.

The participants later memorialized the substance of their discussions with Lica in a sworn exhibit in Cause 732, which identified her by her given name, Alice Hattie East. According to the document, once she'd gathered them in her bedroom, "Alice H. East closed all the doors and stated that she had a lot of things to talk about and tell them about. For the next couple of hours, Alice H. talked about the long history of their family and the unfortunate lack of closeness between Robert and his brother, Tom.

"Robert came into the room once during this conversation, and Alice H. required him to leave before she could continue. Alice H. stated that there were some specific properties that she and Robert both wanted Tom's children to have."

These included La Mula pasture at the Santa Fe Ranch, as well as the Buena Vista Ranch, for Mike. Lica then turned to two more ranches that she and Robert had purchased together after Tom's death. One was the 19,000-acre Lytton Ranch, a part of Sarita Kenedy East's old San Pablo Ranch, which Lica said was to go to Mike's sister, Alice East. The other was the 17,000-acre Santa Rosa Ranch in Kenedy County, which was earmarked for his other sister, Lica Elena, now married to cattleman John Pinkston.

"She wanted to make sure there was enough money available to pay the taxes on the property," the document continued, "but that they [Lica and Robert] were unsure what to do with the rest of the property."

Lica subsequently summoned her nephew Mike to the San Antonio Viejo to personally convey the same information. "When I went out there," he recalls, "my Aunt Lica first showed me the heirlooms, especially stuff that was dated from the 1800s, silver and china.

"We were sitting in the dining room. They had a glass-front cabinet with three doors. It was kind of oval shaped. They had their plates, their china. They had napkin holders. She'd get things out. They had dates on them from the 1800s. She was showing me all this stuff. I guess in her own way she was saying, 'This is here.'"

Rubén Garza, then a young border patrol officer who had spent much of his life on the ranch, says Lica meant for Mike, Lica Elena, and Alice to inherit all the family heirlooms in the house, including guns and jewelry. He recalls that Lica put him to work inventorying all the items in the house that she wished for her nephew and nieces to receive.

"Robert didn't care anything about that stuff," Mike says. "But she did. Then she said, 'I want you to have the Mula and Buena Vista. We want Alice to have the Lytton. And we want Lica Elena to have the Santa Rosa.'

"But she also said, 'In the end, I have no idea what Robert will wind up doing. We've talked about it. But you know how Robert is. But I am going to make sure you get the Mula back.'"

Mike remembers his aunt added that if a foundation was to be established, the model she and Robert both admired was Aunt Elena Kenedy's trust arrangement, under which her ranch remained a family cattle operation, with a preference for Tom and Mike to lease the grazing rights already in place.

Lica told Mike that she and Robert wanted some portion of the ranching profits from any foundation to go toward cancer research, what Hayden Head had referred to as "medical research and health care in South Texas," in his 1985 letter to Robert and Lica.

Also like Aunt Elena's trust setup, game hunting—particularly commercial game hunting—was to be strictly prohibited. It was her single definitive statement on the foundation. She made no mention of a game preserve.

Had brother and sister revised their wills to formally document these estate decisions, including creation of a foundation as Lica described it— or if Lica had outlived Robert—harmony might have prevailed. But they didn't, and she wouldn't, and although Robert later said he still wished for his nephew and nieces to inherit the ranches, he wanted to bequeath them via his will. As far as ever has been disclosed, however, he never had the appropriate papers drawn up.

CHAPTER 19

At approximately three o'clock Saturday morning, February 16, 1993, just five weeks after Old Mama's centennial birthday, Lica called from her bedroom, waking Robert. When he reached her, as he remembered, "She just put her arms around me and grabbed me."

Lica was suffering a fatal heart attack.

Robert immediately telephoned Mike.

"Lica's sick!" he said. "I'm taking her to the hospital!"

"I'll meet you there," Mike said.

Robert was panic stricken but sufficiently composed to telephone Aída Garza in Hebbronville to instruct her to send an ambulance to the ranch's main gate, where he'd bring Lica for the EMTs to transport to the hospital. Aída remembers that Robert continued to call her again and again at brief intervals until sunup.

Elda Molina, widow of the main gate guard, José Molina, had been helping Lica with Old Mama since her cancer returned. Now Señora Molina brought Lica from the house and placed her in the back seat of Robert's car, where she held Lica in her arms.

He tore at 60 miles an hour along the eight-mile ranch road to the main gate, watchful as they sped over the blacktop for white-tails wandering around in the night.

In the wild ride's confused aftermath, Robert would remember the ambulance waiting for them at the highway but nothing of the trip to the hospital, whether he drove or rode in the ambulance with Lica or anything about Elda or her husband, José, who followed them to the hospital in his pickup.

His first clear recollection was of the hospital, where he recalled looking on as Lica's body was wheeled into the emergency room. A nurse checked his sister's life signs. "*Oh,*" the woman said, *"esa mujer ya tiene como veinte minutos, estaba muerta ya cuando vino."* "This lady has been dead for more than 20 minutes."

Robert lacked words to express his anguish. "I didn't know what to do," he later said. "And they told me I could not move her."

Dr. Antonio Falcón was summoned to the ER by a nurse. "Her message was simple," Falcón recalls. "She said that Mr. Robert East was there. 'He's brought his sister in. She's dead. You need to come pronounce.'"

When he arrived at the emergency room, it was immediately evident to Falcón that 72-year-old Lica East had been dead for quite some time, probably before she had reached the ranch gate.

Dr. Falcón turned to Robert. "I went outside and offered my condolences to him," he says. "What I remember very clearly is that I offered to call the funeral home of his choice, and he got very, very upset at me. He wanted us to take his sister and put her in the back of his car. He was going to drive her back to the ranch and bury her. It just really caught me by surprise.

"He was not a little bit upset. He was *really* pissed off. I think he was very angry that he couldn't just get his sister and leave. I don't think he wanted anything to do with anybody there."

Dr. Falcón then thought to contact his brother, Starr County sheriff Eugenio "Gene" Falcón Jr., with whom Robert was acquainted. Perhaps Gene could settle down the poor man.

"It must have been two or three o'clock in the morning," the doctor remembers. "I said, 'You need to get over here. Roberto is here, and he's demanding that we take the body and put it in the back of the car. He's going to take her to the ranch.'"

Dr. Falcón was surprised to learn from his brother that Robert was fully within his rights to do just that.

"'That may be the law,' I said. 'But c'mon Gene! This guy's going to take his sister and go dig a hole in the sand and dump her in there. I think we should try to do something more decent for the lady.'

"So Gene came and talked to him. Took him outside and talked to him for a long time. He also was having problems with Roberto. That's when Gene called Mike."

The confrontation over Lica's body stretched past dawn, moving back and forth between the parking lot and the emergency room. Mike East remembers he was already underway to the hospital when the sheriff reached him on his cell. "He said I better get there, because they were having trouble with my uncle. I got there as quickly as I could. My uncle was very distraught. He wanted to take Lica home.

"I said, 'Robert, you can't take Lica home. We have to make other arrangements for her. She has to go to a funeral home.'"

As Robert later told the story, at that moment, he was reminded how Lica once told him that, in any emergency, he should call his old friend Marty West. Marty would know what to do.

So he called West, from a banking family in Kingsville, who was close to both Robert and Lica. West told Robert that he needed to put Lica in the care of a funeral home. Marty offered to contact a mortician friend for advice on the matter. Robert gratefully accepted and then reluctantly agreed to return to the ranch with Mike. Dr. Falcón recalls that he was still upset when he finally left.

Once West saw to the mortuary preliminaries, he drove to the ranch, where he found Robert "grief struck," he says, "pale and quiet. He felt that vacuum happening, I'm sure. Like the wind had been sucked out of him."

It fell to Robert to inform his mother of her daughter's death, which he did, but Old Mama may not have understood him. For years thereafter, Alice would call mournfully from her bed at night for the missing Lica.

CHAPTER 20

Days before her death, Lica had arranged to remove her father's remains from Kingsville to the San Antonio Viejo for reburial. She did not expect to live to see his reinterment. Marty West completed her work. After helping Mike manage the burial details, including headstones, West saw to it that the senior Tom East was properly exhumed and returned home to rest next to his daughter.

They would be the cemetery's first interments. Lica had chosen a grassy area near the main house for it, shaded by a tall mesquite tree and several palms and enclosed by a nondescript pipe fence painted white. It was the kind of structure Robert would build.

She left instructions that her death notice in the *Kingsville Record* should advise mourners that "memorials may be made to the Cancer Therapy and Research Center at the South Texas Medical Center in San Antonio."

Mike East stayed close to his grieving uncle over the coming days, crying with Robert on one occasion. They frequently walked together the short distance from the house to the new burial plot, sharing old memories, thinking of Lica. Robert ordered that her room be preserved as she left it and that a memorial candle burn there.

Mike recalls that, on the day of Lica's funeral, as he and Robert stood together at Lica's graveside, his uncle first told him of his and Lica's decision to leave La Mula and the three ranches to him and his sisters. "Robert told me in the exact same words that Aunt Lica told me," Mike says. He made no mention to his nephew of a foundation or wildlife preserve. Otherwise, Robert's hopes for the future of the ranch tracked exactly with what Lica had briefly described to Mike just weeks before.

"Robert, that's fine," Mike told him. "We don't have to talk about this now. If you want to talk about it later, that's fine."

After firing Paul Pearson back in 1990, Robert had hired Ronald P. Stasny of Beeville as his new lawyer, then switched to John G. "Buster" Adami, Jr, from a ranching family in Freer, Texas. In 1989, Adami had worked with Pearson and Tom Wheat to successfully defend Robert and Jeannette Holloway on fraud and related charges brought against them by ranchers Peter and Jane Weakly, who claimed East had reneged on a land deal.

Adami had been a star linebacker at Texas A&M for three years, including 1967, when the Aggies won the Southwest Conference football championship. After losing their first four games that season, the team won six straight, including a 10–7 victory over their archrival Texas Longhorns, then defeated eighth-ranked Alabama in the Cotton Bowl. It is a hallowed memory in Aggie sports history.

Adami graduated from Baylor Law School. In 1973, he joined the Perkins law firm, where he was generally regarded as a bright newcomer with a promising future. His mentor at the firm was Kenneth Oden. "Ken was as good as they come," says Tom Wheat. "And he learned from Jake Floyd, who also was as good as they come."

Two years later, Adami persuaded his A&M roommate, Jim Mayo, to leave a banking job in Laredo to become senior vice president at the Alice National Bank, where Mayo was named president in 1979.

Mike East knew Buster Adami from the early 1980s, when the lawyer sometimes drove out to La Parra, the Kenedy ranch, to see Mike's father on legal business. His first direct professional contact with Adami came a few weeks after Tom Jr.'s death.

Adami, who represented the Frost Bank, which administered Elena Kenedy's trust, had drawn up a lease document that Mike came by the law firm to review and sign. The lawyer later negotiated some ranch leases for Mike. Over time, the two became good friends.

Mike and Buster spoke together briefly at Lica's funeral. "I got Buster aside and told him what Robert had told me," Mike remembers. "I said, 'I don't care what Robert does. It's his business. But he told me that he would give me the Mula and the Bueno Vista. He's giving me twice as much as my sisters would get.'

"And I said, 'It might cause problems. If he does anything, whether it's 3 acres or 300 acres or 3,000 or 300,000, it would be better if it was given out equally or undivided.'"

Adami nodded his understanding, then told Mike that Robert had also told the lawyer of his and Lica's plans for the four properties. Whether the inheritance would be divided or undivided had not been settled, Adami said.

Buster Adami represented Robert's interests in the probate of his sister's will. She left him her entire estate as they had agreed, so now it was up to Robert to carry out their mutual intentions toward Mike, Alice, and Lica Elena. But as Lica had told Mike, "You know how Robert is." There was no guarantee that he'd honor their agreement.

With her death, Robert assumed some of Lica's roles at the ranch. These included check writing. Robert immediately complained of how expensive everything was, including Old Mama's care, which had grown more costly when she was put on a feeding tube, requiring more skilled—and consequently more expensive—nurses. Robert's answer to the problem was to assign Ramón Rocha, a young vaquero, to Old Mama's nursing team. Rocha's duties included bathing her. At the same time, Aída Garza, the bookkeeper, was busy dissuading Robert from taking Old Mama with him to work cattle at La Mula, where he planned for them to stay together in the cage as they had for more than a decade.

After Rocha explained to Mike that taking care of *La Madama*'s private hygiene made him uncomfortable, Mike asked Buster Adami to look into the nursing issue. The lawyer found that Alice qualified for Medicare reimbursements, which meant better nursing at reduced rates. It also meant that a grateful Ramón Rocha could return to cowboying, where he belonged.

CHAPTER 21

On the afternoon of November 15, 1993, Buster Adami contacted Mike East from his Alice office, informing the rancher that he'd prepared some important documents that required Mike's signature that day and no later. East was working cattle at the Kenedy Ranch near the coast. He'd be done late that afternoon, he said, and suggested they could save time by meeting out on the prairie, about 14 miles equidistant between Kingsville and Alice at an overpass on State Route 141, near its intersection with US 281.

Mike arrived at the overpass in his pickup just after dark. Adami and his assistant, Laura Ray, were waiting for him with the papers. East did not ask what the documents were about or why the hurry. "All Buster said was that there were some papers to be signed," he later testified in *East v. East*. "I said, 'Okay.' That was it."

Mike signed the pages as he sat in Adami's car. Then the lawyer took about half an hour to explain what the documents were about. He told Mike that, 12 days earlier, he had met with Robert and Jeannette Holloway to discuss the huge tax bill that Mike and his sisters would likely face should they receive the promised ranch properties, as Robert then intended, via his will. The "kids," Adami told Robert, would have to sell some if not all of the land just to pay the tax, thus defeating the bequests' basic purpose—keeping the property in the East family.

From Holloway's diary:

> Buster and I went to Ranch. Buster brought up the possibility of giving Tom's kids some land without paying gift tax. Robert asked me what I thought, and I said I didn't think he should, because it would cause problems. Buster assured us he could leave Robert in control all his life.

Absolute control of his property in his lifetime was a key issue for Robert. Although he distrusted lawyers, he trusted this one and therefore allowed Adami to explore the matter.

Tax law was not Adami's forte. So he consulted with Meadows-Collier, a Dallas law firm that specializes in complex tax matters. Meadows-Collier was already overseeing Adami's work with Holloway on Lica's estate tax with her young associate, Carlos Martínez.

Adami explained to Robert that the Dallas tax lawyers believed he'd be liable for the taxes on Lica's estate under any scenario. But they agreed with Adami that a tax-saving move called a disclaimer should spare Mike and his sisters a heavy hit from the IRS.

Under Texas probate law, Robert could repudiate, or disclaim, all or any part of the land Lica left him in her will and place the acreage instead into a limited partnership with Tom's children. He would serve as general partner, with the final say on all matters, a nonnegotiable point with Robert.

At his death, the partnership would dissolve, and each of the heirs would receive his or her designated ranch or parcel, with no tax consequences. The only catch was that they needed to file the disclaimer within nine months of Lica's death. Hence the November 15 deadline.

Another meeting was held on November 11. Holloway picked up Chuck Meadows and Robert Collier at the Corpus Christi airport and drove them to Alice to meet with Robert and Buster Adami.

"Chuck tried to explain to Robert what could be saved in taxes if he disclaimed some of the property willed to him by Lica," Holloway reported in her diary, "There were discussions about how much the taxes might be when he died, and the probability that Tom's children could not pay the tax necessary to own any of his land. How a private foundation would work, and Robert wanted Mike to run it.

"I don't think the fact that Mike couldn't run it, and graze cattle on it too, was clear to Robert. I wanted protection for Robert that I didn't think was possible. We left with a reminder to Robert that he had until Monday, Nov. 15 to decide, but if he elected to disclaim that was final, and he couldn't change his mind."

Adami told Mike that he'd briefed Robert several times on all aspects of the disclaimer and that his uncle also had been patiently schooled both by Holloway and the Meadows-Collier team.

Jeannette Holloway's misgivings were based, for the most part, on Robert's persistently weak grasp of the subject. No matter how often the lawyers walked him through the details, she could tell that he still didn't get it. Holloway also understood that a disclaimer would diminish her control over his affairs. She spent the afternoon of November 14 with him at the San Antonio Viejo, ostensibly to answer any further questions he might have.

"Didn't you think he should do it?" Holloway was asked at her later deposition.

"I didn't think that it could be done and get the tax result that they were saying," she answered. "Plus, I wasn't sure that, sometime in the future, laws might change and there'd be a problem."

"So you did not think he should do it, did you Ms. Holloway?"

"I didn't think that he would be satisfied with it a few months later."

She added that Paul Pearson also had counseled Robert against doing it.

Holloway recalled that she and Robert spent much of their time together that Sunday reminiscing about his family.

"Did he remind you of all the things that had gone wrong over the years between him and Tom's family?"

"Yes, ma'am. Or he reminded himself."

"Did Robert have any questions?"

"He had a question about whether he should do it or not."

"And what did you say?"

"'That's your decision.'"

"And he was uncertain, wasn't he?"

"Yes, ma'am. When I left the ranch that night, he still hadn't decided."

Robert drove from the San Antonio Viejo to the Perkins law office early on the afternoon of Monday, November 15, and once more discussed the disclaimer with a number of the assembled lawyers, including Messrs. Meadows and Collier from Dallas. Jeannette Holloway watched from another room as he signed the documents without reading them then departed without taking his own set of copies with him.

"Before he signed," Buster Adami later testified, "I looked at Robert, and I said, 'Now Robert, we don't have to do this if you don't want to do it. You can tear up these documents right now.' And he said he wanted to go ahead and sign."

When Adami finished explaining the disclaimer to Mike that night in his car at the overpass, the lawyer added a personal note. "You really need to thank Robert," he said, "because it was very generous on his part to do this. You all be sure and thank him."

East discussed the disclaimer with no one, including his then-wife, Kathy, or either of his sisters, until Thursday afternoon, November 18, when he called his uncle from his truck on his way home to the Santa Fe. They spoke amiably. The call lasted 12 minutes, according to Mike's billing records.

"Robert," Mike recalls telling his uncle, "That was awfully generous of you to do what you did, and I want to thank you for it."

"It's a good deal," Robert replied. "Y'all will get those properties when I die. It's not going to save me any taxes. It will save you taxes. But I'm going to run these properties till I die."

Then he flipped, as Jeannette Holloway expected he would.

Weeks after their telephone conversation of the 18th, Robert telephoned

Mike to inform his nephew that he had done some things he wished he hadn't, and he wanted them undone. Robert made no mention of the disclaimer. "I didn't know what he was talking about," Mike remembers, "so I said, 'Okay. Robert, if you did something you're not happy with, I think it needs to be changed.'"

No one knows just what set Robert off. It may have been as routine as a signature card for the pro forma checking account Buster Adami had established for the partnership. There was a line on the page for Robert's signature, as well as three more for Mike, Alice, and Lica Elena to sign.

"When Robert saw that," Charlie Hury suggests in his manuscript, "he immediately concluded that it was three against one, since there were three of the 'kids,' and only one of him. That [was] not what he wanted, and Buster had somehow and for some reason tricked him."

On the other hand, the lawyer continues, it "may very well have been nothing more than an excuse for him to do what he wanted to do anyway, which was to change his mind and get everything back for himself and under his sole ownership and control.

"Since he rarely had to stand by his word on anything important, Robert developed a habit of changing his mind that was as infuriating as it was predictable, a characteristic that would come up again and again. He also had a terrible habit of remembering only what he wanted to remember.

"That tilted his perception of reality to the point where he couldn't tell what really happened and what did not. By then, he probably could have taken a polygraph and passed it, because he actually believed the half-truths, misconceptions, and lies he had been telling for so long."

Mike was asked in his Cause 732 deposition whether his uncle ever explained his change of mind.

"Well," East replied, "he said he wanted to take and put everything back the way it was. And he didn't want those lawyers giving his property away, that he wanted to give it to us in his will. He didn't want those lawyers doing it for him. And then the remainder of the property he wanted to set up the way Ms. Kenedy had set it up."

"Did he tell you he wanted to give all of that property to you and your sisters upon his death or only some of that property?"

"When he talked to me, he talked about La Mula and the Buena Vista and the Lytton and the Santa Rosa."

"He mentioned all four of those again, and you're sure of that?"

"Yeah. We had a lot of conversations after the disclaimer was signed, and at some of those conversations all four of those properties were mentioned."

"He changed his mind, obviously, from time to time. Right, sir?"

"That's correct."

"Which is something you had known about your uncle for a long time?"

"That's correct."

"And so it was unclear to you, when you would be talking about your uncle after November 15, 1993, what he really wanted to do with those properties?"

"Well, what he really wanted to do was put it back like it was."

"But beyond that, it was not clear to you?"

"That's correct."

CHAPTER 22

Robert stuck to his story, except when he didn't. At one of several meetings convened at the Perkins law firm office to address his complaints, he denied ever approving of the disclaimer in any form in front of Jeannette Holloway, Buster Adami, and Chuck Meadows, three of those intimately familiar with how the disclaimer had been devised and composed according to Robert's specific wishes.

"Funny how three people could all get it wrong, isn't it?" Holloway remarked to Mike East at the time.

Robert blamed everything on Buster Adami and soon replaced him with Paul Pearson, who, to that moment, had played no role in the disclaimer business. One of Pearson's first moves was to accompany Robert to San Antonio, where they paid a visit to Leroy G. Denman Jr., a powerful rancher, banker, and lawyer who had represented the King Ranch for 50 years, as had his father for decades before him. Denman was the same Leroy Denman Alice East mentioned in her long-ago letter of anger and exasperation with the King Ranch management that she sent to Jake Floyd.

Denman, 76, was a noted conservationist whose St. Charles Ranch on San Antonio Bay formed an original part of the Aransas National Wildlife Refuge, noted for its whooping crane reserve. He was also a trustee of the Caesar Kleberg Foundation for Wildlife Conservation.

When Charlie Hury later asked Robert under oath why he had chosen to meet with Denman, he answered, "I wanted to accomplish what I wanted to do and what Lica wanted to do."

"How did you think Mr. Denman could help you in this process?" Hury asked.

"Well, I think Mr. Denman would help me because he knew all of my family, and he knew all the family feuds, and he knew more about my family, I guess, than any lawyer. And I'd known his father, and he was my uncle's lawyer, the King Ranch lawyer. We'd been friends a long time."

"Had you talked to any of your family members before you went to see Mr. Denman?"

"I don't know. I might have talked to Mike. I'm not sure."

"What was [Denman] going to do in all this?"

"Well, he was going to advise me and help me in any way he could. He said that he was very much busy with my relatives. He had 70 he was working for."

"Okay. Did he help you any in trying to get this undone?"

"Well, he and Mr. Pearson had talked. They spoke at that time."

"What was it that Mr. Denman was going to try to do to get this thing straight? What did you all discuss?"

"Well, he discussed that with Mr. Pearson. I don't remember everything that they talked about, but the head of the thing was to dissolve this, what Mr. Adami had done."

"Did they talk to you about how to go about dissolving what Mr. Adami had done?"

"Well, I left it up to Mr. Denman and Mr. Pearson to figure out what to do."

"Okay. At that meeting, did they run any alternatives by you about how to go about getting this thing done?"

"I don't understand that question. Alternatives? What does that mean?"

"Things that you could do to get it undone. Say, 'Well, Robert, you can do this or you can do this or you can do this.' That sort of thing."

"Well, he said about the disclaimer—that's the first word I ever heard about the disclaimer—if that pertains to undone. I was there to see him about it, to undo it."

"Right."

"Yeah."

"And did Mr. Denman tell you how you could go about doing it?"

"Him and Mr. Pearson talked."

"Did Mr. Denman tell you anything about how you could go about undoing it?"

"He said it could be done."

"Did he say how it could be done?"

"Well, I didn't know how it would be undone, but I wanted it undone, and I went to see Mr. Denman."

When Hury asked once more if Denman had shared any concrete ideas with him, Robert answered, "I don't remember, but that was our conversation."

He later told his nephew that Denman said undoing the disclaimer would be as simple as relocating fences around a cattle pasture.

After the trip to San Antonio, Robert called Mike to a meeting with Paul Pearson at the Santa Rosa Ranch, which his late sister had promised to Lica Elena. It was a hot Texas day. The meeting lasted two hours. The ranch house had no air conditioning. Mike remembers Pearson sweating heavily. The lawyer was clearly not enjoying himself.

According to Robert's later testimony, "the purpose of it was to tell Mike [that] Mr. Adami had done things that I didn't want him to do . . . and I told him that I wanted him and Alice and Lica Elena to take care of [running the ranch] because that was Lica's wishes and my wishes too . . . where they could donate for cancer or for different things . . . for anything that was important."

Robert denied that he ever said he wanted to set up a foundation the way Elena Kenedy had organized her trust. "No," he told Hury. "I never did tell her—I didn't tell him that, because I didn't know how my Aunt Elena set up her property."

Hury asked about Robert wanting Mike to run cattle on the foundation property.

"Mike brought that up," Robert replied. "I didn't bring it up. I wanted them to run cattle just so, you know, not to . . . stock it too heavy. . . . Of course, it would be left up to them. I wouldn't be there to tell them what to do."

That was about as succinct as Robert ever was.

Mike remembers Paul Pearson declaring that day at the Santa Rosa in a very earnest voice that, "Robert has no problem with the disclaimer. He understood what was done. What he did not understand was the amount it was for. If you'll get your sisters to relinquish their part, you can have the Mula."

"Well, there would still be tax exposure," Mike replied.

"We can still file a lawsuit where there won't be tax exposure," said Pearson. He added that it would be a friendly lawsuit. Mike said he'd never heard of one of those, and it made no sense to him.

Pearson turned to Robert and said that, as a tax lawyer, it was against his nature to tell a client that disclaimers weren't any good. He did them for clients all the time. They were not a tool for taking land away from people. They were a tool for preserving land by avoiding estate taxes.

"I felt like maybe things could be worked out where Robert would accept what he decided to do, the disclaimer," Mike recalls. "It might become acceptable to him. He hadn't lost any control. He hadn't lost anything. Nobody could bother him about anything. It was something that was done to preserve land and to save taxes."

Mike had a lingering question, as well. Paul Pearson, at one point in their conversation at the Santa Rosa, had described the possible foundation as a wildlife foundation. East had never before heard the word wildlife used in connection with his aunt and uncle's prospective foundation and wondered where it came from. He did not pursue the matter, however.

The three of them met again at the Santa Rosa a week or so later. Pearson had apparently reviewed his options because, according to Mike, he now presented a completely revised agenda. He announced that Robert really didn't understand any part of the disclaimer and wanted it undone. Period.

CHAPTER 23

On a summer day in 1994, Robert appeared unannounced at his dentist's office in Edinburg with Old Mama in tow. Alice had suffered chronic dental problems for many years, but nothing prepared Dr. Jesús Ochoa for what he encountered at a cursory glance at Old Mama's teeth. The dentist told Robert that the job was too big and complex for him. Old Mama needed to see an oral surgeon, he said, and recommended Gary Schwarz.

Robert, in the meantime, had caught sight of Dr. Ochoa's fetching young dental assistant, 19-year-old Carilu Cantú. "Can she take us?" he asked. Ochoa nodded yes, and soon, Robert and Old Mama were out the door and on their way to Dr. Schwarz's office with dark-eyed Carilu from nearby San Juan at the wheel. Robert referred to her by a diminutive that, to many ears, sounded like Scottie. Her days as a dental assistant were over.

Dr. Schwarz recalls that Alice sat impassively in his dental chair, staring straight ahead, saying nothing, as he administered a mild anesthetic before examining his patient. "She was not in good health," he remembers. "Her mind was gone."

Schwarz found that Mrs. East still had a complete mouthful of 28 teeth—her four wisdom teeth had been pulled—but they were all infected, rotting off at the gum line and fused into her jaws by the process of ankylosis. Multiple infections were spreading poison throughout her body. All of Old Mama's teeth required extraction, a major surgical procedure.

"Robert," Schwarz said, "I can't do this in the office. I need to put her in the hospital. I need to put her to sleep."

"'Oh no, no, no!' Robert said. 'You can't put Mama to sleep! You've got to do it here.'

"So I end up getting talked into this against my better judgment," says Schwarz. "Robert wanted to stay in the room, which a doctor should not have allowed.

"She was bleeding like crazy. I looked up at Robert. 'I told you I cannot work safely on your mother here at the office. We need to do this in the hospital.'

"He goes, 'Yeah! Yeah! Okay! Okay! Okay!'

"I hadn't given her much anesthetic, just enough to relax her. But when I stopped the surgery, I couldn't get her to respond.

"Robert had his head down on the desk. He was praying. 'God please don't let Mama die! Don't let Mama die!'

"I'm thinking to myself, *What a legacy for my life! The guy who got caught trespassing on Robert East's property killed his mother!*

"Mama's vital signs were fine. She just wasn't responding. Now I was just praying too. *God! Just please get me out of this. Lord help me!*

"Then, all of a sudden, she just opened her eyes and looked at me and my assistant and indicated she needed to go to the bathroom. It was like she'd been wide awake but [like] she just wasn't talking."

The procedure was rescheduled for the hospital a couple of weeks later. Robert spent the night before at Dr. Schwarz's house, where he was given the room belonging to Schwarz's oldest daughter, Rebecca. Her bed was covered with stuffed animals.

"He thought that was coolest thing," Schwarz remembers. "I said, 'Let me take them off.' And he said, 'No! I want to sleep with them.' Next day everything went well. Mrs. East's health improved. She became more alert for a year or two, a different person."

At about this time, Mike East's estranged wife, Kathy, inserted herself into the fray. In the spring, Mike first noticed a change in Kathy's daily routine. "My wife at that time was leaving real early in the morning and coming in late at night," he says. "I had never seen her be so energetic as she was.

"She had a riding saddle in the back of her car, and she had one of the Santa Fe Ranch hands going with her. This went on about a week. She was too dressed up to be working cattle. Anyway, I asked the hand, 'Where are you going?'

"He said, 'Oh, we're going over to help your Uncle Robert work cattle, but I'm not supposed to say anything.'

"I said, 'Oh really?'

"Prior to the disclaimer, she never had anything to do with Uncle Robert. All she did was make fun of him. As soon as she finds out that he and I are having a problem, however, she gets in the middle of it. That really complicated everything, because, before that, Robert and I were trying to work things out.

"By that time, there wasn't anything left to our marriage. I was biding time before she and I went separate ways. But it was the idea that she went over there and [was likely trying] to influence him against me that rubbed the wrong way."

On her birthday weekend, Kathy announced she was going to Padre Island.

"Then I find out she wasn't at the island," Mike says. When his sister Lica Elena called the San Antonio Viejo to check on Old Mama, the duty nurse told her that Kathy had been at the ranch all weekend.

"Then Paul Pearson called out there, wanting to talk to Robert. The nurse told him that Robert wasn't there, that he and Kathy were out looking at horses or something or other. Pearson told the nurse to have Robert call him the moment that he got in. So Robert called Pearson, and Pearson told Robert that if he wanted to prevail in this disclaimer dispute, he needed to get Kathy out of there.

"I don't think he got her out of there, but they got more discreet.

"Anyway, I didn't care about her going to the island and meeting whoever she was going to meet out there. But I cared about her meeting with my uncle. That set me off."

Kathy came home one day, Mike says, and announced that Robert had offered to make her trustee of all his property. She told Mike that she could then turn around and lease it all to him. Mike and Jeannette Holloway and others had repeatedly explained to his uncle that this was self-dealing and illegal, but Robert stubbornly refused to listen.

"I got mad about it," Mike says, "and it hampered my efforts to try to talk to my uncle anymore on a one-to-one basis to try to resolve this disclaimer."

Mike and Kathy separated in February of 1995. Mike filed for divorce that May.

"So we had this disclaimer lawsuit, and at the same time, I had a divorce lawsuit going," he says. "She knew which buttons to push as far as my uncle was concerned. She told him I mistreated animals. In her deposition in the divorce suit, she said that, when I came back from signing the papers at the overpass, I said that I had the old SOB where I wanted him now. I never said anything like that, and if I had, I sure as hell would never have told *her* that."

CHAPTER 24

The depositions in Cause 732, *Robert C. East v. Michael East*, filed August of 1994 in Texas's 105th Judicial District, were taken from February through August of 1995. Little was accomplished, except that attorneys generated hundreds of billable hours. Tom Wheat remembers that Robert complained, as always, whenever he received an invoice from Kleberg & Head. He threatened to fire Paul Pearson for over-charging him on several occasions. In time, Wheat remembers, Kleberg & Head learned to consult with Aída Garza on Robert's current frame of mind before submitting invoices.

Pearson by then was at work on launching Robert's foundation, which he knew would not happen unless he could undo the disclaimer, and if he did not undo the disclaimer, he likely would get fired again anyway. So the lawyer drew up the paperwork, and Robert recruited several would-be directors, including his cousin, Richard "Tres" Kleberg III; Chris Huff, the game warden; Dr. Schwarz, the oral surgeon; Hugh Terry, a cattle buyer; and others. Aída Garza remembers that a copy of the founding document was placed in Robert's safety deposit box at the First National Bank in Hebbronville. She says it has since been lost or stolen. Pearson apparently did not file the document with the Texas secretary of state, so perhaps all he was doing was stalling for time.

The main problem Pearson faced with the disclaimer case was that under Section 37 of the Texas Probate Code, disclaimers are irrevocable; once filed, they cannot be undone.

Jeannette Holloway mentioned in her diary that she'd warned Robert of this at their November 1995 meetings with Buster Adami. Changing his mind was not sufficient to undo the disclaimer, she told him. Attacking Buster Adami wouldn't get the job done either. Robert seemed not to have listened or chose to ignore his accountant's advice.

So Pearson needed something potentially more persuasive in court. He came up with "loss of capacity," a mental state in which Robert was so emotionally traumatized by his sister's death that he did not know what he was doing when he signed the disclaimer documents.

"Plaintiff," the lawyer wrote in his petition for a declaratory judgment, "was suffering from a temporary condition which prevented him from understanding the nature and character of the transactions in question, and plaintiff did not have the capacity to execute the documents."

However, Pearson went on to argue, Robert had happily recovered his equilibrium and was now ready to reclaim the property that had been taken from him at a vulnerable moment.

A version of this stratagem would resurface 13 years later in the legal fight for control of Robert's estate.

Mike felt there might be a chance to resolve the problem without a lawsuit, despite the situation with Kathy and Robert, until Charlie Hury filed their response to Pearson's incapacity petition on the 9th of September.

"Plaintiff herein had sufficient capacity at the time of executing the series of documents on November 15, 1993," read Hury's counterclaim, "and was possessed of sufficient capacity at the time of filing this cause to have violated the partnership agreement of the parties, either intentionally, knowingly, or with actual conscious disregard to the rights or welfare of the limited partners.

"If the plaintiff suffered incapacity," he went on, "it had to be before or after execution of the relevant documents and at the time of the submission of this case. Accordingly, if there was any such incapacity, defendants seek in the alternative to have the court adjudicate plaintiff to be mentally incompetent to manage his person or property at the time of submission of this case, to remove him as general manager of the San Antonio Viejo Limited Partnership and make such other and further orders and arrangements as may be appropriate to appoint a guardian for the person and property of Robert C. East."

Robert was enraged.

"I knew he was real agitated about it because he called me a day or so later and told me he wanted his ranch key back," Mike recalls. "What seemed to agitate him was the part we put in there that if he was incompetent on November 15th, 1993, he was incompetent before, and he was incompetent after, because he wasn't any different on November 15, 1993, than he was any time before or any time after.

"And I don't know whether somebody misled him on that particular issue, that we were saying that he was incompetent or what it was. But he was very agitated over that, and he said that we were saying he was crazy and [that] we were going to have him locked up."

According to one witness, Robert falsely claimed that he actually was locked up at a psychiatric facility for a week or more.

Robert was not at all bothered that Hury observed "his somewhat notorious relationships with members of the opposite sex also appear to have continued unabated throughout this period," referring specifically to a brief fling following his sister's death. The affair skidded to an end when the young woman crashed Robert's car.

In his later deposition, Robert recalled driving to the law office in Alice on November 15, 1993, in response to Buster Adami's request that he come over to sign some urgent papers.

"I would do what him or Ms. Holloway told me to do because I had faith in them, what they told me to do," he testified, "and I would do it. There were a lot of papers together, and I didn't want to read them. In fact, I couldn't understand them if I did read them. And he said they were real urgent papers."

"What then did you do or say?"

"I signed some papers that I shouldn't have signed, and the reason I signed them [was] because I had great faith in Adami. And I was in real bad shape."

Robert said that Old Mama had called for Lica in her sleep throughout the previous night.

"I hadn't got any sleep. And I was real upset, and she called Lica all night long. I don't know what I signed. Mr. Adami never offered no explanation to me what I was signing. He did like a deck of cards. He just shuffled them. 'Here they are.'"

"Did you ask what they were?"

"I didn't ask Mr. Adami, because I had great faith in him, and he was my friend. He had already explained that they were for the taxes. He said they were tax things, [and] I just had to do it on account of Lica's estate, for the taxes."

"Prior to signing these things, it is your testimony that you never discussed any of those specifics involved with any of those professionals, is that right?"

"Yeah. I told Mr. Adami that I didn't want no partnership, and I wasn't giving any land away until I was dead. Mr. Adami was doing things that I didn't intend to do. He was making partnerships and giving land away, and he didn't have authority to do it. Does that answer your question?"

Jeannette Holloway pictured matters differently. When Franci Neely-Crane, one of Robert's lawyers, asked her if she'd ever said, "Robert was a 70-year-old man who had the mind of a 15-year-old in terms of his decision-making ability," she lied and said no and that she wasn't qualified to make such a determination.

"You knew how very terribly upset Robert East was about [Lica's death], didn't you?" Crane asked.

"Yes, ma'am."

"You knew he was having trouble sleeping, didn't you?"

"Yes, ma'am."

"And he had a great deal of stress in his life that had not been there before, didn't he?"

"Yes, ma'am."

"He was left at that time with the sole caretaking responsibility for his 100-year-old mother. Right?"

"Yes."

"He was having to take on himself some business affairs that he had never theretofore been involved in, like looking over investments and making sure that bills got paid?"

"That's right."

"And that took a big toll on him, didn't it?"

"Well, he didn't like it."

"And it was upsetting to him, wasn't it?"

"Yeah. He was spending money."

CHAPTER 25

Francigene "Franci" Neely-Crane was then a high-dollar litigator at the Susman Godfrey law firm in Houston. Paul Pearson hired her to examine witnesses. Recently married to businessman Jim Crane, future owner of the Houston Astros baseball team, Crane was able and fierce by reputation. The courthouse crowd noted that Ms. Crane was young and attractive as well. They reckoned Paul Pearson made a shrewd choice of lawyer with Robert as a client.

"How are you today?" she greeted Mike East the morning he began his deposition in an Atlas & Hall conference room. Robert and Mike's sisters, Alice and Lica Elena, were among the onlookers.

"I feel like a lamb being led to slaughter," Mike answered with a smile.

"Well, good," Crane said. "This won't take long."

Attacking Mike's credibility was crucial if Paul Pearson was to make his "loss of capacity" argument stick. Crane's job, therefore, was to throw shade on Mike's motives, as well as question his reliability as a witness. To test his composure, she almost immediately brought up the sensitive subject of Mike's wife, Kathy, asking if he'd discussed with Buster Adami her possible role in the creation of the limited partnership in connection with the disclaimer.

"No," Mike answered, staring hard as he spoke, wondering what else Kathy had alleged to the lawyer.

"Are you positive of that?"

"Talk to Mr. Adami about my wife signing a partnership agreement?"

"Right."

"No. What partnership agreement would she sign?"

Crane then asked if, prior to November 15, 1993, Mike had told Adami he did not want Kathy's name on a partnership agreement.

"Of course not," he replied. "Where did that information come from?"

"Are you positive of that, Mr. East?"

"Ms. Crane, I'm under oath." He glowered, then moved his chair down the table toward Crane to sit directly opposite her.

"Okay," she persisted. "And so you are positive that you did not tell Mr. Adami—?"

"Ms. Crane," Mike cut her off. "I'm telling you I am under oath. Do you understand me?"

Charlie Hury intervened. "Mike! Come on back over here," he ordered his client.

"That's all right, Charlie," Mike replied. "I'm in control. But I'm trying to make a point here."

Crane was indignant. "I *really* don't want that to happen again," she said. "I mean, I don't want to feel like I'm going to be physically—" She hesitated, then said, "Maybe we should take a break. Why don't we take a quick break?"

Mike apologized to Crane as he walked away to the men's room, where he encountered Gary Gurwitz from the Atlas firm. Gurwitz complimented East on how he parried the plaintiff lawyer's attempts to rattle him. "It was just an act to get you off balance," Gurwitz said. "You handled it perfectly."

Witness and attorney later squared off over Robert's intentions for his foundation. Crane kept calling it a wildlife refuge on his property. "No," Mike answered. "Robert never said anything about a wildlife refuge. That right there is Paul Pearson talking. That's not Robert talking."

East elaborated on his answer. "My uncle doesn't want any animals sold," he testified. "He wants them taken care of. He wants the house kept like it is.

He wants everything in its place. Talk to him about what he *doesn't* want, and that's what Robert would tell you."

"And," Franci Neely-Crane asked, "he hadn't indicated to you, after your aunt's death, that he wanted to leave this property to a wildlife foundation?"

"No. After my aunt's death, his indication was that he wanted us to have these separate properties individually. He understood that even if he wanted to, he couldn't leave all of the property to us, because we wouldn't be able to pay the taxes on it, and the property would wind up having to be sold because of that.

"He said he wanted to leave that property, to set it up like Aunt Elena did, where there would be no hunting on it. It would be for charitable purposes.

"I know that this idea of some of the money going to cancer research came from [my aunt]. She spoke to me about it because of her situation with cancer. And he said that he wanted some of these monies to go for a charity and [wanted] some of it to go for cancer research. But he specifically said that he wanted me to be able to lease [the San Antonio Viejo] and run cattle on it.

"I don't think a wildlife foundation helps charity or cancer research, either one," he added.

"Well," Crane replied, "I can see you're very opposed to a wildlife foundation, aren't you?"

"I don't have any objection to a wildlife foundation," he said. "A wildlife foundation is not consistent with what he talked about to me at that time. A wildlife foundation doesn't help needy people or doesn't go towards cancer research. I'm not at all opposed to [a] wildlife foundation."

Crane saw an opening.

"Are you trying to suggest that Paul Pearson, some time in 1994, was the person who planted the idea of a wildlife foundation in your uncle's mind?" she challenged East.

Charlie Hury stepped in again.

"I'm going to have to object to the form of that question," he said. "C'mon Franci, he told you what he said. He told you what went on."

"I won't say this again," she replied, "but I will raise with the court these speaking objections, okay?"

Annoyance crept into Hury's response, possibly for real.

"I will [speak] as I deem appropriate," Hury told her, "and I'm not going to take legal instructions from you on what you think is the proper way to make an objection. I told you once before, your opinion as to what the law is [is] only an opinion. It's not of any particular relevance to me. When you become a judge, then you can tell me what the law is."

Crane characterized many, if not most, of Mike's responses to her questions as "nonresponsive" for the record. But as the deposition wound to a close, she touched a nerve—deliberately, no doubt—igniting one last clash with the witness.

"Mr. East," she said, "I'd like you to consider something for me, sir. Please answer this if you would. Give me your very, very best answer. In your heart of hearts, do you feel that it was proper for Mr. Adami, who was your friend and had been your lawyer and was your lawyer, to be advising your Uncle Robert about this disclaimer transaction, sir?"

Mike answered that he didn't think Buster's friendship with him affected his work for Robert any more than Crane's friendship with Morris Atlas's daughter-in-law, Nancy, affected the quality of her work for Robert.

Now Crane was perturbed, as East had hoped. "I *really* object to that as nonresponsive," she said.

Hury intervened. "You asked him in his heart of hearts what he felt, and he's telling you. If you don't want to know, don't ask him."

The admonition stung. "Don't talk to me like that ever again, please!" she said.

"Well," Hury answered, "you've been talking to him like that for two days."

Crane continued to probe Mike's relationship with Buster Adami, asking who advised him and his sisters on the disclaimer.

"Nobody advised us," Mike answered.

"Who told you what was in those documents?" she asked. "And who gave you the reasons why you should sign those documents?"

"He didn't say we should sign them," Mike replied. "He said that my uncle wanted to do this, that he understood it wasn't going to save him any taxes but [that] it would save us taxes. Robert would be in control of this property until he died. What advice could he give us on that, you know? Either you do what your uncle has said he wants to do, or you don't do it. There's no advice to be given."

"You didn't know what your uncle wanted, because you hadn't talked to him about it, did you, sir?"

Hury adamantly objected that the question was argumentative.

"Don't yell at me one more time!" Crane warned him as she deployed a forefinger to begin twisting and pulling a hank of her long hair. Lawyerly decorum was abandoned.

"Well, you're yelling at him."

"No, sir. I'm not!" Twist. Pull.

"Oh yes you are!"

Crane turned again to East. "You don't know about that, sir, because you did not talk to your uncle on November 15, 1993. Isn't that so?"

"The acreage was consistent with what he had told me at Lica's graveside," Mike replied. "All it was doing was saving taxes on those same properties that he had [discussed] at Lica's graveside."

"Nonresponsive." Pull. Twist. Twist. The deposition was nearly out of hand.

"I don't know why anybody would object to keeping the federal government from getting these taxes," Mike went on. "Even Paul Pearson said it was a tool that was used not to take land away from people but to save estate taxes. It was a tool that he used all the time, and it was against his nature to say that a disclaimer was the wrong thing to do."

"Nonresponsive," Crane said. "That's it."

"Ms. Crane," Mike said as she stood to leave, "I have your broom outside, gassed up and ready."

The attorney said nothing. She was nonresponsive.

CHAPTER 26

As the deposition phase of Cause 732 wound down, Paul Pearson and Charlie Hury hired mental health experts to weigh in on the farcical debate whether Robert had suffered a loss of capacity at the time he signed the disclaimer but later regained it. Pearson's bigfoot was Dr. Charles M. Gaitz, 72, a clinical professor of psychiatry at the Baylor College of Medicine and the University of Texas Medical School, both in Houston.

Dr. Gaitz interviewed Robert at the ranch, twice, on August 4 and 9, 1995. In his later recap of the first interview, the doctor wrote, "Mr. East said Mr. Adami did what Mr. Adami wanted to do, not what Mr. East wanted to do. He and his sister had planned to put property into a game preserve or foundation that could support cancer research, support schools, and give out scholarships but still use the land to run cattle. The lawyer set this plan aside and gave the property to relatives. Mr. East said he was very surprised when he learned of this. He has concluded that Mr. Adami was working both sides.

"Mr. East believes that he was in bad shape when he signed the papers. He had been depressed and upset after his sister died and was under a lot of stress with much work and responsibility. It got him down, and his sleeping problem was worse than ever."

Aída Garza, whom the psychiatrist did not interview, probably saw more of Robert in the period following Lica's death than anyone else. She had a simpler take on her boss's mood. "After Lica died," she said under oath, "Robert seemed to be angry at the world. Robert seemed to be angry all the time."

"Distant?" she was asked.

"Not distant."

"Just angry?"

"Angry. I mean, I got the impression he was just angry at the world."

Dr. Gaitz summed up his findings in a cover letter. "Mr. East has led a frugal life, with few or no indulgences," wrote Gaitz. "He has little interest in friendships, hobbies, or socializing. His lifestyle is characterized by his small but functional office in Hebbronville, Texas, and a home on one of his ranches that was built about 50 years ago and [that] is only partially air conditioned. He has no interest in luxuries.

"Mr. East seems to have had little interest in philanthropy, world affairs, or social problems. He values honesty and hard work. He relieved himself of responsibility, beyond working on the ranches, by relying on authority figures, e.g., his sister, attorneys, and accountants. He rarely consulted physicians except for injuries, arthritis, and skin problems.

"In response to his sister's death, having to assume other business responsibilities, concerns about his 103-year-old mother, persistent drought affecting ranching activities, and probably occasional concerns about his own future, Mr. East became very emotionally upset in 1993. This was manifested by depression and suspiciousness. At times, he dealt with stress by withdrawal. He appears to have had much difficulty comprehending and coping with relatively simple and certainly with complex matters that were beyond his day-to-day, hands-on work on the ranches.

"In this mental state, I believe his judgment to make informed consent was severely impaired in November 1993. Mr. East is convinced he signed papers without full knowledge of their content and implications. He believes he was unduly influenced by persons who had a conflict of interest.

"It is critical to remember that Mr. East requires extra time, repetition of facts, and explanations in detail before he can make informed decisions.

When confronted with pressure to make urgent decisions, he seems to fall apart or gives responsibility to the specific authority figures he trusts at the moment to have to make decisions about matters other than hands-on ranching is an area in which he has had limited experience [*sic*]. Authority figures should not assume that submission to authority is to be equated with consent, but [it] is a protective mechanism Mr. East uses when he lacks confidence or self-reliance to persist in achieving a specific goal.

"Impression: Adjustment Disorder with Depressed Mood. (309.0) 21"

Charlie Hury countered Dr. Gaitz's findings with testimony from a psychologist, 40-year-old T. Walter Harrell, PhD, from Houston, then in private clinical practice, as his CV described it, with an "emphasis on evaluation and treatment of cognitive and behavioral disturbances associated with neurological disease/trauma and specific development disorders."

Harrell did not interview Robert but based his analysis on a review of interrogatories and depositions in the suit, together with Robert's medical records and Dr. Gaitz's notes and statements. He took sharp issue with the older man's conclusions.

After acknowledging in his report the "obvious limitations in diagnosing a mental condition by retrospective analysis of documents," Harrell wrote, "my initial impression is that, while Mr. Robert East was suffering from depression, the mental infirmity did not render him incompetent. This opinion is based on several factors. A major depression of a moderate to severe degree is likely to cause difficulties with concentration, attention, and indecisiveness.

"This has been reported by subjective accounts of Robert East, and there are testimonials that it was observed by others. A diminishment in the ability to concentrate and to attend may express itself as bouts of forgetfulness.

"However, it is not likely that the degree of depression experienced by Mr. Robert East would have caused him such a marked degree of functional impairment as to render him unable to act in his own best interest or [to] have such an effect on his cognitive ability that he would not understand or be incapable of understanding the nature and effect of a contract or, in this case, a disclaimer."

Harrell concluded, "To selectively argue that he was mentally incompetent the day he signed the disclaimer yet was competent to carry out other duties and responsibilities as a rancher and businessman is not logical. Further, it is not consistent with what is known about a major depression and its effect on cognition. Nor does it appear to be consistent with the facts in evidence and the records that I reviewed."

In the end, neither side was confident enough of its case to risk a jury trial, so they decided to cut a deal.

Under it, Robert regained the land he'd disclaimed and agreed to return La Mula via irrevocable trust to Mike and his sisters at his death. Mike, Alice, and Lica Elena, in return, agreed "not to challenge or contest any limited partnerships, wills, codicils, living trusts or private foundations, charitable gifts or fiduciary appointments or any other trusts, entities, estates, or estate planning or conveyance documents created or executed by Robert C. East or by his mother, Alice Kleberg East."

Paul Pearson had crafted a document to give himself plenty of room to shape Robert's estate as he liked, going forward.

In case the IRS flagged the settlement, Robert deposited $2,250,000 in an escrow account to cover any possible assessments. Under a mineral exchange provision, after Robert's death, his nephew and nieces were empowered to swap their rights to minerals under the San Antonio Viejo for Robert's rights beneath the Santa Fe. They also were granted so-called executive rights, the authority to negotiate and close oil and gas drilling deals in the Santa Fe without Robert's interference.

Both sides needed a sympathetic judge to make it all happen and found one in the Honorable Bill Burdock of Texas's 105th District Court. "We told the judge about the agreement," says Charlie Hury. "All judges prefer agreements. If there's an agreement, they don't have to decide any issues. We told him what we'd agreed on and said, 'We'll do this, a whole dog-and-pony show, if you'll come to that conclusion.'

"He said, 'I will.'"

The hearing was held in chambers on October 20, 1995. In his final judgment, Burdick found that Robert was temporarily incapacitated on November 13, 1993, was unduly influenced "by one or more persons or entities other than the Easts concerning the transaction" and that he had made "a serious remedial mistake concerning both the nature and effect of the transaction and the amount of property to be disclaimed was made, thereby justifying the invalidation, cancellation, and/or rescission of the disclaimer." The disclaimer was otherwise defective too, Burdick ruled, "and all other relief requests are to be denied."

Case closed.

CHAPTER 27

T he disclaimer suit was no sooner settled than Paul Pearson at last prevailed on Robert to establish a management trust and sign a new will that, with his death, would convey his entire estate to fund what was then to be called the Tom T. East Sr. and Alice K. East and Alice H. East Wildlife Foundation. Notable by his absence from the foundation title was Tom East Jr., Robert's late brother.

The documents identified Robert as the sole trust officer. However, in the event of his incapacity, NationsBank of Texas, Paul Pearson, and Rogelio Garza, a lawyer who'd been raised on the ranch, were empowered "to act as co-Trustees of the trust or trusts created herein for the duration of the incapacity of Robert C. East." Upon his death, the same threesome would act as "Directors or Trustees" of Robert's planned foundation, as well as coexecutors of his estate.

Robert had followed Helenita Groves's advice and invited at least two relatives to serve as a trustee, director, or executor—his nephew Mike and cousin Tres Kleberg—but neither of them ever was named a trustee, director, or executor of Robert's estate or foundation. Among the six or more other friends, family members, and associates whom Robert approached about the positions, only Rogelio Garza was ever actually named a trustee or director, an appointment that later vanished in the flurry of codicils and amendments as the foundation was tailored to Paul Pearson's and others' interests.

Rogelio Garza's father was first hired as a San Antonio Viejo ranch hand in the 1930s by the senior Tom East. The Garza family lived through the 1940s at Casa Verde, where Jesús Sifuentes later tended his goats.

Rogelio, or "Roy," a Vietnam vet, put himself through law school working as a police officer, then practiced mostly criminal law in Edinburg. He was strongly attached to the ranch, however, and enjoyed working weekends there as a cowboy. Garza also did immigration work for Robert and was entrusted with the occasional special assignment as well. These included advising Kathy East in her divorce from Mike.

At the time of the disclaimer settlement, according to Garza, Robert had raised the idea of naming him ranch administrator, a move likely meant to relieve Robert of the business-side responsibilities he'd been forced to assume at Lica's death.

Robert also discussed the foundation idea with Rogelio, as he did with several people. Garza remembers, "Robert, one time, said, 'Rogelio, if I form a foundation or something, I want Mike to be a trustee or something.' I knew by then that Paul Pearson wanted to control the whole thing, the foundation."

Garza also recalls discussing the proposed wildlife preserve with Robert, who, as was typical, wanted nothing fancy or expensive.

"'Okay,' Robert said, 'they want to protect the deer? Why don't they fence the main ranch? Ten thousand acres. Put up a game fence, and that's it.'"

Garza believes that Robert's foundation talk was only that—talk. "I don't think he ever wanted his land to go into the foundation," the lawyer says, "because Robert never thought he was going to die. I'm serious!"

Of Paul Pearson, Robert told Rogelio, "I don't know what he's talking about. I just want to be left alone."

Tom Wheat, who worked on the East estate documents with Paul Pearson at Kleberg & Head, says he made every effort to ensure that Robert understood the documents and gave them his informed approval. According to Wheat, they went over the original management and will documents together, page by page, and these sessions were video recorded. He doesn't know where the tapes may be today.

After signing the estate documents, Robert once more had second thoughts. On November 7, his niece, Lica Elena, heard by telephone from Lupita Vira, one of Old Mama's nurses. As Lica Elena noted in her diary that day, "She says Robert is talking like he is not happy with what he has done.

"He says he doesn't want to leave everything in the lap of Rogelio Garza and Paul Pearson. Realizes he has cut his family away and talks like he'd like to mend fences. Says he wants to call Mike or myself, but Pearson is telling him he can't.

"Pearson says to be careful what he says to me because I am the mastermind. Says he doesn't want [Kathy, Mike's estranged wife] to come around or call."

Lica Elena spoke again with Vira on November 11. "Lupita says that Robert is still saying that what he did wasn't right and wants us to have everything when he's gone," she wrote, "but he has signed documents and put it in the hands of Paul Pearson and Rogelio Garza.

"Every time Robert tells Pearson or Rogelio what he wants to do [about] giving up his property, they talk him out of it. Lupita says that Rogelio boasts that he is going to be the new *caporal* for Robert. He wants Robert to pay him $100,000 a year plus interest earned on the $2 million held in escrow in accordance with the settlement documents. He wants medical insurance for him and his family and wants Robert to fix the old house [headquarters] at the camp.

"Lupita also says that Rogelio told Josie or maybe Norma that, if Lupita's attitude doesn't change, he is going to have her dismissed.

"These people are taking advantage of Robert, and I am not sure what can be done. They have to be stopped."

According to a memo Rogelio wrote, the administrator job discussions with Robert foundered on "his unwillingness to relinquish control of the daily operations and corresponding duties of his ranch. Despite his decision not to employ me as his administrator, our friendship and working relationship never faltered, and, in fact, I continued working on his ranch on weekends."

Paul Pearson, who had conceived a deep animosity toward Buster Adami, was also determined to permanently put Adami out of the picture. On November 12, Lica Elena wrote in her diary, "It's Sunday evening, and I can't sleep. Mike has called to tell me that a lawsuit has been filed on behalf of Robert against Buster Adami and Collier-Meadows. What in the world is going on?

"Does Robert know what he is doing, or are these people (Pearson and Roy Garza) taking advantage of him? I have to know. I thought that, when the settlement was done, the disclaimer went away. What are the grounds for this lawsuit?"

Robert's action, Cause 95-9250, filed in the 101st Judicial District in Dallas, came as no surprise to Buster Adami. He'd alerted the Texas Lawyers' Insurance Exchange to expect it back in August, just days before it was filed.

"I never dreamed they would go after Buster," says Mike East, "because Buster hadn't done anything wrong. He was just trying to help Robert draw up the best possible will that he could for Robert and everyone else."

The suit, filed against Adami and a cohort of other attorneys from both the Perkins and Meadows-Collier firms, alleged a "breach of the fiduciary duties they owed him, their breach of contract, their professional negligence and gross negligence," and so on. Jeannette Holloway was named a third-party defendant as well.

Intimates say Buster long had been leery of Paul Pearson. "Buster did not trust him," says Wanda McDaniels, Adami's longtime legal assistant. "He didn't like him. He was always rather suspicious of him. I don't remember anything specific Buster might have said, but I know that he felt Pearson was doing an injustice to Robert."

In March of 1996, Adami hired his friend, lawyer Tony Canales of Corpus Christi, to file a countersuit against Robert. The document charged that his erstwhile client had "falsely and unjustly" accused Adami "of embezzlement in connection with [Adami's] legal representation of the defendant."

Adami charged that Robert bad-mouthed him for "fraudin'" him, as Robert put it, "at funerals, parties, and other public gatherings" and "upon information and belief" to the family of the defendant, friends of the defendant, employees of the defendant, professional people known to the defendant, and the public in general.

"These words spoken by the defendant were false, malicious, erroneous, defamatory, and slanderous, and the defendant well knew at the time these words were uttered and published that they were and [that] the charge and accusation [were] untrue."

The discord of charge and countercharge was finally settled out of court, but Paul Pearson had achieved his purpose. The episode foreclosed any possibility of Robert and Buster Adami ever working together again, and it left Buster Adami deeply scarred. Mark R. Paisley, one of his colleagues at the Perkins firm, as well as a codefendant in the suit, remembers, "We didn't talk about the suit that much. I think he was mad, angry, depressed, and felt betrayed."

"Pearson was clearly out for himself," says Jimmy Nixon, "and Buster was trying to help Robert, always. There was no self-enrichment going on with Buster. He was an honest man and a friend of the whole family."

CHAPTER 28

Robert's "desire and purpose" in establishing a foundation, according to the trust agreement, was "to further the education of the people of Texas and elsewhere in wildlife conservation and in the knowledge of the breeding and living habits of our wild creatures and in the relationship of wildlife to domestic livestock on our ranches and farms; to afford students and others interested in wildlife betterment and propagation and in the raising of wildlife along with domestic animals, a place for research and an opportunity for the study thereof; and to develop scientifically methods of increasing the wildlife populations of the state and nation for the benefit of future generations of our people who may not have the opportunity to know and appreciate our wildlife, as I have, unless methods of increasing and conserving our wildlife are scientifically developed."

Paul Pearson had cribbed this statement of purpose word-for-word from Rob H. Welder's will, drafted 42 years earlier by M. Harvey Weil.

Harvey Weil's borrowed text notwithstanding, Tom Wheat remembers, as does Rogelio Garza, that Robert never articulated to either man a coherent view of what he wanted the foundation to accomplish. "Robert was not a guy who thought futuristically," Wheat remembers. "Robert lived in the now. He liked women. He liked roping and cattle, and that was what was important to him. He looked for ways to do something about that every day. He did mention that he wanted to memorialize his parents. He told me he was very proud of his parents."

Page five of the trust agreement directed that Old Mama, should she survive Robert, was to have "exclusive benefit" of the main house and all its contents "for so long as she lives." Thereafter, the house was to serve as a meeting place for the foundation's executives "and as a museum of the mementos collected by Grantor's family over the years." This section further ordered that "these items [are] not [to] be distributed to any other person or entity," although, one day, they would be.

The same clause designated 1,000 acres surrounding the main house as "residential property," to be surveyed in the form of a rectangle, with an easement for access to the main gate.

Page eight provided that the original three trustees could, at their discretion, "name two more persons as additional Directors and/or Trustees with primary consideration to be given to Grantor's nephew, Mike East, and Grantor's nieces, and thereafter one or more of their descendants."

Mike, Lica Elena, or Alice and, thereafter, one or more of their descendants were also to receive preference if they bid for ranch grazing rights, a provision directly in line with Elena Kenedy's earlier designation of Tom and his son, Mike, as preferred lessees of her grazing land. "[They] shall have the right of first refusal to lease the surface estate," the document read, "if he (they) match the best offer received from any other prospective tenant for the original lease term or any renewal terms of said lease."

CHAPTER 29

Alice Kleberg East, Captain Richard King's last surviving grandchild, died at age 104 on September 6, 1997. Her grandson, Mike East, who had not spoken to his uncle, Robert, since the disclaimer debacle of 1995, attended Old Mama's burial next to her husband, Tom, and her daughter, Lica. But Mike had no words for Robert that day and refused even to enter his house.

He remained silent until October 3, 1998. That night, Mike hosted a gathering at the Santa Fe ranch, hiring a mariachi band for the occasion. Shortly after ten o'clock, as most of his guests were making their way to their cars, it abruptly occurred to him that, in two days, his Uncle Robert would turn 79.

Mike's anger toward Robert "had started mellowing out," he says. "It was time to make amends. Robert probably didn't even remember that I'd been mad at him. Once he got what he wanted, he forgot there had been any 'friction.'"

Mike decided that, since he had a mariachi band still warmed up and ready to go, that he'd begin making amends with a surprise. He grabbed two men who knew Robert well, Rogelio Garza and his friend Juan López, an insurance executive, and invited them to come along for an impromptu birthday celebration at Robert's ranch.

Mike's divorce was final by now, and he was seeing Letty García, a nurse from Rio Grande City he'd met at a Ninfa's Mexican restaurant. Letty joined the birthday emissaries that night as well. It turned out that her grandfather, Félix García, and his uncle, Bernardo, for whom Letty's father is named, once worked as foremen on the San Antonio Viejo for Tom, Sr. His son mentioned Bernardo in his 1935 diary. Mike recognized their names. They were among the ranch's most experienced vaqueros. Both had quit when Robert took over. Félix later lost his life in a train accident.

Letty was also cousin to Oscar Ozuna, a cowboy who was raised on the ranch and worked there on the weekends. Oscar soon would become a principal villain in Robert's story.

The mariachi band members were happy to play a second gig that night. They packed their violins, guitars, trumpets, *vihuela*, and *guitarrón* into their van and followed Mike down the highway to his uncle's ranch.

It was past eleven when the party arrived at the San Antonio Viejo. Romanita Alaniz, the night nurse, opened the front door for Mike, who went straight to his uncle's bedroom to awaken Robert and wish him an early happy birthday.

The mariachis tuned up and began what Letty remembers was a five- or six-song set. Robert, a bit groggy but beaming, walked out to the living room to enjoy his favorite music along with his surprise birthday visitors. Robert recognized Letty as Oscar Ozuna's cousin and Félix García's granddaughter.

He opened an old trunk filled with photographs and started sorting through them in search of a picture of Letty's grandfather. He found one from the 1940s of the two of them standing together, backs to the camera, with the ranch *remuda*. He gave Letty the picture as a present.

The birthday party broke up just after midnight. Robert summoned one of his ranch hands to fill the mariachi players' gas tank. Mike drove Letty, Juan López, and Rogelio back to the Santa Fe by two o'clock. The long estrangement was over. Weeks later, for Mike's 55th birthday, Robert sent his nephew a surprise in return, four horses to help Mike celebrate the day.

CHAPTER 30

Carlos Martínez had first come to Dryden & Holloway as a part-time employee in the 1970s. One of his duties was to assist in preparing the annual East Brothers financial audit. At the time, "Tom was in charge," he remembers, "then Lica and then Robert. Robert was always in the background. I very seldom saw Robert."

When Jeannette Holloway retired in 1996, Martínez, with another employee, Ann Lockhart, took over the firm and renamed it Martínez, Lockhart, & Company. He personally replaced Holloway as Robert's CPA and gradually became a familiar face at the main house, as well as the ranch office in Hebbronville, where Martínez worked closely with Aída Garza.

Another frequent presence was Ron Davidson, a wealthy rancher retired from the oil and gas business. Davidson was an enthusiastic big game hunter. He is remembered for first appearing at the San Antonio Viejo with a hunting party, hoping to get a shot at a big white-tailed buck, for which Robert charged as much as $10,000—per bullet.

The guide that day was Rubén Garza, who had worked for Robert since his school days, in summers and after class, taking care of Lica's dogs, helping feed the horses, driving Robert to his doctor appointments, and working cattle. Garza also took an interest in helping contend with the ranch's poachers:

going on poacher patrols, looking for cut fences, and learning from the old cowboys how to track down the bad guys.

In the 1980s, Rubén joined the border patrol but continued to spend a significant amount of time at the ranch, he says, helping deal with poachers during hunting season. He developed a close relationship with Robert.

"I grew up as a little boy with him," Garza says. "He was like a father to me, because my father had passed away real young. Any issues I had we could discuss. He was my go-to with anything."

Rogelio Garza—no relation to Rubén—remembers how Ron Davidson worked hard to ingratiate himself with Robert. "Robert would say something like, 'I wish I had a power plant.'

"'You don't have a power plant?'

"'No.'

"So maybe if one of the little houses needed one, Ron bought him one."

Davidson, for example, supplied the gas tank and lighting apparatus for Casa Verde, Jesús Sifuentes's goat shelter.

"Maybe a gas generator or air compressor. Whatever Robert mentioned, Ron would get for him," Rogelio remembers. "He always had a cigar. Robert this, and Robert that. He would tell Robert what he wanted to hear.

"I remember Robert was going to run some lines with PVC pipe. Ron ordered them and paid for them."

Robert's cowhands report that Davidson was nearly a constant presence at the ranch, where he often stayed in the main house with Robert for extended periods of time.

Two of Robert's old acquaintances, formerly frequent visitors to the San Antonio Viejo, remember that the ranch's character began to change about this time, and they no longer felt welcome there. It was clear to them that Ron Davidson was carefully ingratiating himself to Robert with the ulterior motive of receiving a significant portion of Robert's land upon the old man's death.

Davidson denies any such schemes.

"I really cared a whole lot about ol' Robert," he says. "He was a different kind of fellow, but he was always good to me. He always looked forward to me coming down there. He'd have all his mail held up. He'd say, 'I want you to read all that, make sure I ain't getting in a bind with something.'"

Rubén Garza remembers a phone call with Davidson, who had taken an interest in the plans for a foundation. "He explained to me what needed to happen with the foundation, okay?" Garza recalls. "He said that Robert wanted me to be the wildlife security guy, to handle all the wildlife stuff. He [Davidson] would handle all the oil and gas. Carlos [Martínez] would handle all the financial, the CPA stuff."

Oscar Ozuna, then a weekend regular at the ranch, was going to run the cattle operation.

"That was it," says Garza. "And he goes, 'We need to get rid of Aída.'"

"I said, 'Who are you to be making these decisions like this? I mean, you people are making decisions. Do you know how long Aída has been here? Do you know that she's my aunt?' And he basically said, 'We cannot have a woman running this.'"

"Do you know how to tell when Rubén's lying?" Davidson asks. "Whenever he opens his mouth."

On April 28, 1998, Robert gave Ron Davidson limited power of attorney to negotiate on his behalf "seismic permits, surface use agreements, lease options, lease agreements, and other agreements and contracts relating to oil, gas, and other minerals or the development of same." Paul Pearson notarized the document.

In his new capacity as Robert's oil and gas man, Davidson one day pointed out that there were considerable amounts of toxins in the ranch ponds adjacent to old Exxon exploratory drilling sites. He explained that Robert might be liable for the cost of a cleanup.

In truth, Exxon had already paid Robert to do the cleanup himself. He did a halfway job. Nevertheless, according to Mike East, Davidson urged Robert to sue the oil company for remediation and won a settlement.

At about the same time, Oscar Ozuna gradually began to assume a key role in the ranch's cattle operations, moving decisively to fill a power vacuum as age and infirmity began taking their toll on the old *patrón*.

Ozuna was born in Rio Grande City, one of three children in the family of Sabas Ozuna, who, for decades, headed up the three-man team that maintained the San Antonio Viejo's 100 or more windmills. It was vital work in sun-scorched country lacking rivers or any permanent standing water, as well as one of the more dangerous jobs on the ranch. Sabas Ozuna discouraged his son from coming near the towers.

Oscar lived at the San Antonio Viejo into his early 20s. His older cousin, Rogelio Garza, remembers him as a shy and sheltered kid with whom he killed frogs with their slingshots.

Ozuna developed into a burly, athletic horseman, by reputation the best roper on the ranch. He also was one of Robert's favorites. "Him and his mom and Lica, they raised me," Ozuna recalled shortly before his death in 2019. "They kept me under their wings."

In a famous San Antonio Viejo ranch episode, a particularly ornery and agile old bull refused for years to stay penned. "Every time we put him in the pen, he would jump out and run off," Oscar explained. "That year, Robert said, 'Catch him.'

"We went over and got after him. He stumbled, and my horse stumbled over him, and I jumped off. The bull then got up and started going straight at my horse.

"I was trying to drag myself away from him. But when the bull tried to hit my horse, he stepped on my right leg and broke it."

The horse survived. The bull ran off once again. Ozuna sustained a compound fracture of his right shin and ankle. He was injured on a Thursday and taken to the hospital, where he was put into a full-leg cast and kept overnight. According to Oscar, when he returned home on Friday, he noticed his right foot was turning black. So he cut off the heavy plaster cast and went back to the hospital for an inflated-air model.

Ozuna drove a truck with an automatic transmission, so to operate it, all he had to do was hoist his right leg onto the passenger seat and manage the pedals with his left foot. After resting on Saturday, he returned to working cattle on Sunday, telling Robert he was okay to ride if he got a boost into the saddle.

The cowboy had spent 32 years as a tick rider—*garrapatero* for the US Department of Agriculture. Tick riders patrol the left bank of the Rio Grande, on the lookout for Mexican cattle carrying fever ticks into Texas.

Mondays through Fridays, he intercepted ticky Mexican cattle for the USDA under the direction of his Uncle Tomás, one of the tick program bosses. He had considerable free time, so he took Robert's horses to work with him and gentle them during the week. As before, Oscar worked cattle at the San Antonio Viejo from Friday nights through Sundays, when Robert regularly shipped them to auction in San Antonio.

American ranchers near the river believed that Oscar was occasionally diverting their animals to his own profits. He was also accused of rustling Mexican cattle. His Uncle Bernardo García, Letty's father, then an investigator for the Starr County district attorney, received a number of complaints that his nephew was a thief.

As Kleberg County sheriff Richard Kirkpatrick recalls, Oscar also was thought complicit in the border drug trade, as well as the lucrative traffic in smuggling Mexican nationals into Texas.

Oscar's opportunity to refine and diversify his illicit enterprises would arrive when Robert's chronic knee problems turned acute, creating the need for a ranch foreman to replace *el patrón* out on the range.

For more than half a century, Robert had acted as his own foreman, so the necessity of stepping aside was a galling reminder of the mortality he had defied for decades.

His earliest available medical records date from July of 1957, when he was treated for "mild anxiety and poor sleep," lifelong afflictions. His doctor put him on Seconal, a barbiturate, and chloral hydrate, a sedative no longer prescribed today. Robert's blood pressure was a satisfactory 120/82.

In 1994, as he was driving south from San Antonio on his way to the ranch with one of Old Mama's nurses, he suffered a dizzy spell near Tilden, Texas. He turned the wheel over to the nurse.

"I got kinda mixed up," he later said.

A similar bout of dizziness overcame him as he drove through a bump gate. A doctor gave him "little white pills," he said in his deposition for *East v. East.* "I don't know what they call them pills. It seems like they helped me with them spells."

After he complained of insomnia in the aftermath of Lica's death, Mike put him in touch with Omar Garza, a semiretired medical doctor and friend who often came to the Santa Fe for horseback riding. Garza prescribed Prozac, an SSRI (selective serotonin reuptake inhibitor), in 20-milligram doses, as well as Doral (quazepam) sleeping pills. Dr. Garza also put Old Mama under his informal care.

Letty García remembers a morning in Rio Grande City when Carilu Cantú Leal (she had recently married) and Romanita Alaniz arrived with Robert in his gray Ford Crown Victoria at the clinic where Letty worked. The two women said Robert had been suffering seizures, apparently related to his use of Xanax (alprazolam), a sedative widely prescribed for anxiety and panic.

Dr. José Gutiérrez, who had prescribed the drug, had recently taken Robert off Xanax. Worried that he might have suffered a stroke, the doctor ordered a CT scan of Robert's brain. It came back negative, and he was sent home with Carilu and Romanita. Letty recalls Carilu was at the wheel, and that Robert departed with a wave and a big smile.

They returned Robert to the San Antonio Viejo, where he again went into seizures at about 4:30 that afternoon. Alaniz once more contacted the clinic, where Dr. Mario Jiménez prescribed a small dose of Xanax and asked Letty to go check on Robert. The seizures subsided.

Medical emergencies such as the Xanax scare would become commonplace with Robert as his overall health declined. He also had a long history of injuries sustained while working cattle. In one of the worst of these mishaps, his horse fell on top of him, breaking his jaw and shattering a couple teeth. Robert, who like Oscar Ozuna had a very high tolerance for pain, rode several more horses that day before asking to be taken to the hospital. In another of his notable riding mishaps, he cracked five ribs.

His nephew says that Robert put himself in jeopardy whenever he rode. "For one thing," Mike explains, "he never would tighten up a saddle on a horse. He didn't want to hurt the horse. But it's more uncomfortable for a horse to have a saddle rolling on its back than for it to be snug and firmly in place. He'd leave them so loose that if he was doing something fast or happened to lean, the whole thing would roll. I saw that happen several times. Of course, he'd fall off."

In 1976, when Robert was in his mid-50s, his primary care physician for many years found "considerable degenerative disk disease" in his cervical spine. Robert was administered a course of cortisone in his shoulder.

By the 1980s, Robert's blood pressure had edged up to 150/94, and he developed his first serious problems with arthritis, the bane of his later days. In May of 1980, his left knee swelled so painfully that it warranted a prescription for Darvocet, then a popular combination of an opioid and acetaminophen, since banned.

Four years later, his doctor gave him Percodan (oxycodone hydrochloride and aspirin) and Darvocet for severe right chest pain.

In March of 1986, a Dr. Sanders in San Antonio diagnosed degenerative arthritis in both Robert's knees, "with marked narrowing of the medial compartment and marginal spurring."

The doctor reported on subsequent examination that Robert had fallen "on both knees. The left knee is markedly swollen and tender. The right knee has a large hematoma subcutaneously over the medial aspect of the knee, apparently from a rupture of the saphenous vein," the longest vein in the human body, which returns blood from the nether reaches of the leg.

"This patient has been trying to walk around for two or three days and has become steadily worse. I will place him on strict bed rest for 48–72 hours. Knee braces ordered." The doctor also prescribed Medrol (methylprednisolone), a steroid to take down the swelling.

In 1987, Robert's cholesterol level was 247.

CHAPTER 31

Edilberto López, known as Eddy, arrived in South Texas from his native Mexico in December of 1997 and found work at the San Antonio Viejo, where his father, Lupe López, was then the camp cook.

Eddy first was assigned to the main house as a dog minder. Then he was brought to the cow camp kitchen to work as an assistant to his father and to learn how to cook himself. Among his duties was delivery of the hot meals Lupe López prepared for the hands working in distant ranch pastures.

Eddy says that Robert, at the time, still got around in his battered red Silverado pickup. "Robert was the main one," he recalls. "He ran the show. No one moved until he gave the orders."

By 2002, however, it was clear that Robert's arthritis, particularly in his knees, had become more than a painful distraction. It was now necessary for the cowboys to help him up and down from his horse each day. The physical rigors of working cattle exhausted him.

"He would walk, and then his legs would give in," Aída Garza remembers. "He would end up on the floor."

The only answer, his doctors told him, was double knee replacement surgery. East agonized over whether to have the surgery, which he dreaded. "He tried so hard not to have it," Garza says.

He finally relented, but the procedure was no help, because Robert would not stick with his rehab. "He refused to stay for it in San Antonio," Aída says. "Instead, they got somebody from the Valley to come and give him rehab at the ranch. When he didn't feel like doing it, he didn't do it."

Hiring Oscar Ozuna full time, therefore, became less of an option and more of a necessity. If Robert was going to replace himself, he favored Oscar for the job, at least at first.

Oscar, who earned $50,000 a year working for the USDA, told Aída Garza he wanted at least twice that much from Robert, far more than the old man ever had paid any employee. He also insisted that the terms of his deal be kept secret.

"When he signed his first contract," she says, "Oscar insisted the deal be cut and the documents produced at Paul Pearson's office in Corpus Christi. Only Robert was allowed to join the discussion. Ron Davidson and Carlos Martínez were kept in the dark."

Oscar agreed on $10,000 a month until his USDA pension kicked in, when Ozuna's monthly salary would drop to $7,000. "He also was supposed to get an annuity of $400,000, maybe a little more," Aída continues. "And he did not get it. By that time, Robert was not pleased with him. Robert told me that Oscar was doing things that he was not supposed to do. What that was, I didn't ask. He wanted to fire him, but when he went to Paul Pearson, he was told he could not because of the contract."

CHAPTER 32

B esides arranging professional nursing care for Old Mama, Buster Adami did legal work for all the Easts on their joint mineral holdings beneath the San Antonio Viejo and the Santa Fe ranches. Robert resisted mineral exploration out of habit. His nephew and nieces wanted a more active program.

Almost all oil and gas production on the two ranches had been controlled since 1933 under a lease originally held by Humble Oil and Refining Co., later to become Exxon and then, in 1998, ExxonMobil.

The giant oil company wanted to farm out some of its production, but ExxonMobil needed permission from Tom East Jr.'s heirs to do so. So Hidalgo County attorney Cullen Looney was hired by the family to draft a state-of-the-art oil and gas lease that permitted the drilling while also protecting their mineral rights.

Spartan Energy, an exploration company, was hired to probe deep into the subsurface for hydrocarbon deposits, using a new technology called 3D seismic. Coastal Corporation, founded by oilman Oscar Wyatt, took over the old lease, but Coastal then was sold to the El Paso Corp., which did the actual drilling—29 wells in all, on a stretch in Brooks County that an Exxon engineer once dismissed as a "goat pasture."

El Paso's first well, the Tom East No. 1, was drilled in early 2001. The bit hit a huge pool of gas at 15,000 feet down into the highly productive Lower Vicksburg Sands, and a sea of natural gas gushed to the surface. The Tom East No. 1 was, for a time, the most productive gas well in the United States, if not the world.

Robert held two-thirds of the East family share in Tom East Field gas profits, while his brother's heirs held the rest. By 2004, the field had produced about 177 billion cubic feet of natural gas, which is commonly measured in multiples of a thousand cubic feet (Mcf). In the period between 2001 and 2004, Mcfs at the wellhead sold for between about $3 and nearly $20. The field continued to produce for years afterward. According to one estimate, Robert's monthly royalty income from the Tom East Field reached $12 million for a time.

Aída Garza remembers Paul Pearson calling to say that a check for about $3 million was on the way. She says Robert never paid attention to incoming checks, but he did this time, asking her to bring it to the ranch before she deposited it. "Let me see that check," he said. "Don't take it to the bank before I see it."

"He looked at it," she recalls. "I remember he was smiling. He said, '*Never* did I dream of seeing a check in this amount.'"

In the summer of 2005, Robert asked Garza to tell him how much cash he had in the bank. According to her later affidavit, she found $138 million in his various accounts.

"Robert grew up being pretty tightfisted and worth in the range of $5 to $10 million," says Tom Wheat. "In the '90s, Robert was about a $12 to $15 million guy, with a whole bunch of land. Then all that revenue changed, and I don't know how many hundreds of millions of dollars he ended up with."

Robert never indicated a grasp of what the huge sums meant. It occurred to Mike and his sister, Lica Elena, for example, that whatever tax burden they faced would have been easily covered had Robert simply left them the four ranches in his will, as discussed.

Neither of them, however, was about to mention the fact to their uncle. Mike didn't discuss money with Robert. Lica Elena presumed Robert would distrust anything the family told him at that point.

The logical person to explain to Robert in concrete terms what the Tom East Field bonanza meant to him was Paul Pearson, whom he should have been able to trust. But Pearson's agenda never included enlightening his client, nor promoting East family solidarity. Robert therefore remained in the dark, and that was fine with his lawyer. All of a sudden his campaign for control of Robert's estate took on real urgency.

CHAPTER 33

Pearson amended the management trust agreement five times: on October 17, 1995, the day after Robert first signed it, and again on April 24, 1996; March 12, 1997; December 18, 1997; and January 12, 1998. Then he waited almost five years, until November 26, 2002, when Carilu Cantú Leal drove Robert to Corpus Christi, to sign a sixth amendment, which revoked the first five. These early amendments all appear to have been lost, perhaps deliberately.

Page one of the sixth amendment changed the name of the foundation to include Tom East Jr., so the new title read: the Tom T. East Sr. and Alice K. East and Alice H. East and Tom T. East Jr. Wildlife Foundation. Robert's name was overlooked or excluded.

With Old Mama's death, the trustees were instructed that the main house and all of its contents were still to be "retained at the expense of the management trust and that all of the grounds surrounding same shall be maintained."

The house could be used for periodic meetings of the trustees, but it was not to be opened to the public for any purpose. The document also directed that "an area within one mile of the main house still shall be an absolute sanctuary for animals, and there shall be no hunting allowed, even for educational, research, or maintenance purposes.

"The Trustees shall also maintain the gravesite of Grantor and his mother and sister on that site." This directive made no mention of Robert's father, the East family patriarch, whose remains Lica East had brought from Kingsville for the purpose of reinterring Tom Sr. with his family at the San Antonio Viejo. The exclusion may not have been deliberate but was nonetheless lamentable.

The sixth amendment also shrank the "residential property" after Robert's death to "640 acres surrounding said residence. [It] shall be surveyed as a distinct tract in the form of a rectangle, with an easement for access to the main gate." The amendment further provided that a fund be set aside to cover "the perpetual maintenance of this property."

With gas revenues streaking, Pearson dropped two trustees, Rogelio Garza and NationsBank, and replaced them with Ron Davidson and Carlos Martínez. Both were to serve, along with Paul Pearson, in the case of Robert's incapacity or his death.

He also took steps to wall the estate away from Robert's nephew and nieces. Although the original trust agreement stipulated that Mike, Alice, and Lica Elena and their descendants were to receive a preference in the selection of future trustees, this provision was now cast aside. "Under no circumstances," the amendment read, "shall any descendant of Grantor's father or mother or anyone related to such a descendant by blood or by marriage ever be appointed as a Trustee or successor Trustee hereunder."

Such a draconian prohibition might have been understandable had the intrafamily enmity of the mid-1990s still governed Robert's thinking. But there is no evidence that he still bore his relatives any active malice. As Mike observed, once the disclaimer fight was through, Robert likely forgot what it was about.

The amendment also directed that "under no circumstances shall any Trustee or anyone related to a Trustee by blood or by marriage hunt or kill any whitetail deer on Foundation property; any Trustee may be removed by the remaining Trustees immediately upon determination that this provision has been violated."

The hunting prohibition is a mystery, inasmuch as only one of the trustees, Ron Davidson, was known to enjoy the sport.

The trustees were directed to administer a monthly retirement benefit to six employees, beginning on each employee's 65th birthday and lasting until their death, provided they were in Robert's employ on the day of his death. They were to receive between $200 and $2,000 a month, the amount earmarked for Aída Garza, identified in the document as Robert's office manager, whose employment also was guaranteed at least until she turned 65. However, her position would grow increasingly untenable.

That day, Robert also signed a fourth codicil to his will, the previous three having been revoked. Under the new codicil, Davidson and Martínez replaced Rogelio Garza and the bank as coexecutors, just as they'd replaced them as trustees.

Rogelio says he knew nothing of the change until Mike East informed him of it five years later. The codicil provided that, if for some reason all three "shall die, resign, be removed, or otherwise fail or cease to serve," The Trust Company N.A., a financial services firm Pearson had founded and operated, would serve alone as successor independent executor.

The codicil reiterated Robert's "primary desire" that "my overall ranching operations and business affairs be conducted in the way I have always conducted same with a minimum of personnel and in a manner to minimize the overall costs impacting the businesses conducted by me prior to my death."

Robert that day also designated Ron Davidson as "guardian of [my] person in the event of later incompetence or need of a guardian." Martínez was first alternate, Oscar Ozuna second, and Paul Pearson third. He also named Davidson as guardian of his estate, with Carlos as first alternate and Pearson second.

The new codicil pointedly disqualified Evelyn and all her children and grandchildren from guardianship of Robert's person and his estate. Nor did either the sixth amendment or fourth codicil mention a preference for Mike or his sisters Alice and Lica Elena in granting grazing leases. They weren't mentioned at all.

Thus Robert's wish that Mike or his sisters lease his lands for grazing after his death—attested to under oath by Jeannette Holloway, incorporated into a 1990 letter from Paul Pearson to Robert, and included in the 1995 estate documents that Pearson drew up—suddenly vanished from the estate papers, never to reappear.

"I think the lawyers were doing this," says a prominent Texas estate attorney who has reviewed all the East estate papers described here. "I don't think Robert was doing this."

Robert was losing his grasp, emboldening Pearson to ignore his clearly expressed desires for his estate's future. His signatures on the two documents were noticeably shakier than on the 1995 originals.

CHAPTER 34

I t had been 12 years since Robert had banished Paul Pearson from a ranch pasture for disturbing him at work and then fired him. But the attorney had patiently contended with Robert's moods and quirks to maneuver himself into control of Robert's estate via the trust agreement and will, in the event of Robert's looming incapacity or death. It was now only a matter of time. In the process, Pearson had ruthlessly maligned both Buster Adami and Mike's family, effectively isolating Robert under the pretense of protecting him from his enemies.

As Carlos Martínez recollects the situation, "Paul Pearson sets up a charitable foundation. Robert did not understand any of it. None of it. He just wanted to keep the land together. Whether he wanted to leave it to Mike and his two nieces, I don't know. It seems like he did, okay? It seems like he would have."

So what was Pearson's objective?

"I'm not really sure what Paul's agenda was," says Martínez. "I think Paul Pearson was a conniving little guy. I don't know what his purpose was. He wasn't in it for himself. There was nothing in it for him, you know."

Pearson left Kleberg & Head in 1997 to start his own practice, taking along Robert as one of his most important clients, as well as fellow lawyer

Paul Oliver Price as his partner. In April of that year, the two established Pearson & Price in Corpus Christi.

By 2003, with the latest amendment and codicil in place, and the Tom East Field's gas production swelling the value Robert's estate almost by the day, Pearson must have felt his goal, whatever it was, nearly was at hand. Then, on July 2, fate short-circuited Paul Pearson's schemes when his heart abruptly gave out while he was exercising on his home treadmill. Pearson was 55. He left behind his wife, Beverly, six children, and an estate appraised at $612,000.

He was not universally mourned. "I remember Mike called me and told me Pearson had dropped dead on his treadmill," says Charlie Hury. "I started laughing. Mike said, 'Charlie, don't laugh! The man's dead.' I said, 'I know he's dead! That's why I'm laughing.'"

When Tony Canales heard the news, he called Buster Adami. "'Buster,' I said, 'I just heard that Pearson died.'

"He said, 'Good.'"

Tom Wheat remembers discussing Robert with Paul Price, Pearson's partner, who had billed hours on the disclaimer case and also drafted Oscar Ozuna's employment contract under Pearson's guidance.

According to Wheat, the two Pauls worked as a team at Kleberg & Head. "To me, Price played a secondary role," he says. "Pearson would meet the clients, discuss the situation, then come back and sit down with Price and say, 'I think we can do this, this, this, this.' And then Price was the guy who dotted the i's and crossed the t's and franked the documents.

"They had a very strong Christian connection. Both were on the fringe of right-wing Christianity, not quite evangelical Christianity but right before that."

As Wheat and Price spoke following Paul Pearson's death, Wheat said, "'I need to go see Robert and see how he's going to get through all this.' I hadn't been with him for a few years.

"Price said, 'I wish you wouldn't.'

"I said, 'Why?'

"And he said, 'Well, we're trying to help Robert now. I'm afraid, if you jump in there, you're going to end up taking the business.'"

Wheat obliged him.

Paul Price was born March 23, 1950, in remote Birigui, Brazil. By his teen years, he was living with his family in Carrollton, Texas, a Dallas suburb, where he graduated from R. L. Turner High School in 1968.

According to his senior yearbook, *The Roar*, Price was a member of the math and chess clubs, the National Honor Society, and the tennis team. He was named most valuable player in his senior year. From there, he enrolled at Wheaton College, then a men-only Evangelical Protestant liberal arts school in Wheaton, Illinois, self-described as "explicitly Christian."

Price graduated magna cum laude with a bachelor's degree from Wheaton in 1972, then returned to Texas for law school at Southern Methodist University in Dallas.

In 1998, Paul Price's 20-year marriage to his wife, Lynn, ended in acrimonious divorce. It was the same year Mike and Kathy East split.

As he had hoped, Price succeeded Paul Pearson as Robert East's attorney. On April 21, 2005, he altered Robert's will with a fifth codicil through which he replaced the deceased Pearson with himself as a coexecutor of Robert's estate and added Oscar Ozuna as well, so that there were four coexecutors, including Davidson and Martínez.

The six employee pensions established in the sixth amendment were all reduced to single lump-sum payments of between $4,000 and $6,000 each.

These changes in Robert's estate documents continued without the knowledge of any other member of the family, just as Paul Pearson's periodic revisisons had been produced under the radar.

Price continued Pearson's process of cleaving Tom East Jr.'s side of the family away from the estate, attending to details such as removing Tom Jr.'s name from the foundation's title, which became the Tom T. East Sr. and Alice K. East and Alice H. East and Robert C. East Wildlife Foundation.

The attorney also brought Oscar Ozuna into closer control of Robert's affairs and his estate's future. In a seventh amendment to the management trust, also dated April 21, 2005, Price replaced Paul Pearson with himself as a trustee and added Ozuna. Both became codirectors as well.

Robert affixed his wobbly—but still legible—signature to the papers in Corpus Christi. On the same day, Oscar Ozuna received a three-page "medical power of attorney." In the event Ozuna was "unable or unwilling to make health care decisions" for Robert, Paul Price was his designated replacement.

The document designated Oscar Ozuna "as my agent to make any and all health care decisions for me, except to the extent I state otherwise in this document."

It's major provisions:

"I would like to continue to live in comparatively the same manner I now enjoy, and under no circumstance do I want to be put in a rest home or nursing home, no matter how luxurious or comfortable.

"I also realize, of course, that illness may be so severe that hospitalization would be required, and my prohibition against being placed in a rest home or nursing home is not intended to preclude my placement in a hospital or similar facility. If absolutely necessary to preserve my life, my Agent shall make all necessary arrangements for me at any hospital, hospice, convalescent home, or similar establishment and assure that all my essential needs are provided for at such a facility but only until such time as I can safely and comfortably be returned to my personal residence."

Under "limitations on the decision-making authority of my agent," the document directed that "whether I have either a terminal condition or merely an irreversible condition, for so long as there is possibility of my recovery to a meaningful and sentient life, even if only for a matter of weeks or even days, I request that I be kept alive using available life-sustaining treatment."

Whatever his future state of health, he asked that saline solutions be administered as needed to forestall his possible death from dehydration, "and I do want medication to alleviate pain."

The directive also provided that "My physician and I will make health care decisions together as long as I am of sound mind and able to make my wishes known. If there comes a time when I am unable to make medical decisions about myself because of illness or injury, I direct that the following treatment preferences be honored:

"**My Medical Treatment**

"I believe that life is very precious, a gift from God. I deserve to be treated with dignity and respect. If I cannot speak or decide for myself, I want the following requests carried out:

"I want to be fed and hydrated by mouth if possible.

"I want to be kept warm and clean at all times.

"I do not want to be in pain. My doctor should give me medication to control my pain, regardless of whether that makes me drowsy or whether I sleep more than normal.

"If one or more physicians who have personally examined me reasonably believe that I am likely to die within two weeks as a result of disease or illness, despite receiving all appropriate medical treatment, then I want all burdensome procedures that would prolong the dying process to be withheld or withdrawn.

"I forbid any form of physician-assisted suicide, euthanasia, or any other action done with the intent of ending my life.

"I want to be given food and fluids as long as I can swallow. If I am unable to swallow, *artificial* nutrition and hydration must be administered even when other interventions are withheld or withdrawn.

"If my doctor and one other physician reasonably determine that my death is likely to occur with two weeks, and life-sustaining treatment will only prolong my death, I want life-sustaining treatment if my doctor thinks it will help, but I do not want life-sustaining treatment if it does not improve my condition or help my symptoms.

"If my physicians and one other qualified physician familiar with my case decide that I am permanently and severely brain damaged (meaning I cannot speak and cannot respond to my environment) and they do not expect my condition to improve and life-sustaining treatment would only delay my death, I want life-sustaining treatment if my doctor thinks it will help, but I do not want life-sustaining treatment if it does not improve my condition or help my symptoms.

"If my doctor and one other qualified physician familiar with my case decide that I am in a coma or that I am brain damaged and they do not expect me to wake up or recover and they do not expect my condition to improve and life support would only delay my death, I want life-sustaining treatment if my doctor thinks it will help, but I don't want life-sustaining treatment if it does not improve my condition or help my symptoms.

"Other Considerations
"I wish to die in my home if at all possible."

CHAPTER 35

Oscar Ozuna also went to work at once to broaden his scope of control of the San Antonio Viejo itself.

"Things weren't right from the beginning," says Ramiro Palacios, who, at great personal peril, would secretly record the horrors that awaited *el patrón*.

"When Oscar started working," Palacios recalls, "it was right after Robert got his surgery. Robert kinda talked to him about helping, not run the ranch but just to work the cattle while he was recovering. Right after that, Oscar was giving orders left and right."

Ozuna clamped down on the movement of people and information in and out of the ranch. Even before he was officially named foreman, he changed all the ranch locks and very carefully meted out the few keys he did not keep to himself. Even Robert waited a month for his own set.

Stifling the flow of information first of all meant silencing Lupe Maletta, who was then taking care of Robert. Maletta knew almost everyone who worked on or visited the ranch and shared a great deal of ranch gossip with all of them. So Oscar banished him from the main house to the Sauz ranch and then to the Buena Vista, neither of which had electricity or telephone service. Ozuna only relented when it was necessary for Maletta to teach Eddy López how to care for Robert.

"At this time," says Eddy, "Robert could do very little for himself. I was responsible for taking care of his needs, making sure he didn't fall. He was still riding horses, but he would get very tired from riding and come home very late, six in the evening, and very tired."

Romanita Alaniz, Robert's night nurse, was promoted in 2003 to take over as cook and perform "such other duties as Employer may assign to her," according to her contract. Alaniz's base salary was set at $3,600 a month for her full-time presence at the house Mondays through Thursdays and all holidays.

She was one of Mike East's few remaining sources inside the ranch, discreetly supplying him with news of Robert's health. When she incautiously told Robert that Oscar was stealing cash from the house safe, Ozuna accused Alaniz of being the thief. She was soon gone.

"It has been alleged," Charlie Hury later said to Carlos Martínez while taking the accountant's deposition, "that Oscar systematically removed everybody that was close to Robert, so that Oscar could consolidate his control over Robert."

"That's correct," replied Martínez, who himself would be jettisoned in the purge, only to be rehabilitated as it served Paul Price's purposes. "I feel that totally."

"Why?"

"He was there more than anybody else, and Robert would listen to Oscar quite often, and Oscar would misrepresent to Robert what was happening; against me, against Ron, against Rogelio, against Aída."

"Why?"

"To make us enemies, to make Robert think that we were his enemies."

"So that he could get rid of you?"

"To get rid of us."

"And consolidate his control?"

"Correct, and he was doing it systematically starting with Romanita, who happened to be the care provider at the ranch."

"Tell me about Romanita."

Martínez explained to Hury that significant sums of cash at that time were routinely sent from the office in Hebbronville to the ranch with no accounting control. He said he asked Aída to set up a ledger sheet, to track where the money was going, which she did.

"Romanita tried to do that at the ranch," he went on, "but Oscar wouldn't allow it. He would tell Robert that [it] really was none of anybody's business what happened to that money, and he didn't have to do it.

"We made Romanita somewhat in charge of that money, to be accountable. If Robert took it, she was just to put on that sheet that Robert took it. If it got paid to somebody as a loan or to pay for supplies, just put in there 'paid for supplies'—some type of accountability versus none."

"Oscar didn't like that?"

"Oscar didn't like it at all."

Alaniz was fired per a letter from Paul Price on his office stationery on September 20, 2004.

Had she lasted through the end of the year, she was due $55,000 in a onetime supplemental payment. Instead, she was given a prorated fraction based on her date of discharge.

Oscar went on to falsely accuse Aída and Carlos Martínez of stealing $3,000 a month from the Mexican nationals' pay packets in apparent imitation of Robert's old practice. Aída countered his accusation with a meticulously maintained paper trail. She claims that she could accurately account for every dollar, down to the exact number of the bills the hands received in their pay packets, by number and denomination, plus change. However, being able to demonstrate that Oscar was a thief was not a path to job security.

Ozuna was not subtle. To neutralize Rubén Garza's influence on Robert, he began inventing stories about the younger man. "Oscar was accusing me of a lot of things," says the border patrol officer. Among them were stealing cattle feed for resale, poaching deer, and smuggling drugs and immigrant Mexicans, all crimes for which Ozuna himself was suspected.

"Every time I'd go to the ranch," Garza later testified, "Robert would say, 'Oscar said you came in here last night.'" Rubén then explained to Robert that he could not have come to the ranch the previous night because he'd been on the midnight shift and had just gotten out of work.

Eventually, Rubén Garza sued Ozuna for defamation and won a nominal $25,000 judgment. He claims that Ron Davidson persuaded him to file the defamation suit. Davidson later testified against him at the trial.

Robert gave a half hour of videotaped testimony in the case on February 8, 2006. Seated in his wheelchair, wearing an open-necked shirt, he took questions in English that an interpreter translated into Spanish. He'd then answer in a low, halting voice in both languages, which made for some confusion in the proceedings. Robert drooled and coughed and seemed short of breath on the video.

He testified that Oscar was hired on a handshake deal and that, in his memory, no written contract was ever signed. When shown a copy of Oscar's employment contract, he stared at it until Emeraldo "Lalo" Salinas, a ranch cowboy, handed him his reading glasses, which didn't help.

"I can't see too good," Robert said as he handed them back.

He couldn't remember the last time he had ridden a horse. Asked who prepared his meals and took care of his daily grooming and personal hygiene, he answered that he did so himself. He repeatedly glanced into his lap as his testimony wound to a close. According to Garza, Robert wet himself in court that day.

The lawsuit cost Rubén his relationship with Robert, thereby accomplishing Ozuna's objective. Garza would next see Robert on his death bed, to say good-bye.

His aunt, Aída Garza, became another of Oscar's targets, mainly because she complained to Robert that the foreman spent lavishly and refused to produce a record of his dealings. When Ozuna declined to include sales slips and invoices with his expense reports, she went to Robert. The foreman argued that all the extra paperwork was unnecessary, then retaliated against Garza in a familiar way, leveling a number of accusations against her, including the novel allegation that she'd stolen a ranch stove.

Aída recalls that, in August of 2005, she was presented at the ranch office in Hebbronville with a one-page letter from Robert. The document instructed Garza to open two new accounts for two new business entities at the First National Bank of Hebbronville. She says the new crowd at the ranch came to her steadily with such documents for her to act on, and she had developed the habit of checking with Robert before she did so. Often, according to Aída, Robert countermanded whatever Paul, Oscar, Ron, or Carlos wanted done.

She says that, in this case, she suspected Robert's signature was forged, so she filed the document without acting on it. Then, on the afternoon of September 7, Garza drove to the ranch in her minivan with her assistant, Verónica Rodríguez, known as Vicky, to see Robert personally.

At the ranch gate, as Aída wrote in her later incident report to the police, she encountered Tino Canales, who, "wrote my license number on his hand and told me he had instructions not to let me in. According to Mr. Canales, those orders came from Oscar Ozuna. I told him he was not the boss. He said he knew but that he had to protect the property."

There followed a confrontation during which, the gatekeeper later claimed, Aída rammed him with her vehicle. She denied it, which Vicky Rodríguez confirmed in her statement. Both women said they'd seen Canales walking normally after suffering the alleged injury to his leg. Rodríguez later amended her account, saying it was possible Garza had hit Canales as he claimed.

When Aída and Vicky at last made their way into Robert's presence that day, Aída asked him if he'd recently authorized any new bank accounts, without mentioning why she wanted to know. When Robert said he had not, she told him about the letter with the suspect signature.

"Call Price now!" he told her. Aída replied that it was past five. The lawyer would be gone from work, and she did not have his cell number. Robert agreed she could telephone Price in the morning, which she did.

She recalls the lawyer listened as she repeated her conversation with Robert the previous afternoon, then spoke. "Well," he said, "he told me he wanted it."

The next day, Price and Carlos Martínez appeared at the Hebbronville

office, she says, with a single-page typewritten letter on East Brothers stationery from Robert for her.

"You are hereby notified that your employment is terminated today," it
read, "effective immediately.

"I appreciate your service in the past," it continued. "However, the incident that occurred earlier this week, as well as various other problems over
the past couple of years, have necessitated that I terminate your employment.
Sincerely, Robert C. East." This time, Aída recognized Robert's sketchy signature that ran over and through his typed name. (See Appendix A.)

CHAPTER 36

In the spring of 2006, Oscar moved to rid himself of Carlos Martínez. According to the accountant, Paul Price simply informed him one day that Robert had ordered him fired. There would be no discussion of the matter.

The abrupt dismissal was trademark Ozuna, executed without courtesy or excuse, which violated Martínez's employment contract. Determined to take up the matter personally with Robert, he grabbed his contract and drove from Corpus Christi to the ranch's main gate, where he met up with Tino Canales.

"I'm here to see Robert," he told the guard.

Canales replied that he was under orders not to let the accountant past his gate.

"Orders from whom?" Martínez asked.

"From Robert."

"Did you hear it directly from Robert?"

"No," Canales answered. "I heard it from Oscar.'"

Martínez pulled out his contract.

"Look at what it says," he told Canales, "that Oscar cannot keep me out, okay? It's signed by Robert. The only way that you can hold me back is if Robert himself told you, and you just admitted to me that Robert didn't tell you."

Canales still would not let Martínez past the gate, but he did let on that Robert was at the ranch. Martínez then suggested to the guard that he call Robert. Canales dialed the main house, but the telephone had been disconnected at Ozuna's order. Martínez turned around and drove home.

About three weeks later, Carilu Cantú Leal delivered Robert unannounced to Chuy Ochoa's dental office in Edinburg. The old man was suffering from an emergency dental issue, but they learned on arrival that Dr. Ochoa was undergoing heart bypass surgery.

Carilu then drove Robert a few miles north to the strip mall office of another dentist she knew, Dr. Joel Hernández, who was immediately available to treat Robert. The dentist's wife, Hermelinda, known as Lyndy, was an accountant who operated the storefront Quick-E Income Tax Service next door to her husband's office.

As Dr. Hernández finished up with Robert's treatment, Carilu recollects, "Lyndy came in and introduced herself.

"'A girl!' Robert said. 'Okay, she's hired. I want her.'" With that, Lyndy Hernández replaced Carlos Martínez as the ranch accountant.

CHAPTER 37

Paul Price performed major surgery on Robert's management agreement and will in the summer of 2006 and presented his work for East's signature in Corpus Christi on September 8. Verónica M. Loa, Price's assistant, notarized the documents.

They revoked amendments seven and eight in their entirety—both of which had been his work—leaving only one of Paul Pearson's original amendments, the sixth, still in effect. Price also rewrote article four of the agreement, once again liberally lifting text from Rob Welder's will, as Paul Pearson had.

He restored the original provision for maintenance of the main house and its contents, established an "absolute" game sanctuary everywhere within a mile of the house, and ordered the trustees to "maintain the gravesite of the Grantor and his mother and sister," again overlooking that Tom East, Sr. lay at rest with them, just as the first Paul had done.

Unchanged was the prohibition against any of Tom Sr.'s and Old Mama's descendants "or anyone related to such a descendant by blood or marriage ever being appointed as a Trustee or successor Trustee hereunder." The clause was aimed at Tom Jr.'s descendants and, presumably, also covered any of Robert's possible offspring, should there one day prove to be any. It guaranteed that the East family would almost certainly never participate in the East Foundation, whatever it was named.

The previous prohibition against trustees killing white-tailed deer was left in place, with a single exception. "Ron D. Davidson of San Antonio, Texas," it read, "may hunt and kill one whitetail deer per hunting season on the Wildlife Foundation property for so long as Ron D. Davidson provides oil and gas consulting services to the Wildlife Foundation."

The document further appointed Davidson a director of the foundation once it was formed, along with Price and Oscar Ozuna. All three also would become trustees in the event of Robert's incapacity or death.

Robert's illegible signatures on the documents looked like the track of a drunken ant stumbling across the pages. His initials on the pages' bottom right corners appear to have been executed by more than one hand.

"Looking at his signatures and initials on some of these things, it's a question to me whether he really had capacity," says an estate law expert who reviewed the documents for this book. "It sure puts lawyers in a bad light, doesn't it?"

There was more to come. Approximately three months later, on Wednesday, November 15, 2006, Carilu called Iza Palacios to ask if she could prepare a lunch the next day at the main house. Señora Palacios's husband, Martín, was the ranch mechanic. Iza helped out from time to time with the cooking at the main house.

Robert expected some visitors, Carilu told her. The occasion was to be yet another document signing. Iza agreed to prepare the lunch. She'd serve up a hearty meal of chicken with zucchini (*pollo con calabaza*), pork chops (*chuletas de puerco*), rice (*arroz*), and beans (*frijoles*).

Paul Price, accompanied once more by Verónica Loa, would bring with him a 10th amendment to the trust agreement that shuffled the foundation board yet again. The new amendment removed Ron Davidson as a director. He also lost his deer-a-year ranch hunting privilege. The only holdover was Oscar Ozuna, who was joined on the board by the newly appointed Carilu Cantú Leal and Tino Canales, the gateman. All three also were named trustees in the event of Robert's incapacity or death.

The 10th amendment's companion document, a seventh codicil to

Robert's will, named Ozuna, Leal, and Canales its coexecutors. Verónica Loa notarized both documents.

Each of the three also was assigned a general power of attorney that day, to take effect in the event of Robert's disability or incapacity. Their authority to act in his stead extended from real estate transactions to stocks and bond trades, claims and litigation, tax matters, insurance, annuity transactions, and so on. Although they knew as little about these subjects as they did about overseeing a multimillion-dollar foundation, they were empowered to wield, as the document itself proclaimed, "broad and sweeping" control over Robert's affairs.

Price saw to his own interests as well. The document further directed "that my Executor(s) retain the services of legal counsel representing me personally at the date of my death to represent the Executor(s) of my estate." That almost certainly would be Paul Price.

"This was a full-employment program for lawyers and the foreman and everyone else who was around Robert," observes the consulted estate law expert. "It wasn't for his benefit. Much of the documents are trying to limit liability for the fiduciary."

Oscar Ozuna had recruited three acquaintances to witness the seventh codicil: Dr. Ochoa, the dentist; Fausto Salinas Jr., the hay merchant from Rio Grande City; and Gus Pérez Jr., who operated Border Enterprises, a farm and ranch store, also in Rio Grande City.

Pérez recalls that he and Salinas arrived at the ranch together at about eleven that morning. Iza Palacios was on hand to oversee the meal, along with Lupe López and his son, Gerardo, Edilberto's brother, who was in charge of Robert's care that morning. Oscar and Carilu attended as well.

Pérez and Salinas were seated at a table in the kitchen for lunch with Dr. Ochoa, Oscar, Lalo Salinas (no relation to Fausto), and Robert, who came last to the table.

"I didn't know Robert well, personally," Pérez says. "Around a crowd like that, he looked kinda tired. I feel he didn't like the commotion, especially in his own house."

Fausto Salinas recognized Paul Price, who was seated next to Verónica Loa at the main dining room table. "He was kinda controlling things," Salinas recalls. "He came in and told Robert to go over there and sit with those people. Robert said, 'No. Let them have lunch over there.'

"I was told somebody had been there earlier in the morning doing an evaluation on Robert, to make sure he was of sound mind. Whether he was or wasn't, I don't know." As Salinas recollects, the visitor was said to be a psychologist or psychiatrist from Kingsville.

Iza Palacios remembers watching the stranger, who was dressed in a suit and accompanied by a female assistant, pass through the kitchen into the dining room where he closed the door. Less than 10 minutes later, they left, accompanied by Lyndy Hernández, carrying a large envelope.

After lunch came the documents. Salinas was sitting next to Robert at the dining room table when Robert, for no apparent reason, fell into Spanish, forcing Fausto into the role of translator. The odd scene was similar to Robert's deposition earlier that year in Rubén Garza's defamation suit against Oscar Ozuna.

"Price would ask him a question in English," Salinas recalls, "and Robert would ask me, in Spanish, 'What did he say?'

"I'd answer, 'He said you're changing your will,' or whatever. 'And you're naming this person and that person and this person.'

"In Spanish, Robert goes, 'Tell him yes.'

"Then I'd say, 'He says yes,' and Price would nod his head. There was tension between them. I got the impression he didn't like Price.

"One of the questions was, 'You're giving these people control of the ranch X amount of years. Do you want them to start right now, or when you die?'

"When I told Robert that, he said in Spanish, 'When I die? I'm still alive. As long as I'm alive, I'm running this place.'

"I translated it, 'As long as he is alive, he's the boss. Once he dies, that's another thing.'

"Price was kind of getting a little bit annoyed. The girl with him was smirking."

Salinas, like Gus Pérez and Dr. Ochoa, signed the codicil as witnesses but did not watch Robert as he scratched four primitive marks and two *RE*s on the three documents that day.

Gerardo López, who, at the time, had little or no English, understood only the Spanish parts of the conversation and did not know what all the papers were about. Ramiro Palacios, Martín and Iza's son, says he was told that day that Robert was empowering Oscar Ozuna to sign checks for him. In fact, Oscar had been signing checks on Robert's accounts since he engineered Carlos Martínez's dismissal the previous spring.

Palacios later questioned López on the day's events.

"Can you remember if Robert was having a good or bad day?" Ramiro asked.

"He was not 100 percent," Gerardo answered. "He had not slept well that night."

"Was he alert?"

"He was not."

"Can you describe the scene?"

"The lawyers were sitting down, and Carilu was standing next to Robert. I was standing near the fireplace. I was there in case Robert needed something."

"Who did most of the talking?"

"Carilu and Oscar."

"Really? Not the lawyers?"

"No. The lawyers didn't talk too much."

"Do you remember any of the Spanish words that were said?"

"Robert would say, 'No. Not signing. I can't sign. I do not want to sign.'"

"Did he say it more than once?"

"About twice. Then Carilu convinced him by sweet-talking him."

"What kinds of things did she say?"

"Carilu would tell Robert it was best for him. She would tell him, 'Look, Robert. You need to sign it for your own good.'"

"How about Oscar? What did he say?"

"Sometimes I couldn't understand Oscar. He would mumble. But he also would tell Robert to sign."

"Do you remember anyone mentioning Mike or any members of the family at this meeting?"

"Yes, I remember them telling Robert that Mike wanted to take his ranches away from him."

"Did you actually watch Robert write his signature? Did you watch him do it?"

"Yes, I saw him sign with Carilu's help."

"She moved his hand?"

"Yes."

"So she directed his hand as he signed?"

"Maybe because he would shake, tremble a lot. So she guided him to sign."

"She moved his hand all the way across?"

"Yes."

"Did she do that on all the documents or just some?"

"She helped him with about three documents that I can recall."

"How long did this take in all?"

"More than two hours as I remember."

"So, did he resist every document every time they made him do it? That's why it took so long?"

"They would explain to him what the documents were about without him reading them. And he was reluctant to sign. That's why it took so long."

"Did Oscar and Carilu leave at the same time as the attorneys left?"

"They all left about the same time I took Robert to his room."

"Was Robert very tired after the meeting?"

"Yes, he was very tired and very quiet and pensive."

In a separate conversation, Gerardo López's brother, Eddy, told Palacios that visits from the attorneys often left Robert confused and disoriented, and afterward, he sometimes hallucinated in his sleep. On occasions when the mental issues persisted or worsened, Eddy said they would take him to Dr. Francisco Peña, a family physician in McAllen, who would examine Robert and adjust his meds as needed.

After the November 16, 2006, meeting, Eddy told Palacios, "He got very sick, very disoriented two nights in a row."

Robert hallucinated that Old Mama was calling for him and tried to get out of bed. López did his best to calm *el patrón* as he waited for dawn, when he could call Lalo Salinas to drive Robert to see Dr. Peña. As it was, they had to wait until Monday morning. Eddy recalled that the doctor checked Robert out—he was still disoriented—and instructed Eddy to temporarily increase Robert's daily sleeping medication from half a pill to a whole one until the sleep disturbances eased.

CHAPTER 38

Following the impromptu nighttime birthday fete of October 1998, Mike made time to help out his uncle whenever he came to work cattle at La Mula or over at the Sauz ranch, near Port Mansfield on the Laguna Madre.

These were usually low-key encounters. Robert was increasingly less sure of himself on horseback and tired easily. He still asserted his authority, however, always in charge of directing which animals were to be shipped or were possibly in need of medication or were to be kept with the herd.

Mike also regularly visited Robert on holidays, when the old man was often left alone at the ranch. As ever, on these occasions, his nephew avoided discussing business. "Even before the disclaimer," East says, "he'd tell me stuff he wanted to do. I'd just listen and say, 'Well, Robert, you do whatever you think you need to do.'"

Mike noticed that Robert often seemed wary and cautious on these visits. Although he was always cordial, his warmth and spontaneity, which had been restored after the birthday party, faded, as if he was holding something back.

They'd go for drives out across the San Antonio Viejo pastures, one of Robert's favorite pastimes, which often would put him in mind of the old days. He might show Mike where his father had once roped a bull or reminisce about the times Tom Jr. and his friends had roped speedy pronghorns from open-top hunting cars.

They sometimes chased the animals—capable of up to 60 miles an hour at full gallop—into Aunt Sarita's San Pablo ranch. "He said that my father kept trying to get him to go with them," Mike recalls, "but he wouldn't go, because, if Uncle Arthur found out, he'd get awful mad."

Still, the coolness persisted for years, until February of 2003, when Robert announced his intention to work cattle at La Mula. He asked if he could use Mike's cattle pens at the pasture's Cantinas Camp. He also said he was interested for the first time in engaging a helicopter for the work, a move he'd long resisted.

Mike was ready to help. He made his portable pens available, brought some of his men to the roundup, and hired a helicopter pilot, Peter McBride, a onetime foreman of the King Ranch's Encino Division.

On the appointed day, February 5, Mike and his men, along with McBride, arrived at La Mula to find no Robert, no Oscar Ozuna, nothing. Not until after ten that morning did the San Antonio Viejo crew finally show up.

This day Robert wasn't just remote; Mike found him hostile, in a very dark mood that would not improve throughout the day. He was obviously angry about something. At lunch, he turned down the beef ribs Mike had ordered up specially to please him and, instead, sat in his truck with Rogelio and ate the bagged lunch he'd brought from home.

When Letty asked him if he'd like some ribs, he replied, "No thanks," then provided the day's single light moment when he added, "I'll kick Rogelio out, and you can come sit in the truck with me."

Robert was unable to walk the approximately 40 feet from his truck cab to the chute to sort cattle, so Mike drove him over in his truck and helped his uncle climb into one of the pens. Robert, however, was no longer equal to the job. "He couldn't tell the difference between a bull and a cow," Mike remembers. "It was the last roundup I ever did with him and probably his last roundup ever."

Only on later reflection did Mike figure out the likeliest reason for Robert's ill humor. Oscar, he realized, had probably made up some story about him that morning, which set Robert off. At the time, however, Mike still had no notion of all that was transpiring at the San Antonio Viejo or what Robert was hearing about him daily from Oscar and others.

Mike had not seen the videotape of Robert's faltering deposition of February 2006. Or told of the scene in court. For him, the onset of his uncle's rapid physical and mental decline was first noticeable on a Sunday the following August, when he visited Robert at the San Antonio Viejo. He brought along a friend, Ascención Bañuelos, a noted horse trainer. Robert took them on the usual ranch tour. Before they headed out, however, Eddy López warned Mike that his uncle could no longer move his foot between the truck's gas and brake pedals. He'd need to sit in the middle of the truck's bench seat so he could reach down to the left to move Robert's feet for him.

The three men bounced along for a while until they encountered a group of Robert's hands enjoying a few beers on their day off. *El patrón* stopped and told the men that he wanted some cattle fed. They replied that they'd already fed them. When he repeated the order, the cowboys said no more and proceeded off on foot, as if to do as the old man ordered.

As they walked around the truck, Bañuelos noticed with alarm that the transmission stick was in drive and Robert's foot was resting on the gas pedal. The trainer nudged Mike, then directed his attention to the gear shift and gas pedal. Slowly, Mike reached over to gently ease the transmission into park, preventing injury and possible death for any number of the ranch vaqueros walking in front of the truck.

Mike still had no inkling there was something very much amiss at the San Antonio Viejo. He'd heard rumors that Oscar was enriching himself via supplier kickbacks, drug and human smuggling, white-tail poaching, and various types of chicanery that Aída Garza was at a loss to combat. Mike also heard that Robert's physical care, overseen by Ozuna, was poor. He refused, however, to believe most of what he was hearing, dismissing it as typical ranch chatter.

Then came another warning sign. In the early autumn of 2006, Mike started to encounter trouble trying to contact Robert. Often as not, there'd be a busy signal on the main house landline, and Robert's cell phone didn't answer. "Then the landline didn't work at all," he says. "You couldn't get through any-more. So it was getting harder and harder to communicate with Robert.

"Thanksgiving was coming around. I called out there to let Robert know I was coming to see him. Carilu answered the phone. She said, 'Oh, that'd be great because we're having a little meal for him the day before. So there won't be anybody on Thanksgiving. It'd be great if you came.'

"But I couldn't get through. So I called Rogelio Garza, who gave me a mobile number for Lupe López, the cook. I told Lupe that I was going to come see Robert the next day.

"He said, 'Well, have you told Oscar you're coming?'

"I said, 'No. I've never had to tell him before. Why should I start now?'

"Lupe got real nervous. He said, 'Well, did you tell the girl that you're coming?'

"'What girl?'

"'You know, Oscar's girlfriend.'" López meant Carilu Cantú Leal.

"Why should I tell her?" Mike answered, then told the cook to inform his uncle he'd be coming to see him the next day.

"An hour later, Oscar called to tell me that Robert didn't want me coming on Thanksgiving. I said, 'If Robert doesn't want me there on Thanksgiving, he's going to have to tell me himself. I'm going.'

"That was the end of that.

"I showed up out there on Thursday. Robert was missing. Oscar had hauled him to Hebbronville.

"I waited anyhow, and they finally came back. Robert wasn't real lucid. He seemed to be just a bit out of it.

"Oscar left. I stayed, and we had lunch. I asked Robert if everything was okay.

"'Well,' he said, 'I don't have any money.'

"I gave him a hundred-dollar bill, which he shoved into his shirt pocket with a big grin. I remember thinking how odd it was that a guy who was cashing monthly royalty checks for millions of dollars didn't have a dime on him.

"'Let's go back to Mama's room,' he said after we finished eating.

"I said, 'Okay.'

"He knocked on her door and said, 'Mama, you have a visitor.'

"When there was no answer, he knocked again.

"'Mama, you have a visitor,' he repeated.

"I said, 'Well, Robert, she's not here anymore.'

"'Where is she then?'

"'I imagine she's in heaven, because she's not here anymore.'

"'Oh! That's right,' he said.

"So we go in there and sit down, and he turns the TV on. He starts talking, and then he starts crying, and he starts telling me, 'These people are making me so mad! They treat me like I'm crazy!'

"I didn't know what he was talking about. These people just treat him like he's crazy? 'Robert,' I told him, 'don't pay any attention to these people, whoever they are. They're the ones who are crazy. Just don't pay any attention to them.'

"When I got up to go to the bathroom, he told me, 'Don't leave! Don't leave!'

"I said, 'I'm not leaving. I'm just going to use the bathroom.'

"So I stayed there with him until he fell asleep in a chair. Then I got up and left."

CHAPTER 39

Ramiro Palacios joined Robert's caregiver rotation in late November of 2006. On night duty weeks later, he was awakened in Old Mama's room by the familiar sound of Robert's phlegmy cough. *El Patrón* went silent as Ramiro walked through the bathroom to his bedside. Then he coughed again, opened his eyes, and shouted, *"¡Abrele a la vaca!"* "Let the cow out!"

After another brief silence, Robert yelled, "Ya-ya-ya-ya-ya-ya!"—the sound he made when working cattle. He coughed once more and called for ranch hand Lalo Salinas, then repeated "Ya-ya-ya-ya-ya!"

As he shouted, East tried to pull himself out of bed. Ramiro gently restrained him, whispering low to the old man that he was only dreaming. Robert made one more effort to leave the bed and awakened briefly before sinking back to sleep.

The incident shook Palacios, adding to the apprehension he'd felt from the moment he began taking part in Robert's care. The central problem was Oscar Ozuna, who, with hundreds of thousands of acres to oversee, still played a direct role in every detail of Robert's care and spent an unusual amount of time with him.

Robert placed uncommon trust in Ozuna, no doubt because of their long association and his admiration for the foreman's cowboy skills. But Oscar also expertly manipulated the old man.

"He was a very smooth talker," Palacios explains. "He always told Robert what he kinda wanted to hear, and he did it well.

"If he didn't want him to go the doctor, Robert wouldn't go. If he wanted Robert to go to the doctor, he made him go. But he would make Robert think it was his decision.

"For example, Robert needed to go to the doctor for a checkup on his ear, but Oscar didn't want him to go.

"'Hey, Robert. How's your ear?'

"'Well, it feels good. It hurts every now and then.'

"'Does it hurt more like it was hurting a week ago?'

"'No.'

"'You're feeling better?'

"'Well, it still hurts a little bit.'

"'Does it hurt like it did a week ago?'

"'No.'

"'Do you want to go and spend all day in town?'

"'No.'

"'Do you want to go?'

"'No.'

"If he wanted him to go, it would be, 'Don't you want to feel better?'

"'Yeah.'

"'Don't you want to get better?'

"'Yeah.'

"'You want to start feeling like you were feeling a week ago?'

"'Yeah.'

"So, Robert would go."

Another ranch employee who saw and heard much was Juan Molina, a gate guard employed by the oil companies, as his father had been. Molina was on a first-name basis with two of Robert's regular female visitors.

"The first one was Molly," he says. "She was from Floresville. She would come down and stay for the weekend. This went on for a couple of years. Then, all of a sudden, she didn't come anymore. I never asked him what happened with her. Then, one day, he called me and said, 'I'm going to have a friend over. Her name is Janet.'

"Young! A pretty little girl. She must have been in her early 20s. She would drive all the way from San Antonio, spend a couple hours with him, and then head back."

Molina says that, before Oscar Ozuna became ranch foreman, he was just another guy he saw come and go. After a couple months as foreman, however, Molina remembers Ozuna reorganizing the ranch to suit his priorities.

"All the business Robert would do was in Hebbronville," he says. "Oscar started moving everything over to Rio Grande City.

"He also could make Robert do whatever he wanted. He kept him under medication.

"I'd ask, 'Where are you taking him?'

"'Oh, I'm taking Robert to the dentist in McAllen.'

"That was his story. Every time he brought him back, Robert would be asleep in the vehicle."

Ramiro Palacios, who also had first-hand knowledge of how Ozuna controlled Robert, wanted to expose Oscar but wasn't certain where to turn with what he knew. Ramiro had come to the United States as a young child. Not until 2012 would he and other so-called dreamers gain protection against deportation conferred by the DACA (Deferred Action for Childhood Arrivals) legislation. He considered contacting the police but decided that was too risky. He had become friends with Tino Canales, the gate guard, but wasn't sure he could trust him. He knew that Robert had a nephew, Mike East. He'd seen him at the ranch. But Oscar had said that he and Mike agreed on everything, so that choice didn't look promising, either.

For the time being, Ramiro would keep his own counsel while continuing with a practice he'd inaugurated on the January night of Robert's startling dream blitz. It occurred to Palacios at that moment that he should preserve the strange interlude should Robert fall from bed and hurt himself while working cattle in his mind. He realized people might not believe him if he didn't have proof and might possibly hold him responsible if Robert injured himself during such an episode. So Ramiro had flipped on his cell phone's audio recording function. Then the young man thought better of it. He was concerned that others might misuse the recording as evidence that Robert was losing his mind. He switched off the cell phone recorder at three minutes and twelve seconds.

But an idea took hold. Ramiro spent hours each day with Robert and was so familiar a figure around the old man that others hardly noticed him. He realized that, with some caution and a little stealth, he could deploy his recorder as a covert means to substantiate what he was witnessing in Robert's room, catching Ozuna and others in their incriminating conversations, oblivious to his presence.

Occasionally, he caught his subjects in surprisingly intimate encounters. Carilu Cantú Leal, for example, can be heard with Robert in his room, indifferent to the caretaker's presence.

"Well hello, dear," she says. "You're awake. I got here a while ago. I didn't want to bother you. You were snoring like a horse."

"What?"

"I already did all the chores in the morning."

Unintelligible.

"You don't want these people."

"Who?"

"The people that have been coming. You know what's going on. They probably just came to see how you were doing. They say you're not doing good. You're not there in your mind. But they got the surprise, because you're doing excellent. You're all in your right mind and in your health. You rather have us taking care of you?"

Unintelligible.

"Noooooo! Your health comes first. Your health is very, very important. How do you like the little tank that helps you breathe? That oxygen tank, is it helping you?"

Unintelligible.

"You like when the nurse comes to visit you?"

Gasp. "I don't think I need them."

"You need to get better, so we can keep talking and be good friends. Promise me you'll be okay. What's the matter?"

"Be careful."

"Aw! Thank you, sweetie. I'm gonna give you a big hug."

"Come to bed with me."

"No, Robert! I don't have time for that," she said, explaining that she was leaving to pick up her daughter. "Good night, Robert. I'm taking off."

He took secret photographs too. Palacios also collected damning evidence of how Robert was being manipulated, neglected, and abused.

Robert suffered for weeks from a painful middle ear infection, as well as a sore tooth. All that was available in the house to relieve his discomfort was a bottle of Aleve, a nonsteroidal anti-inflammatory drug.

He also developed a persistently painful bedsore. Ramiro remembers that a nurse from San Isidro had tried to treat the oval-shaped, two-inch lesion with alcohol patches, but Oscar fired her before she could work any improvement.

Robert was still capable of rallying once in a while, Palacios documented. On January 27, 2007, for example, Robert directed the young man to call his friend Rose for him. A short while later, she and another girl arrived at the ranch in a rental car.

Robert entertained the two women in his bedroom, then fell asleep at about 7:30 p.m., his usual hour. Ramiro cooked dinner for the women, who spent the night in Lica's old room.

The next morning, as Palacios recalls, his mother, Iza, cooked breakfast for Rose and her friend. Upon their departure, it was discovered their car had an underinflated tire. Ramiro pumped some air into it, filled their gas tank, and they were gone by 9:30 a.m.

Rose later sent Robert a thank-you note.

CHAPTER 40

Not even the tearful November 2006 scene with Robert stirred Mike East to suspect that anything was seriously amiss at the San Antonio Viejo beyond his uncle's failing health. It would take several more shocks to finally persuade him of Robert's peril.

Sandy Kale, a friend of Mike's ex-wife, Kathy, was a physical therapist who treated Robert on occasion. Ramiro Palacios remembers Kale asking him how Robert had fallen into such obviously poor condition. He replied only that Oscar Ozuna supervised Robert's care, stopping short of making more direct accusations against the foreman should Kale pass them along. If Ozuna perceived him as a threat, Ramiro knew, he wouldn't hesitate to denounce him to the border patrol.

Kale took her concerns to Johnny East, Mike's son, and passed along Ramiro's cell phone number, suggesting that Johnny have his father call Palacios.

"So my son Johnny came to me again," Mike remembers, "telling me that the young man who was taking care of Robert at the time believed the family needed to look into Robert's condition, because things weren't right for him out there. I guess I'm pretty dense. I was still convinced that it was probably just stories. People were mad at Oscar.

"Johnny said, 'You need to call Ramiro. I have his phone number. You need to call him and talk to him. That's all I ask you to do.'

"I didn't know Ramiro, but I called him. He said, 'Yes, there are a lot of times Robert needs medical attention and they refuse to take him to the doctor. Things aren't right for him. He isn't getting the care that he should be getting.'"

Mike listened but wouldn't attempt an intervention based on Ramiro's word alone. Johnny kept after him to act. Mike said he wanted proof.

After Dr. Peña refused the Corpus Christi attorney's request that he certify Robert as mentally competent, he was soon without the patient. Carilu Cantú Leal's handwritten record of Robert's doctor visits indicates his final appointment with Dr. Peña was at 9:30 on the morning of January 30, 2007.

Peña ordered blood drawn, X-rays, and an electrocardiogram. Then, at his recommendation, on February 5, Robert began hyperbaric treatments for his bedsore, administered by Dr. Eduardo Mariel, an internist.

Dr. Mariel would have him sit in a hyperbaric chamber, inhaling enhanced concentrations of oxygen under elevated pressure to promote the lesion's healing. The sessions lasted from 76 to 106 minutes each. Ramiro Palacios recalls the treatments seemed to help, although Robert disliked them and finally refused to continue after his tenth visit to Mariel's clinic.

There are no further mentions of doctors in either Carilu's or Ramiro's notes until March 14, 2007, the first day of what would be Dr. Jetta Marie Brown's brief career as Robert's next physician.

The Florida-born Brown graduated from the University of Texas Medical Branch in Galveston in 1977. She received her doctor's license that August, followed by a one-year internship in general surgery. In 2007, at age 54, she was working as a general practitioner and was available for house calls. Dr. Brown, like Sandy Kale, was acquainted with Kathy East, who introduced her at the ranch.

The doctor, who did not respond to numerous interview requests for this book, would direct Robert's home medical care for approximately two months. Part of that time, she resided at the ranch, sleeping in a west wing bedroom.

At about six o'clock on Sunday evening, March 18, 2007, Mike East received a call at home from a worried Rogelio Garza. The attorney informed him that Robert had not eaten in four or five days and was growing very frail. Lalo Salinas also called Mike to report that Oscar and Carilu were neglecting Robert, spending much of their time together at La Mula.

Oscar now came by the main house only occasionally to check on Robert, Lalo said, once or twice a week at most. After Robert had signed the final estate documents in November 2006, Ozuna was less concerned with monitoring his health.

Mike dialed Robert's cell phone. His uncle, at that moment, was resting in his recliner in Old Mama's room, watching television with Ramiro Palacios, who answered and quickly confirmed what East had learned from Rogelio and Lalo. "Things are not going well here," he said.

He handed the cell phone to Robert. Mike asked his uncle if he wanted to go to the doctor.

"Yes," Robert answered. "If you'll take me."

Mike said that he and Letty would come over immediately. According to Ramiro, Robert seemed pleased at the news.

Mike and Letty left the Santa Fe ranch together in Mike's pickup at about six thirty that evening. They agreed that, if they found Robert in extremis, they'd drive him to the emergency room at Starr County Memorial Hospital in Rio Grande City at once. If he seemed stable, they'd let him rest until morning, then take him to the hospital's family specialty clinic, where Letty once worked.

Oscar, meanwhile, telephoned Robert.

Ramiro answered, held Robert's Nokia to his mouth as he listened to their conversation and recorded it as well. They spoke mostly in Spanish.

"Mike's on his way," Oscar told Robert. "He said he was going over there because you wanted him to take you to the doctor."

"Is he on his way?"

"Yes, he's on his way. Do you know that he's going to take you to the doctor?"

"If he thinks it is a good idea."

"Do you feel sick [enough] for him to take you to the emergency?"

"No."

"He's going over there to take care of you. He says it's his responsibility to take care of you. It's up to you. What do you think?"

"I'm all right."

Oscar then told Robert that, in the morning, he would finally take him to see Dr. Eugene Mackie, an ear, nose, and throat specialist, to treat his ear infection. "I think you're going to need antibiotics for your ear, okay?"

"What time do you get here?" Robert asked.

"Tomorrow." Oscar then switched to English. "But if you need me right now, I'll go right now, Robert."

"You don't have to come."

Palacios detected a nervous edge in the foreman's voice. They discussed Robert's ear. Ramiro explained he had given Robert drops and Tylenol that day. Oscar suggested Aleve worked better for pain.

"If Mike takes him to the doctor, you call me," he ordered Palacios.

"I sure will," Ramiro answered. "Is this man Mike going to take him?"

"No! No! Robert said no. But you never know what Robert thinks."

Ramiro asked if Mike was going to spend the night at the ranch.

"He's not going to stay over."

"All right."

"Anyway, just call me later on to see what happened."

"*Adios*."

Mike and Letty arrived at the San Antonio Viejo to find Robert already asleep, so they went to bed at the ranch.

Oscar got busy overnight. In the morning, Mike and Letty learned that Robert would not be going to the clinic in Rio Grande City or be examined by Dr. Mackie. The foreman instead had made an appointment for him to see his new doctor, Jetta Brown, in Edinburg.

Dr. Brown had an unusual professional history. In 2001, the journalist Berkeley Rice, writing in *Medical Economics*, a professional journal, described her as "a solo GP in Edinburg with no hospital privileges, no office practice, and no listing in the local telephone directory."

"In recent years," according to the article, "Brown has spent much of her time reviewing malpractice claims for local plaintiffs' lawyers. In a deposition taken about a year ago, she disclosed that she charged $300 for reviewing each claim and $500 an hour for testifying as a medical expert. At that time, she estimated that she'd reviewed about 700 cases in recent years."

In a 1999 case, she was hired as an expert witness by 224 former patients of Dr. Francisco Bracamontes, a thoracic surgeon, along with the McAllen Medical Center. As part of their case, the plaintiffs alleged the medical center was negligent "in hiring, retention, and supervision of Dr. Bracamontes" and offered Dr. Brown as their expert in the matter.

The medical center countercharged that Dr. Brown was not qualified to comment on the case's issues. The lawsuit wound up in the Texas Supreme Court, which found for the medical center.

The justices wrote, "The curriculum vitae the plaintiffs submitted for Dr. Brown was a model of brevity. It lists where she went to high school and college but not medical school. It discloses a 'general surgery internship,' but not when it took place or how long it was.

"For employment, it shows two years practicing emergency medicine (1978–1980), 20 years in solo family practice (1980–2000), five years 'specializing in medical-legal issues' (1995–2000), and a 'house call business in general medicine' since 2000. It lists no hospitals where she is on staff or has been for 20 years, although, in her reports, Dr. Brown says she has worked as a 'surgical assistant' and attended 'heart catherizations' [sic] regarding some of her patients. There is nothing else in either the CV or the reports to suggest she has special knowledge or expertise regarding hospital credentialing."

CHAPTER 41

At about nine on Monday morning, March 19, 2007, Mike and Letty joined Robert for breakfast at his kitchen table, along with Lalo Salinas and Ramiro Palacios. Robert was attempting, without success, to feed himself some cereal from a bowl. He couldn't grasp his spoon. Letty asked him if she could help. He nodded yes. She noted he was having difficulty swallowing. She also remembers that, when she asked if he'd like Mike to come help run the ranch, Robert nodded yes once more. Their interchange went no further.

After breakfast, Ramiro and Lalo put Robert between them in Palacios's pickup, while Mike and Letty climbed into their truck. They all left the San Antonio Viejo for the one-hour drive to Edinburg, where they were to meet Oscar and Carilu at the H-E-B store on the corner of McColl Road and Freddy Gonzalez Drive. The supermarket was a short distance from the small, three-bedroom residence and office where Dr. Brown and her husband lived with their daughters.

From the H-E-B parking lot, Oscar led them about four miles south on McColl Road, where he turned left onto East Esperanza Avenue and stopped in front of number 905, a single-story brick address for Upper Valley Interventional Radiology, PA.

By the time Mike and Letty arrived, Robert was already inside. Lalo,

Mike recollects, urged him, "Go inside! Go inside!" which he did, where he was introduced to Dr. Brown, a large woman in a white doctor's coat, standing with Oscar, Carilu, and Robert. As Mike joined them, he recorded two impressions. Dr. Brown seemed familiar with Robert's state of health, and from her stare and body language, she was deeply hostile toward his nephew.

Nevertheless, Mike thought, *Maybe if I talk to this doctor about getting professional nurses to take care of Robert, it will solve a lot of medical issues.*

"Dr. Brown," he said, "you don't know me, but I'm Robert's nephew. As his next of kin, I would like to see my uncle have some nurses around him."

According to Mike, Brown patted Ozuna on the back and replied, "You may be his next of kin, but this man has your uncle's durable power of attorney. He's responsible for all of Robert's medical needs, so you have no say-so."

Startled to hear that Oscar was now in charge of Robert's health decisions, Mike turned to the foreman. "Oscar," he said, "you know Robert needs nurses. Why don't you get him some nurses? It's not like Robert couldn't afford it."

"Robert doesn't want any nurses," Ozuna answered.

"Oscar, I don't think that's right," Mike said. "Robert would like to have nurses around him, especially if they're pretty."

"No," Ozuna insisted, "Robert doesn't want to have nurses."

Mike would later learn from Ramiro Palacios and others that Oscar and Carilu had warned Robert not to engage professional nurses because they would suggest he go to a nursing home. He should just let the people at the ranch take care of him.

Mike spent a few moments alone with Robert in a separate room. His uncle rested on a couch as they spoke. His speech was garbled.

"You couldn't understand anything," East recalls. "I *think* he told me that he needed help at the ranch, but I couldn't tell what sort of help he meant."

Only when Mike urged Robert to get professional nursing care did his uncle manage to make himself understood.

"Well, I don't need nurses," he said.

Back in the main room, Mike once again approached Oscar. "I hope you're not doing something you're not supposed to," he said. "You know that man needs nurses."

"He doesn't want nurses," the foreman repeated again.

"It's pretty obvious there's something going on that really shouldn't be going on," Mike continued, unsure of what he was witnessing but still not grasping the full extent to which Robert already had been manipulated. "If there is, you're not only going to embarrass yourself. You're going to embarrass your whole family."

It didn't yet occur to East that criminal behavior might be the problem, that Oscar's behavior could have far more serious consequences than spoiling his family's good name, that law enforcement might take an interest in how Robert was being treated.

The brief confrontation concluded. Jetta Brown had asserted Oscar's authority over Robert's health issues, questionable though it was, and Mike was left to wonder just how much power the foreman had accumulated.

"I left that imaging center with a bad feeling," he says. A little research on Jetta Brown confirmed Berkeley Rice's information. "I found out she didn't even have a practice. She did house calls, but she didn't have an office. She was a licensed doctor, but her biggest role in life had been testifying against other doctors in malpractice suits. That's who they had taking care of Uncle Robert."

Mike called Charlie Hury with the news that Oscar apparently held Robert's power of attorney. "I called Paul Price," Hury writes in his manuscript, "to ask how it could be true that Oscar ever achieved the rather lofty legal status of actual legal guardian without anybody in the family ever being notified about it.

"Price assured me that all Robert had [signed] was a standard health-care power of attorney giving Oscar the right to make medical decisions for Robert if Robert could not, but that Robert was perfectly capable of making all necessary decisions on his own. Price essentially minimized the whole incident as a misunderstanding of legal terms, but something just did not ring true about it at all."

A little past one that afternoon, Letty García received a call from her father, Bernardo, who had heard from her cousin Oscar that Robert was fine and had enjoyed a Whataburger for lunch that day.

Later, Ramiro called Mike with the news that Dr. Brown had diagnosed Robert with a urinary infection.

CHAPTER 42

April 18, 2007, dawned breezy and cool at the San Antonio Viejo. The temperature hovered in the low 40s, and a 15-mile-per-hour breeze wafted in from the north–northwest. In Lalo Salinas's opinion, the day wasn't warm enough for *el patrón*'s usual morning shower. Lalo and Ramiro sponge-bathed Robert instead.

They rolled him out to the kitchen at 9:30, when Salinas headed for the cow camp, and Ramiro prepared Robert's morning meal of grits with raisins, cold cereal, and chamomile tea. But Robert showed no interest in his food. He seemed to sag into his chair, bowing his head. Both hands fell into his lap.

"I tried to wake him up by rubbing his back and arms," Ramiro recalls. "I got really close to him, and that's when I noticed the left side of his mouth and his left eye were drooping, and he was making a fist in his lap with his left hand. I had been with him since eight o'clock that morning without noticing anything, so this must have occurred right at the breakfast table. It looked really bad."

Ramiro called Oscar at once. No answer. Then he reached Dr. Brown. He remembers she told him to give Robert an aspirin and some Gatorade, put him back into bed, and hook him up to his oxygen machine. She said she was going to prescribe a medicine as well.

"I did that right away," he says, "except for the aspirin. We didn't have any."

Robert fell asleep for another hour as Ramiro made calls from his room, speaking once more with Dr. Brown, as well as Oscar and Carilu. He also asked Lalo to inform Mike, who once again was in Fort Worth with Letty, at a cutting horse competition.

The situation confused and frustrated Palacios. He believed Robert might have just suffered a stroke, and he expected Dr. Brown to rush out to the ranch and take charge of his care. "With Robert's symptoms, I thought Jetta Brown was going to be calling an ambulance," he says, "and I'd have to try to get him to the ranch gate."

Juan Salazar, one of the hands, arrived as usual at 11:30 from Hebbronville with the ranch mail. Dr. Brown's prescription was not ready when he went by the pharmacy, so Lalo was dispatched to bring it out.

According to Ramiro's notes, Dr. Brown called at 11:41 to check on Robert's condition. He was sufficiently awake by then to complain that he felt tired. At Dr. Brown's direction, Ramiro gave him some water and, at 12:30, performed a 10-minute bronchodilator treatment via a nebulizer for Robert's pneumonia.

She asked him a number of questions, including whether Robert was experiencing seizures. He wasn't. When Ramiro asked if she thought Robert might have suffered a stroke, she discounted the possibility. "Oh, no," Ramiro remembers Brown saying over the phone. "He's probably just feeling weak."

The doctor arrived at the ranch at about two and would spend the night. She ordered Robert placed back on his oxygen machine. At about two thirty, Robert consumed roughly a quarter of his lunch of fish soup, Jell-O, and green tea. Later in the afternoon, Dr. Brown sent Lalo Salinas northeast to the town of Falfurrias for IV equipment in case Robert required it.

Mike East, in Fort Worth, missed Lalo's first call that day but finally spoke to him at 9:45 p.m. Letty wrote of their conversation, "Lalo tells Mike that Robert has an obvious mouth deviation and drooping left eye."

The next day, Mike and Letty arrived at the San Antonio Viejo. From Letty's notes: "We were greeted by Carilu, who tells us Robert is sleeping. She takes us to Robert's bedroom. Upon seeing Robert asleep, I noted a left mouth deviation with left eye closed and right eye open. I ask Carilu if Robert had a stroke. She says she doesn't know. Have to ask Dr. Brown. She wakes Robert up, and Mike greets him."

Mike noticed a clear plastic IV bag suspended above Robert's bed. "It had big letters stenciled on it that read *EXPIRED*," he says. "Of course, we questioned that right away. Dr. Brown said she just used that to threaten Robert. If he didn't eat, she was going to give him this IV.

"'Okay. What about his mouth being crooked?'

"She said, 'Oh, that was a fall. A horse fell, and he broke his jaw.'

"I said, 'Dr. Brown, that happened about 60 years ago. I was there when it happened. His mouth wasn't crooked after that.'" Mike explained to her that Robert's lower jaw was wired so that it would heal correctly.

"Do you remember when you broke your jaw?" he asked his uncle. "Horse fell and rolled over on top of you. Remember that?"

Robert said nothing.

Letty asked the doctor if she needed help. Brown replied that there was some medical gear she needed. Letty agreed to go get it.

Despite the business with the IV and Brown's misinformation about Robert's jaw, the conversation was civil and businesslike, focused on Robert's eating problems. Ramiro Palacios quietly walked into the room with his recorder.

"He's always been a big eater," Mike said.

"Right," Dr. Brown replied. "We are feeding him five, six times a day: strained fruits, a pack of raisins, and he will take them." But, she continued, when they tried to give him meat, he refused it.

"Hey, Robert!" she suddenly raised her voice. He said nothing.

"He won't talk much," she shrugged.

The next day, Friday, April 20, Letty and Mike drove to the ranch to deliver the equipment she had purchased for Dr. Brown. One instrument was a suction machine for removing phlegm from Robert's mouth and throat. The other was a pulse oximeter, a small device that is clipped on a finger or toe to measure a patient's pulse and blood oxygen levels. They arrived at the San Antonio Viejo shortly after 6 p.m.

Letty saw that Dr. Brown seemed nervous and upset that evening, and for good reason. She told them that, in the morning, Robert had developed an irregular heartbeat, atrial fibrillation, or AFib, and so far, she had been unable to reestablish a normal rhythm. AFib can be very dangerous. It may lead to blood clots and strokes and other complications, including heart failure.

Brown said she had tried to orally administer Calan, a so-called calcium channel blocker, used to control a patient's heart rate. Robert had spit it up. She also contacted a pharmacy that carried injectable digoxin, also used to control heartbeat, and was waiting for Oscar Ozuna to return with the prescription.

Robert was asleep. Mike and Letty recall him as gaunt and wasted. His breathing was shallow and rough. Dr. Brown told them that his blood pressure was 80/40, very low. She had him on a dextrose drip. Letty noticed that the bag was expired and lacked a regulator. Brown was also giving Robert oxygen via a nasal cannula.

According to Letty, Dr. Brown's hands trembled as she inserted the batteries into the pulse oximeter. Once she had it working, the device measured Robert's oxygen saturation at 93 percent and his heart rate at 72. The latter figure couldn't be trusted on account of the AFib.

They discussed calling an ambulance. Dr. Brown said she was worried that Robert might not survive an ambulance ride. Letty and Mike told her they had with them in their car an automatic external defibrillator (AED), a portable device that monitors a patient's pulse. If the heart stops, the AED delivers an automatic external electrical jolt to restart the organ. Mindful of his father's cause of death, Mike kept such AEDs handy in his ranch vehicles should any of his cowhands suffer similar cardiac emergencies.

They offered Brown use of the AED. She refused. A feeding tube was also discussed. To Letty's practiced eye, Robert was showing signs of cachexia—the wasting of flesh from disease. Dr. Brown said she read Robert's notarized directive that he was not to be put on a feeding tube, and she meant to honor his wishes.

Letty, who had not read the directive, questioned that, pointing out to the doctor that Robert had kept Old Mama on a feeding tube for months.

Mike was incredulous as well. "I don't believe that," he told Dr. Brown. "Until I see that directive, I'm going to withhold my judgment."

He said he could arrange for an air ambulance. Dr. Brown, who struck both Mike and Letty as uncertain how to proceed, replied that she doubted that the "peons," as she called them, at regional hospitals would admit Robert. She possibly had in mind the fact that she had no hospital admitting rights, as Berkeley Rice had pointed out in 2001.

It was now well past dark, and Mike was peeved. "When we first got there, I walked into the dining room," he recalls. "There was a big piece of furniture there that came off Captain King's steamboat, and his portrait had always rested on it. I discovered on this visit that the captain's picture had been replaced by one of my ex-wife, Kathy, standing next to a horse. That didn't set well with me, because I knew Robert didn't put it there. He was bedridden by that time."

According to Ramiro Palacios, Kathy East had presented the picture to Robert some weeks before. He says that it lay in Robert's room until Carilu replaced the picture of Captain King with it, expecting to provoke Mike when he saw it, which it did.

"So we're sitting there, waiting, and the longer we waited, the more I thought about that picture of Kathy being up there, and Captain King's picture not being there, and the madder I got.

"Finally, I asked Ramiro, 'When's Oscar going to show up?'

"'He's not going to come until you leave,' he answered.

"'How will he know when I leave?'

"'She'll call him.'"

Mike and Letty decided on a ruse. They left the house as if to drive home but only went so far as the cow camp and waited. Soon enough, Mike received a text from Ramiro that Oscar had returned to the ranch with Robert's medicine from the pharmacy.

They drove back to the house, where Mike confronted Ozuna in the living room. "I told him I thought it was pretty disrespectful of him to take Captain King's picture down and have Kathy's picture put up there in its place.

"He said he didn't do that.

"I said, 'Well, you're supposed to be the man in charge. You allowed it to happen.'

"He said no. He started making excuses.

"I guess we might have gotten pretty loud, because Letty came in and told me that we just needed to go."

Mike grabbed Kathy's picture—he'd return it the next day by certified mail—and departed with Letty about midnight. Oscar followed them to their vehicle. "You know," Mike remarked to the foreman as he opened the door, "this is going to end up in court."

"I know," Ozuna answered.

Robert awoke about an hour later. He asked Ramiro, in Spanish, if his nephew was still there. At this point, according to Ramiro, Dr. Brown administered the digoxin that Oscar had brought from the drugstore. The medicine did not work. He also listened as Ozuna and Dr. Brown warned Robert that Mike and Letty had a dangerous electric shocker machine they intended to use on him.

Despite the late hour, Mike thought it prudent to call his sister Lica Elena from the car to inform her of the evening's developments at the San Antonio Viejo. He also suggested that she and their sister, Alice, pay a call on Robert. Lica Elena agreed that they would.

The next morning, according to Ramiro Palacios, Dr. Brown consulted a medical textbook and decided to apply nitroglycerin patches to Robert's chest and arms instead of continuing with the digoxin. He says that it was a couple days before Robert's heartbeat was temporarily restored to normal.

He texted Mike and Letty that Ozuna and Dr. Brown were indignant over their visit and told them how Brown borrowed his printer to compose a letter she faxed overnight to Paul Price.

Ramiro spent that night with Robert in his room.

Ozuna also slept at the ranch that night—unusual for him. Palacios says the foreman stayed at the main house because he was afraid that Mike was waiting for him out on the highway.

CHAPTER 43

Ramiro listened quietly the next morning as Oscar, Dr. Brown, and Carilu discussed how Paul Price was to bring with him a letter he composed for Robert's signature. It would bar Mike from the ranch.

Palacios relayed this news to Mike, then bathed Robert, gave him his meds, and helped him into his underwear, a pair of Levi's, and a good shirt before wheeling him out to the kitchen for breakfast. He remembers that Robert seemed disoriented and showed little interest in his serving of Ensure, a liquid nutritional supplement that is high in protein. Robert then retired for his morning nap.

Mike's sisters, along with Lica Elena's husband, John Pinkston, arrived as planned and visited Robert in his room for about 10 minutes. Ricky López, Carilu's cousin and Robert's sometime caretaker, was there. Lica Elena remembers that Carilu was also in the room, as was Dr. Brown, who, at one point, grabbed one of Robert's bare feet and ran her fingernail down its sole. The old man, although he was silent, responded with a sudden knee jerk and an angry frown. Lica Elena assumed the doctor's purpose was to keep Robert awake and alert in anticipation of the expected visit from Paul Price.

She then went for a stroll with her sister and husband to the ranch cemetery, where the sisters' grandparents and aunt were already arranged in a row south to north: Old Mama, Tom East Sr. A space was reserved for Robert on the north end, next to his sister.

On their return, Ramiro Palacios remarked to the group that their brief visit seemed to have brightened Robert considerably.

"Y'all ought to come more often," he said.

Oscar Ozuna materialized about noon and went to Robert's room. Palacios accompanied him, his audio recorder rolling.

"The lawyer will be here in a little bit," Oscar is heard to say on the recording. "So you can give him the okay, so they won't come bother you anymore. He is just going to come visit you and ask you if it's all right to keep Mike out. Mike won't be bothering you and everybody can leave you alone.

"¿*Ta bueno?*" "Is that okay?"

"Fine," Robert replies.

"Rest anyway. When he comes, I will let you know. Remember we're all here for you to help you, okay? We definitely don't need your health to be disturbed by someone like that. I'm glad you're doing much better.

"Mike came last night and made a circus with me and Dr. Brown. We tried to stop him at the gate. He cannot come here and tell you what to do. All this is yours, okay?"

Silence from Robert.

"Don't worry. I'll take care of this, and I'll take care of you too, okay? That's all we want for you, to be healthy and nobody to bother you. Don't worry about anything. You let us do that."

Paul Price arrived with his document for Robert to sign, as did Carilu Cantú Leal, who joined Ozuna and Price in the bedroom with Robert and Ramiro and Ricky López.

At about one thirty, Ramiro clicked on both his mini tape recorder and the cell phone in his shirt pocket. Hoping not to call attention to himself, he placed his laptop in plain sight across the room on a dresser, then made himself as inconspicuous as possible at the foot of Robert's bed.

The first audible voice on the recording is Carilu's. She was seated on a stool near the head of the bed, on Robert's left, where she was feeding him canned fruit from a ceramic bowl she kept on a rusty, old metal-frame table on wheels, along with his water and juice and various utensils.

"Some more?" she asked, spoon in hand. Robert did not respond.

Price glanced at Ramiro's laptop on the dresser. Evidently assuming it was Robert's, he remarked, "That's pretty cool, Robert. You've got a laptop if you want to watch movies—cool."

The lawyer, standing near Palacios at the foot of the bed on Robert's right, produced a gift for his client, a CD of Christian music. Price awkwardly suggested that Robert could listen to it on the road "in your pickup," as if Robert East would ever again drive a vehicle of any sort.

The eerie cries of the ranch's raucous peacocks and peahens are audible in the background as Price gets down to business.

"Robert," he says, "I know you've had a tough time the last month or so, but I'm glad to hear that you are getting better. Dr. Brown tells me you are getting better. I'm glad to hear that."

"Do you hear Mr. Price talking to you, Robert?" Carilu asked.

Robert remained quiet, expressionless, as Palacios recalls.

"I just wanted to come down and visit with you and talk to you about what's been going on. But I don't ever want to bother you. If it's a bad time for me to be here, I'll come back another time."

Robert hawked up some phlegm, gasping for air as he had been doing for weeks.

"I had a real good talk with Dr. Brown. She's a real good doctor. She really enjoys working for you.

"Robert," Price said, "there was a little ruckus last night out here. Do you want Mike to keep coming out here to visit you? Or would you rather him not be coming out here?"

"I have no problem," said *el patrón*. Mike and Oscar's brief tiff had taken place four rooms away from him. He'd heard nothing.

"What was that, Robert?" Carilu asked.

"I have no problem."

"Is that what you want? You want them to leave you alone?"

"Robert is frustrating," said Price, as if speaking of a child. "[He's] trying to talk to us and having a hard time. Try it one more time. So would you rather Mike not come up here? Or do you want him coming up here? You're the boss."

"I don't have a problem," Robert repeated.

Carilu nevertheless asked once again. "Are you comfortable with him coming out here, Robert?"

"Yes."

"Yes?"

"Yes," Price added. "Yes. I want you to be able to see whoever you want to. I don't want anybody coming out here to bother you. If I ever bother you, you tell me, and I'll leave."

He chuckled, then began anew.

"The reason I'm asking you this, Robert, is that Dr. Brown is a little bit concerned. She doesn't think it's a good thing for people to be out here causing a ruckus, you know, right now while you're trying to get your health back. She was a little bit concerned last night that Mike and Mike's girlfriend were causing a ruckus.

"Would you rather Mike just to come out alone without his girlfriend? Because we're going to do what you want to do. She was kinda walking all over your house. I guess Mike took your picture of Kathy.

"I know Mike's your nephew, and if you want to visit with him, that's fine. If you don't want his girlfriend out here, then we'll tell him to come alone."

He turned to Ozuna. "What I understand, Oscar, is that is what Robert is saying right now: Yes to Mike. He would like Mike to be able to come out."

At that moment, and to Price's evident displeasure, Lica Elena, Alice, and John Pinkston opened the bedroom door and walked in.

"Can you leave us alone for a little bit?" Price asked. "I'll talk to y'all later."

"I'm sorry," Lica Elena answered. "We're actually leaving. Saying goodbye to him. Robert, I gotta go.

"You all right?" she asked her uncle.

"Yeah."

"Do you need anything?"

"I'm fine."

"All right."

Alice said good-bye, adding, "You take care, okay?" and then addressed Ramiro in Spanish. *"En una chanza, le mando el libro para que se lo pueden leer ellos."* "Once I get a chance, I'll send him that book so they can read it to him."

"Bye, Robert," John Pinkston said. "If you need anything, you call. Okay?"

Price showed all three to the door as Carilu asked, "Are you all right, Robert? You need a little bit more food?"

She picked up Price's narrative.

"Robert, what Mr. Price was saying is that last night was a big fight between Mike and Oscar, who didn't approve of Mike's girlfriend walking all over the house. They took the picture Kathy gave you. Robert, you know you don't like people to take things that belong to you without your permission.

"What we were asking you, and what Mr. Price is going to ask you, is instead of popping out from nowhere and coming unannounced, would you rather Mike come just him by himself and not his girlfriend? What do you think? Do you like people to go through your stuff?"

Another throat rattle.

Oscar interrupted her to claim that Mike offered him Kathy's photo. "I said, 'It's Robert's. It's not yours or mine.' He said, 'Well, I'm gonna take it.' I think he was wrong. If he took that picture, he can take something else."

Then Ozuna invented a bizarre and far more sinister threat from Mike and Letty. "Last night," Oscar said, "his girlfriend wanted to *shock* you. Dr. Brown and I stood up and said, 'No.' Because if they shock you, then you can die right there, and you don't have to.

"So we need to be very careful with them, because if they come and we're not here, there's nobody to stop them from giving you treatment like that, and you can die."

"Robert," Price stepped in again, "would you rather Mike just come when someone else like Oscar is here? I want you to do what you want to do. I know Mike's your nephew. If you'd like to see him, then you should be able to see him. If you don't want to see him, then you shouldn't have to see him.

"His girlfriend is a nurse. She's trying to tell Dr. Brown how to take care of you, and that's not good. Dr. Brown knows better."

The barrage continued.

Ozuna warned Robert once more about Letty and her death machine. "If we're not here, we can't stop them from doing the treatment like that on you," he said. "She might do the wrong treatment for you, and we don't want that."

Carilu: "We *care* about you, Robert, and we don't want anything wrong or bad to happen to you, okay?"

"That's right," Price agreed. "Robert, we want to protect you. We also want you to be able to see your relatives, if you want to see 'em. If you want to see Lica Elena, Alice, and you want to see Mike, we want you to be able to see them, but we want you to see them in a safe way.

"If you want to think about it, you don't have to decide now. You think about it. I can come back down again."

Carilu: "Would you like to think about it?"

"I can handle it," Price interrupted her.

Carilu persisted. "What would you like to do, Robert? We're here for you."

"Letty wanted to give you a treatment that is given to heart patients," Price warned him. "Dr. Brown says it only should be done in a hospital."

Mike and Letty had with them a portable machine for remote use.

"Dr. Brown doesn't believe you need that treatment now. Dr. Brown thinks you're getting better. Your pneumonia is gone—"

Robert coughs again.

"—and you're responding to some heart medication, and you're getting better."

Carilu steered the subject back to the previous night. "Why did they have to come?" she asked the room. "They just came. Mike and his girlfriend? They just came unexpectedly last night. Wanted to visit you.

"They brought some machine. They thought you were really, really, really ill. His girlfriend, Letty, wanted and he wanted to put this machine that they use for patients that have heart failure."

Price: "[A] machine that goes in your heart [and] gives you little shocks to help get it going . . ."

Carilu: "Like, a shocker is, like, actually to revive . . . the beat."

Price: "Dr. Brown doesn't use it. She uses medication first."

"Right," Carilu agreed. "That's what she's doing. She's using medication. Dr. Brown is using medication because she doesn't *need* that machine.

"Last night, when they came, the girlfriend went around the house and was looking, and they took the picture that Kathy had given you. Mike didn't like the idea of that picture being there. So he took it! And I know you don't like for anybody to take things that belong to you. Is that correct? Is that right?"

"Uh-uh!" Robert finally responds. "I don't like it."

"You don't like it. I know that. She was going through the rooms, through *all* the rooms. She was going into Dr. Brown's things in the bedroom where she was staying. And we're asking you if it's okay. You still want her to keep coming, if she's going to be doing these things? Only you can say if you do or you don't.

"We're here for you, Robert, and we want to take care of you. We don't want things done to you [that] don't need to be done to you. Is that okay?"

"No," he answered.

Carilu ignored his response, asking again, "Can we keep taking care of you in this way?"

Oscar butted in again, claiming that Mike had wanted to fly Robert to the hospital.

Carilu said she even knows the destination. "He was going to take you to Corpus in the helicopter."

Oscar: "Uh-huh."

"But Dr. Brown said you weren't sick. You were stable. You're okay. You didn't have to. Would you have wanted to go to the hospital?"

"No."

"I thought so. In order to avoid this . . ."

Price took over. "Robert, let me ask you something. Do you want to stay out here at the ranch house and have Dr. Brown taking care of you? Is that what you want? You want to be here at the ranch. Is that right?"

"No."

Price plowed ahead.

"What Carilu is explaining to you is that Mike and his girlfriend keep on wanting to take you to the hospital and get you into that environment. Dr. Brown doesn't think that's necessary right now, but if you wanted that, I'm sure she could arrange that. If you'd rather be here at your ranch, have Dr. Brown caring for you here, that's what Dr. Brown will do."

Oscar echoed Price in Spanish. "*¿Quiere que siga la doctora Brown viéndolo aquí? ¿A usted mejor? ¿En lugar de llevarlo al pueblo? ¿Cómo cree usted? ¿Lo que usted quiera, si quiere que ella siga viéndolo aquí? A qui la dejamos que lo mire, para que no lo tenga que meter a un hospital.*"

"You still want Dr. Brown taking care of you here, instead of taking you to town? What do you think? However you want to, if you want for her to keep taking care of you here we'll let her continue to take care of you here, so you don't have to be taken to a hospital."

They're relentless.

"Robert," said Carilu. "Would you rather be taken care of here at the ranch, or in a hospital? At the ranch with Dr. Brown? Do you understand what I'm asking you, Robert?"

"No."

"Do you want Dr. Brown to keep taking care of you here?"

"I don't understand."

"Okay. Mike and Letty wanted to take you to the hospital last night, but you didn't need to. Would you rather go to the hospital and be treated in the hospital? Or do you want to stay here at the ranch, and keep Dr. Brown taking care of you, being your doctor here?"

Oscar reverted once more to Spanish. "*Ya aliviándose, no necesita ella estar aquí nomás los muchachos, ya que se alivie usted. ¿Está bueno?*"

"Once you get better, she doesn't have to be here. Only the boys. *¿Ta bueno?*"

"Robert," he continued, "would you like for me to tell the gate guard for Mike to call before he gets here?"

"No."

Ozuna offered another approach.

"It's better if his girlfriend doesn't come," he said, "because I think you feel a lot safer for yourself and us. Would that be all right with you—"

Robert made an unintelligible sound.

"—for Mike to come by himself? Better? You feel better, right?"

Oscar and Price paused to confer in low voices. Then the lawyer told Robert they could exclude "just the girlfriend."

He turned to the others: "Is that okay with you, Oscar and Carilu?"

"Yeah" and "Uh-huh," they agree.

"In case they come," Price said, "it's better if he comes when, like, Dr. Brown is here, right? I can't tell him to call and make an appointment first. He comes in and upsets Robert. Not a good deal."

Price tried again.

"Robert, what I can do is call Mike's lawyer and tell him that Robert doesn't want to cut off Mike. He wants Mike to go visit with him at the ranch but wants to do it in a way where it is not a danger for Mike or Robert."

Oscar: "Right."

Price didn't specify what the threat to Mike might be.

"So," he said, "I can convey that to Mike's lawyer if that'll make an impact, and then I can tell the lawyer that Mike needs to call a day ahead of time."

Carilu gave Robert more water from a cup. He sipped some and coughs.

"Do you want to finish the plums and apples?" she asked.

"Yeah."

Price then raised two new topics: appointing a guardian for Robert and transferring his estate to his management trust, which the lawyer was eager to see done as soon as possible. He would press his point at length.

"Robert, while you're eating, I'm going to talk to you about a couple of things going on," he began. "I want you to be in a place where you can have control of your own life. I want to protect you from anybody coming in and taking control of you that you don't want. The reason I'm bringing this up is that Mike East's lawyer talked to me about it, and that's what got me to thinking about it.

"There's a legal proceeding for someone to come in and find that they don't think that you are capable of handling your own affairs anymore, and they can go to court and ask the court to appoint a guardian over you.

"You know, the first people they would look at would be the next of kin, which would be Mike and Alice and Lica Elena. But *you*, if you want to—and you've done this in the past—you can sign a document called a declaration of guardian, where you specify who you would like to be appointed if a court ever decides you ever need a guardian. You can specify now who you want those people to be.

"You signed a document like that back in 2002—back five years ago—and, in that document, you specified Ron Davidson, Carlos Martínez, and Oscar. And so, you know, some of that's changed, so that document you may want to change.

"It's something you might want to think about. We can decide at another time. But I can draw a little document—a one-page document—that you sign that names who you want it to be. If you don't want any of your relatives appointed—if you don't want it to be Ron or Carlos, if you want it to be Carilu or Oscar or someone else, you can tell me that, and I'll put it in the document, and you can sign it."

Price also wanted Robert to transfer his estate to his management trust where, by virtue of the documents he had signed in November of 2006, Oscar, Carilu, and Tino Canales would assume control in case Robert lost capacity or died, two near-term possibilities.

"We've already done a trust for you, a management trust," he said. "During your lifetime you can change it. You can revoke it. You're the sole trustee of that trust. You have complete control over it.

"Right now—today—that trust does not have any assets in it. It has nothing in it.

"All your assets are in your individual name. So some of my clients like to go ahead and convey their assets into their management trusts. With you being the sole trustee, you're in complete control. What [that] means is that if someone has to declare you incapacitated, you have trustees you appointed [who] would be in control of those assets, not a guardian.

"You can have three people right—"

Cough.

"—now that you have named. These people would be in control of those assets, not somebody else who got to the courthouse and got a guardianship."

Cough.

"That's another protection that, you know, I could put in place for you if you wanted me to.

"So, you don't have to decide that tonight. I kinda have a sense you may be tired, and you've already had visitors here for a long time.

"I'll come back another time. Maybe first thing in the morning, or something like that? I can come back down next Friday or something if you want me to, and we can do these things.

"I'm concerned for you. I want you to be in control of your affairs. I want you to decide if there ever is a need for someone to step in. For example, if you did have to get hospitalized at some point in time and were unconscious for a period of time and that's when your agents and your power of attorney, the trust is in your management trust, that's when they would take effect.

"But if you had a guardian appointed by the court, they would override your agents and your power of attorney and your trustees and your management trust, unless you've already put your assets in the management trust.

"So, I'm gonna leave a letter here with you that goes through all that. I don't wanna, you know, wear you out right now with it. But just wanted you to know I'm workin' on that, thinkin' about that, and I'll do whatever you want to do."

It's unclear from Price's comments whether the letter was the one Oscar expected, which would bar Mike from the ranch, or whether, as Price said, it would establish a guardianship lest someone such as Mike seek a court appointment as guardian, a possible step toward undoing his years of reworking the estate documents.

"*¿Le entendió Robert? ¿Un poquito? ¿Sí?*" Oscar asked. "Did you understand Robert? A little bit? Yes?"

"No."

"*¿Está cansado?*" Carilu asked. "You tired? You wanna rest?"

"Yes."

"All right, Robert," said Price. "Good to see ya. Adios. I'll be praying for you. Would you like to pray a little before we go? Want me to say a little prayer with you?"

"Yeah."

"Okay. Lord, we come before you right now. We wanna pray for Robert East. Lord, I thank You for him. Lord, I pray that You will heal his body. I pray that You will give him comfort, peace in his heart. I thank You that You love him, and I pray that You will be with him tonight. I pray in the name of our Lord Jesus Christ. Amen."

Carilu: "Amen."

Oscar: "Amen. All right."

Carilu concluded the evening. "*Lo vamos a dejar descansar y dormir. ¿Está bién?*" "We're going to let you sleep. All right?"

CHAPTER 44

T hree days later, Mike East and his two sons, Thomas and Johnny, drove out to the ranch to see Robert. They were turned back at the gate by Tino Canales, who said he was operating under Oscar Ozuna's orders.

Mike asked the guard to call the foreman, which he did. In a three-way conversation, Ozuna told East he was being kept out of the ranch at the direction of "the attorney," presumably Paul Price. Since Robert signed nothing on prayer night, the foreman and lawyer seem to have decided to exclude Mike from the ranch on their own say-so.

Robert's deteriorating health and Jetta Brown's suspect performance as his physician, plus the odd story Paul Price gave about Oscar Ozuna's power of attorney, had led Mike to discussions with Charlie Hury of a possible legal intervention before his uncle was beyond medical help. One of his first thoughts was to contact Texas Adult Protective Services (APS).

Hury vigorously opposed that option. He said it was a matter of common sense and practicality.

"Adult and child protective services are two of the biggest broken bureaucracies in the world," he argued. "I'm not a big fan of getting the government involved in anything, because it hardly ever works."

Mike reluctantly deferred to his lawyer, who favored pressing a legal action against Ozuna and Price and their allies via the courts, such as seeking a guardianship, which would entail the addition of more legal firepower to counter whatever strategies Price and his group pursued.

Rogelio Garza recommended that lawyer Tony Canales in Corpus Christi be hired to form a legal team with Charlie Hury. Canales had a reputation as a killer advocate in court. Hury, who worried that provisions of the 1995 disclaimer agreement might cost Mike legal standing to participate in any guardianship hearings, suggested that they recruit some Klebergs, who had no part in the 1995 proceedings, as intervenors to bolster their immediate issue, which was access to Robert.

Tres Kleberg agreed to join the suit as a plaintiff, represented by Ned Hartline and Scott A. Morrison of Oaks, Hartline, & Daly in Houston. So did Helenita Groves and her daughter, Carolina "Cina" A. Forgasen, represented by Ed Hennessy and Sharon B. Gardner of Crain, Caton, & James, also in Houston.

In an email to Tony Canales in which Charlie Hury reviewed possible causes of action, he raised the idea of alleging criminal false imprisonment. "Even slavery charges are possible," he wrote. "Getting somebody hauled off in handcuffs or at least having them think that might happen . . . is a powerful motivator, and we might want to consider that in the defining and refining of the actual causes of action pursued."

Still another possibility was to charge undue influence, as had been successfully argued decades earlier in the long, long fight over Sarita Kenedy East's estate. If Mike's objective had been to secure Robert's fortune, seeking a legal determination that his uncle had been unduly influenced was a practical if expensive and time-consuming alternative. Getting to see him and getting him proper medical care were emergency issues.

Hury was at Tony Canales's Corpus Christi office, taking a statement from Carlos Martínez, Robert's former accountant, fired by Oscar Ozuna, when Mike East telephoned to say he and his sons had just been turned back at the San Antonio Viejo gate. Hury advised Mike not to elevate the encounter with the gate guard into a confrontation, lest he be falsely accused of precipitating a physical confrontation, as Aida Garza had been—or worse.

After speaking with Mike, the lawyer then turned back to Martínez, asking about rumors that Oscar had recently purchased several new personal pickups at Robert's expense.

"Is that correct?" he asked.

"I believe so, yes," Martínez replied.

"Did he purchase a vehicle for Carilu?"

Martínez replied that Oscar had indeed purchased vehicles for Carilu. He said that he once approached Robert to ask if *el patrón* knew whether Oscar had recently bought Carilu a vehicle. He didn't.

"Oscar had purchased it using Robert East's credit," Martínez explained. "The routine was to go buy the vehicle at a dealership and have the dealership bill the office and have the office write a check for the full amount and pay for it."

Carilu says she required the vehicle to perform part of her job, hauling provisions for the ranch.

When the time came to account for purchases for tax purposes, Martínez said he told Robert that the car had to be treated as a gift, since Carilu wasn't working for him at the time. There would be a gift tax for anything over the $10,000 exclusion.

Oscar, Martínez said, "adamntly" refused, saying he wanted to handle the money as a loan. The two men were standing together in front of East when Martínez asked Robert, "What do you want me to do?"

"Do what you need to do," Robert replied.

"Well, then," Martínez told him, "I think it's a gift, and you need to report it as a gift. We'll need Carilu's full name, social security number, and her address."

According to the accountant, "Oscar got furious with me to a point where we were about to have a fist fight right there in Mr. East's bedroom."

"How," Hury asked, "did Oscar get to the point from just an ordinary employment contract as a foreman to signing checks and controlling everything?"

"Well," Martínez answered, "because he had Robert's ear, and I think during this time—though I can't prove it, other than hearsay—Oscar was telling Robert constantly bad things about me and about Ron. That we were after his money. I was billing too much. And Robert would believe that."

"Those were hot buttons that Robert was likely to believe?"

"Well, yeah. Very hot. Exactly."

"And Oscar knows that?"

"And he will use it against somebody. You know, Robert was always conscientious about bills. I think it's no secret that Robert was frugal with his spending and also with paying.

"At some point, we were talking about Paul Price's bill. He was on a retainer. During certain times of the year, Paul would go beyond his retainer, and that bothered Robert.

"Paul asked me to ask Robert, 'What about paying that excess?' and Robert said, 'We are on a retainer, and that's the way we're going to have it set up.'"

"Did you ever see anybody assist Robert in signing something?" Hury asked.

"Oh, yes."

"How so?"

"We were at the office one time in Hebbronville. I forget what document Robert was signing. Oscar was standing over him. Robert was kind of holding his hand like he was going to sign but wasn't doing anything. So I saw Oscar go over to his hand and kind of like—"

"Hold his hand and move his hand to make the signature?"

"Yeah, to some degree. I even saw where he finished the signature by crossing the *t* or dotting an *i*."

"Right. Did you ever see anybody other than Oscar do that?"

"No."

"Okay. Did Paul Price see this stuff?"

"I'm not sure whether Paul Price was at that meeting."

"Okay."

"I don't think he was, but he was told, and he said, 'That's not a big deal.'"

Hury returned to the question of how Oscar operated.

"Well," Martínez said, "I often wondered how we hired Oscar Ozuna to perform ranch operation [but] he was always at the [main house.]

"He has to ranch 250,000 acres of land. He doesn't have time to go visit the boss, but he often did. I presume he was just there to get Robert's ear and have trust built. Of course, at this time Robert needed physical help.

"Robert, a lot of times, wanted to go [out on the ranch] with Oscar, because he wasn't able to go on his own. Oscar would take him, and Robert was very much grateful.

"[But] it got to the point where Oscar just didn't want to take him. So he came up with excuses not to take him."

"And nobody else would take him?"

"Occasionally, when Ron went out there, Ron would take him."

"And that was the beginning of what, for lack of a better word, would be Oscar's imprisonment of Robert?"

"Exactly. It got to the point where Aída would call to talk to Robert to ask whether he knew if Oscar was doing certain things, and the phone would be disconnected, or she'd be told Robert was asleep. We couldn't get through. Nobody could get through."

Tony Canales asked what Martínez knew of Robert East's physical and mental condition.

"From what I hear, he hasn't been doing too well. He hasn't been functioning too well."

"Can he walk?"

"He's not able to walk from what I hear."

"Is he able to speak?"

"What I hear is he's able to speak, but you cannot understand him."

"Do you know whether or not he is able to write?"

"Robert had very limited writing capabilities even when I saw him. To write his own name, he would struggle a lot."

"Have you received information within the last six months that would indicate whether or not Mr. Robert East is suffering from any type of mental incapacity?"

"Yes. I have received [information that] Robert has been bedridden, not in his complete mental [faculties], medicated, and not able to eat."

"Do you know whether or not Mr. Robert East is capable of handling his financial affairs?"

"Mr. East hasn't been able to handle his financial affairs for years. That's why he hired me and those people."

CHAPTER 45

Two days later, on April 25, 2007, Charlie Hury composed another letter to Paul Price, advising the attorney that "Mike East and his family are seriously concerned about the qualifications of the physician currently attend[ing] Robert East, Dr. Jetta Brown."

After reviewing the East family's multiple issues with Brown, Hury concluded in the letter that Mike and his sisters "have no choice but to insist that Dr. Brown be immediately removed as the attending physician of Robert East and that he be provided with the kind of highly qualified and equipped care [that] he needs and to which he is entitled."

When Mike heard that Chuy Ochoa was put in charge of controlling who was allowed to visit Robert at the ranch, he called the dentist to arrange a visit, only to be told that he could not see his uncle because he had yelled at the old man and upset him.

That Mike was a threat to his uncle's peace of mind was also the major theme of an affidavit prepared by Paul Price and signed by Dr. Brown, who was identified in the document as Robert's primary care physician, with "over 1,000 active patient files."

Robert was depressed, Brown asserted, "and tends to shut down and refuse to communicate with any but his closest caregivers.

"Disruptive visits by Michael East, in my opinion, have resulted in Robert C. East feeling threatened, anxious, and overwhelmed," she claimed. "After the visits by Michael East and his siblings, Robert C. East has refused to eat and, in general, has tended to withdraw and become further depressed."

The doctor elaborated. "His most recent depressed condition has worsened dramatically and has resulted in an inability, at the present time, for Robert C. East to engage in discussions and communicate responsible decisions to other professionals and advisors who do not see him on a daily basis. Robert C. East appears to be overwhelmed at the present time and unable to deal with changes that occur or to process and make major decisions, particularly decisions that require him to address conflict."

Brown's analysis closely tracked Dr. Gaitz's impressions of 12 years before.

Among Robert's medical problems, she continued, he had "just recovered from pneumonia that had kept him bedridden and left him weak and debilitated. Robert C. East suffers from [atrial] fibrillation, a heart condition. Robert C. East had several teeth extracted and that, together with problems arising from a fracture to his jaw many years ago, makes it difficult for him to chew and unable to eat certain foods."

All these issues notwithstanding, Dr. Brown concluded her statement with an upbeat health forecast for Robert, again echoing Dr. Gaitz. "I estimate that this incapacity will be temporary," she wrote, "and Robert C. East will recover after treatment."

In an email to Ed Hennessy, Charlie Hury shared what Mike's sister, Alice East, had told him about Dr. Francisco Peña, Robert's former physician, who had refused to certify his patient's mental capacity the previous autumn. Apparently, Dr. Peña hadn't changed his mind. "The indication I got from Alice East," Hury wrote, "was that Dr. Peña does not think that Robert had been competent to handle his own affairs for maybe as much as the last year."

Paul Price had closed down the law office he once shared with Paul Pearson and joined prestigious Branscomb PC as a partner in the early months of 2007. Branscomb arranged for Dr. Michael A. Arambula, 54, a San Antonio psychiatrist, to come to the ranch office in Hebbronville on the morning of April 26 to undertake what Arambula called a "forensic psychi-atric examination."

On hand for the examination that morning were James T. Clancy, a Branscomb PC lawyer, as well as Paul Price and Dr. Brown, Oscar Ozuna, Carilu Cantú Leal, and Ricky López, plus Vicky Rodríguez, Aída Garza's suc-cessor as the ranch's office manager. The psychiatrist spoke individually with each of these people, save for Clancy, before conducting his clinical session with Robert, which would last about 90 minutes. Arambula later wrote in his report to Clancy that he'd reached a number of opinions "to a reasonable degree of medical certainty."

"Robert East has a history of anxiety/depression, currently untreated, and which has adverse effects upon his mental state," he wrote. Robert's pneumo-nia, Arambula continued, though "currently in remission," still had "residual adverse effects upon his mental state," which the doctor did not specify. He felt "Robert East's convalescence will be enhanced by the continued presence and assistance of staff familiar to him."

Like Dr. Brown, Dr. Arambula wrote that he'd concluded Robert's men-tal issues were temporary, although the course of his convalescence would likely be gradual. He found Robert had "reasonable mental capacity to make decisions regarding his most basic interests, but he will need the assistance of a guardian to manage his more complex decisions until such time in his convalescence that his mental capacity and future guardianship needs can be more definitely evaluated."

The similar prognoses from Brown and Arambula of incapacity likely to give way to capacity strongly reminded Mike East of 1994 and 1995 when Paul Pearson, Paul Price's old partner, argued that Robert had lost capacity in the wake of his sister's death and was therefore not competent to have signed the disclaimer. However, having regained capacity—according to his psychiatrist—he wanted the transaction undone. Both Brown and Arambula's observations could have come straight from the Paul Pearson playbook.

Arambula reported to Clancy that Robert remained in his wheelchair throughout the session. "He looked downward most of the time, but it was obvious that he was alert and listening. His eyes tracked staff members when each spoke; he also tracked objects that were moved around him.

"Mr. East recognized his mother and sister (in a photo), and his eyes welled with tears. He was substantially more relaxed and behaviorally interactive in the presence of his staff. He exhibited extended periods of behavioral involution—withdrawal—when the subject of his nephew or a potential stay in a nursing home was brought up (by me) as two examples."

The word from one of the witnesses in the office that day was that Robert refused to answer any of Arambula's queries and that "he also would not talk to Price."

The next day, Tuesday, April 27, at about midday, Ramiro Palacios was with Robert in his ranch bedroom, texting on his smartphone. As Palacios remembers, Jetta Brown strode into the room, red faced and furious. "Everything that's happening in this house has been heard someplace else!" she shouted at him.

Perplexed by her outburst, Palacios guessed Brown was talking about the steady stream of intelligence that he and others had been providing Mike East and Charlie Hury. When she saw him on his cell, he thought, she probably believed she'd caught him whispering household secrets.

There was, in fact, an effort afoot to confuse and anger Oscar and his circle. They were being sent anonymous texts from "burners"—prepaid cell phones—sometimes repeating to them the content of a recent private conversation, sometimes warning them against harming Robert. Oscar believed the house was bugged.

He responded by wheeling Robert into the bathroom and turning on the shower to mask their conversations. No help. At one point, Ozuna pushed the wheelchair out onto the grass and disassembled it, looking for a microphone.

Dr. Brown may have finally figured out Ramiro's role in this cowboy espionage and psyops program. According to Ramiro, Robert was awake in his bed as Brown stepped up her tirade and followed the drama with his eyes, saying nothing because he was unable to.

Brown tried to grab Palacios, he says, but he backed away, more concerned about the cache of incriminating microcassettes he had hidden in Old Mama's room than by any physical threat Brown posed. Palacios otherwise would have welcomed a chance to defend himself.

His mother, Iza, was also on hand, housecleaning, when the doctor raged through the door. As her son moved through the bathroom to Old Mama's room, Señora Palacios stepped between Ramiro and the doctor, who grabbed her right elbow and shoved her out of the way. Not sure what else the furious Brown might try, Iza knew Ramiro could fend for himself, but she worried about her two-year-old daughter, who she grabbed from her crib as they fled Brown's wrath.

The doctor did not follow Ramiro into Old Mama's room, giving him time to stuff a few belongings, the audiotapes, and his cell into a backpack. He also grabbed the 12-gauge shotgun Palacios kept ready for coyotes and other varmints looking to make meals of Robert's peacocks and other yard pets. Then he walked back toward the kitchen and garage, heading for his pickup.

Dr. Brown intercepted him in the living room, where he intended to leave Robert's Nokia on the table. She looked like she was ready to go at him again.

"Go ahead. Try it, bitch!" Ramiro says he taunted her as he walked past her and out the door to his truck.

Ramiro reached his father, Martín, in Zapata County, who told him to head there. They discussed whether Oscar might call the border patrol. If so, the tapes would be in danger of confiscation. So Martín Palacios told his son that one of his uncles would meet him on the road to Zapata and take the recordings for safe keeping.

The plan worked. After handing off the microcassettes, Ramiro continued on to Rio Grande City, where he met Mike East, Letty, and Mike's son Thomas. Mike advised Palacios to come with them to the Santa Fe, probably the safest place for him at the moment.

His uncle delivered the tapes to Ramiro's father, who entrusted them to Lalo Salinas, who drove them to the Santa Fe, where Mike first heard the Prayer Tape that evening. Although East had known of Ramiro Palacios's clandestine tapes for quite some time, he'd never listened to any of them.

Ramiro had captured approximately 40 conversations of varying lengths, audibility, and pertinence, each identified by number. The most remarkable feature of the conversations was Oscar's repeated condemnations of Mike and his sisters.

Recording number 10 picked up Ozuna in the kitchen, talking to Ramiro and his mother. The foreman bragged that Robert just received a check for $368,000 in cattle sales. "We're doing good, financially," he says. "It's just that these people, they see that we're doing well. Their fear is that the old man will not leave anything to no one. That's their fear."

"I don't think Robert will do that," said Iza.

"You never know with Robert," Oscar replied. "He will do as he pleases."

Number 29: Another kitchen tirade.

Oscar: "They haven't come to see Robert since the [disclaimer] fight, when they took everything away from him. They went to court. Robert got it all back. At that time, they were fighting, they went so low to look in the trash. Lica Elena is a poison.

"They would come because he sees me like a son. I stayed two nights. They can't stand me."

"If Robert wasn't right in his head," said Iza, "he would not have recognized his nieces."

Ramiro remarked on how happy Robert was that they visited him. "He was asking when they would be back to have lunch ready and cook ribs for them."

They discussed Robert.

"He's doing really good," said Oscar.

Iza noted, "He is eating a little bit more; not good, but a little more, better than previous weeks."

"Yes," Oscar agreed. "It's normal for him at that age. The doctor knows because all she does is see elderly. She's been doing it for years. She says it's very normal for his age."

Ramiro: "Yes, good days and bad days."

Oscar: "Yes, when they come these people say he is not eating. They're looking to see what Robert's going to leave them. All they want is to put him in a nursing home or a hospital, so they can have control. But the thing is, they were blown away when they found out that I have power of attorney. I have all the power to take care of him. They can't do anything, because I'm not in favor of it . . .

"These people are going to say that we are not taking care of him, and say, 'We are going to take him.' They can't do anything, but we care for him really good.

"Just like I told Mike that day. He told me we were not taking care of him, but I told him, 'Look, we take care of him the best we can, because it's to our benefit for Robert to live a lot more years.' I told him, 'It's to your benefit for him to die now. Y'all are just after what he has.' He got very upset with me. Mike says he doesn't need what Robert has.

"The more you have, the more you want. I told him that the rich always want more. I told him, 'You're not going to lecture me on how you people function. I've known your kind all my life. It's the truth.'"

Mike listened to the tapes in the agonizing realization of the physical and mental ordeal his uncle must have suffered for years. What had Robert thought to hear Oscar's fantastic assertion that Mike and Letty were threatening to kill him? Likewise for Carilu's weird allegation that Letty had rummaged through Dr. Brown's personal effects?

After years of ignoring the multiple warning signs that something was deeply amiss at the San Antonio Viejo, Mike was at last confronted with clear evidence of how an "essentially rudderless old man," as Charlie Hury described Robert, was kept isolated and ignorant and poisoned against his family. Mike finally understood his uncle's strange anger on the day of the last cattle roundup and then his tears of anger and frustration that Thanksgiving night in Old Mama's room.

But the truth so far was only half revealed. Soon would come the second revelation of Oscar's chronic thievery, dwarfed as it was by the two Pauls, who, by their legal handiwork, quietly repurposed Robert's estate toward a future he could hardly imagine, let alone embrace.

The American Bar Association cautions lawyers about both the appearance of impropriety and undue influence. A lawyer's legal skill and training, together with the relationship of trust and confidence between lawyer and client, create the possibility of overreaching when the lawyer participates in a business, property, or financial transaction with a client. Attorneys who encourage clients to name them as a trustee or cotrustee do so at great risk. Attorneys sometimes, jokingly, refer to these arrangement as "retirement annuities," as Paul Pearson apparently once did.

CHAPTER 46

Paul Price betrayed his scheme on the afternoon of April 21, the day of the Prayer Tape, when he mentioned to Robert how the conversation he had with Charlie Hury "got me to thinking" about a guardian for his client.

The lawyer did not wait for Robert to name one. Nine days later, Ron Davidson filed an emergency application for appointment as Robert's temporary guardian. Davidson, who had given up his appointments as a trustee and executor and was relieved of his special ranch deer-hunting privilege, was suddenly back on the Price team.

Dr. Brown's affidavit, initially drafted in the Branscomb office and edited by Paul Price, was attached as an exhibit to the oil man's application. Vicky Rodríguez, now the San Antonio Viejo ranch bookkeeper, notarized it. Also attached was Robert's declaration of November 26, 2002, prepared by the late Paul Pearson, which named Davidson as guardian of his person, as well as his estate.

Price may have acted so soon out of concern that Charlie Hury was about to file his own motion to have Mike East named his uncle's legal guardian. The Davidson application warned that "If Michael East were granted a temporary restraining order or [was] appointed temporary guardian of Proposed

Ward, . . . such appointment would seriously jeopardize the fragile health of the Proposed Ward."

There was no proof of the now-familiar allegation, that Mike had "entered into Proposed Ward's house unannounced and uninvited on several occasions over the last couple of weeks, creating disturbances and interfering with the medical care of Proposed Ward's attending physician, causing anxiety and deepening the depression of the Proposed Ward. Michael East has delivered threats to personnel at Proposed Ward's ranch of filing litigation against Proposed Ward and his employees."

Davidson asked for $500,000 from Robert's bank accounts to finance his proposed agenda. His wish list ranged from "the authority to obtain and audit all records relating to Proposed Ward's assets" to "the authority to employ attorneys, accountants, appraisers, consultants and other professional advisors, as well as administrative staff and other staff, as needed to help administer Proposed Ward's assets."

The next afternoon, Charlie Hury countered in the same district court with an "intervenors' petition for emergency appointment of temporary guardian and thereafter permanent guardian" for Robert on behalf of Mike and his sisters.

After extensive consideration and debate, Hury and East had settled on Carlos Martínez as their choice, agreeing that Martínez's loyalties were uncertain but that he'd been fired by Ozuna, and Price spoke well of him in their deliberations. Hury did not mention the accountant by name in the filing.

Hury writes that his first concern after questioning Carlos Martínez with Tony Canales was "the removal of Oscar Ozuna and his associates, including that physician, so that qualified doctors would be free to give Robert the kind of medical attention he so desperately needed."

Another concern was the number and nature of any estate planning documents, including a new will, that Paul Pearson and Paul Price might have prepared for Robert's signature over the years the two lawyers represented him. Mike and his sisters and their lawyers knew nothing of the numerous estate documents that the two Pauls had produced for Robert's signature for more than a decade, but by this time, they put nothing past either attorney.

Mike asked Carlos if he knew whether Paul Price had done anything that constituted undue influence. Martínez said that he did. East then floated a possible deal. He told Martínez that if Price undid whatever he had done—put everything back the way it was—he could walk away, no questions asked. Nothing came of the conversation.

Hury excoriated Oscar Ozuna and Dr. Brown in his guardian filing.

"As soon as he was hired," Hury wrote, "Oscar Ozuna and persons associated with him began a long and deliberate plan to isolate Robert Claude East and to remove anybody and everybody that was close to Robert Claude East, so that Oscar Ozuna and his associates could control the flow of information to Robert Claude East and consolidate their control over Robert Claude East. In so doing, Ozuna and those persons have dismissed or otherwise alienated long-time bookkeepers, lawyers, accountants, oil and gas consultants, employees, and household staff.

"They have further taken it upon themselves to falsely allege a detrimental effect upon the health of Robert Claude East as an excuse to exclude family members—Mike East, his sons, and his sisters—from access to Robert Claude East and have refused to obtain adequate medical care for Robert Claude East despite specific requests by Intervenors to do so.

"When the health of Robert Claude East began to deteriorate in recent weeks, Oscar Ozuna also falsely represented that he was the sole legal guardian of Robert Claude East and had the sole authority to make all decisions for him, and, as such, he retained the current attending physician, Dr. Jetta Brown, even though she is unqualified and unequipped for the task, and she has no office open to the public, no equipment for home hospitalization, no hospital privileges at any hospital, and no certifications of any kind, and she accepted the false representation of Oscar Ozuna that he was the 'legal guardian' of Robert Claude East without verification or objection.

"Since 2001, the assets of Robert Claude East have also been, at best, mismanaged and, at worst, plundered by Oscar Ozuna and his associates. Upon information and belief, the estate is believed to have decreased in excess of a million dollars as a result of those acts and omissions."

The figure was just a guess. Then, as later, the total amount of money possibly missing from Robert East's accounts was unknown.

Ron Davidson retaliated with a "motion to strike a plea in intervention."

Then Oscar Ozuna entered his own bid. He hired Preston Henrichson, a board-certified personal injury and civil trial attorney in Edinburg, whose filing denied that Robert was in any way incapacitated, temporarily or otherwise. However, the document continued, "if this court finds to the contrary that there is an imminent danger that the Proposed Ward's physical well-being may be impaired or the Proposed Ward's estate may be wasted because Proposed Ward is unable to make reasonable, informed decisions concerning his health or his estate, then Applicant requests that he be appointed temporary guardian of the person and estate of Robert C. East."

Whatever might be said of Oscar Ozuna, he did not want for nerve.

Newlyweds Tom East, Sr. and Alice all smiles at one of the stone buildings near La Perla, their first home. *Photo courtesy of the East Family.*

Tom East, Sr. and Alice share a hug on the rocks. *Photo courtesy of the East Family.*

Former Texas Ranger Walter Russell, head of ranch security, meets with Alice and Lica at La Perla in the 1970s. *Photo courtesy of the East Family.*

La Perla's abandoned ruins in 2019. *Photo © by Letty García.*

Tom East, Jr., in his 20s, working cattle at the Hebbronville railroad pens.
Photo courtesy of the East Family.

After the hunt: Lica with dog (far left) and Robert with dog (far right), bobcat in the middle, likely early 1930s. *Photo courtesy of the East Family.*

Lica with her dog and shotgun, festooned with the day's kill. *Photo courtesy of the East Family.*

Dinner time at Lica's deer diner. *Photo courtesy of the East Family.*

Tom East, Sr., at his desk, wearing his all-purpose, all-occasion business attire. *Photo courtesy of the East Family.*

Tom East, Sr. and Alice out for a ride in the late 1930s. *Photo courtesy of the East Family.*

Alice with Robert in 1940. *Photo courtesy of the East Family.*

The original San Antonio Viejo headquarters, since demolished, with a deer at the door. *Photo courtesy of the East Family.*

Felix García, Letty García's grandfather, a San Antonio Viejo foreman. García and other veteran vaqueros departed the ranch when Robert took over as patrón in 1943.
Photo courtesy of the East and García Families.

Tom East, Jr. rolls his own. *Photo courtesy of the East Family.*

Lica, Tom East, Jr., and their mother Alice (called Old Mama) with a ranch truck and a dog in the early 80s. *Photo courtesy of the East Family.*

Frank Yturria and "Mr. Bob" Kleberg. *Photo courtesy of the Yturria Family.*

One of Robert's antique wagons Letty García rescued from a San Antonio Viejo trash dump and took away to be restored. *Photo © Ramiro Palacios.*

La Mula pasture shelter Robert built in the 1980s for Lica and Alice, and its current occupants. *Photo © Ramiro Palacios.*

Old East Brothers' branding irons Robert once displayed along the San Antonio Viejo headquarters fence. *Photo © Ramiro Palacios.*

The East Family diamond brand Robert ordered built as a camp kitchen chimney adornment at La Mula. *Photo © Ramiro Palacios.*

Alice (Old Mama) and Lica together outside the San Antonio Viejo brick headquarters in the early 1990s. *Photo courtesy of the East Family.*

Robert welcoming guests to Alice's (Old Mama) 100th birthday fête in 1997.
Photo courtesy of the East Family.

Left to right, Lyndy Hernández, Vicky Rodriguez, and Carilu Cantú Leal with Robert, marking his 87th and final birthday in October 2006, at the San Antonio Viejo cowboy camp. *Photo courtesy of the East Family.*

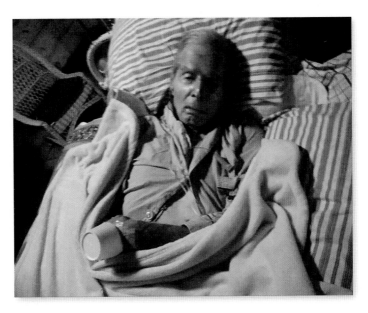

Robert on his deathbed with a styrofoam cup covering an IV at San Antonio Viejo. *Photo © Ramiro Palacios.*

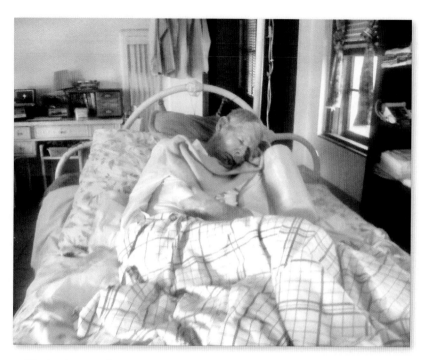

The last known photograph of Robert, on his deathbed, in the spring of 2007.
Photo © Ramiro Palacios.

Oscar Ozuna.

Ramiro Palacios.

CHAPTER 47

After his telephone conversations with Robert Hunter in early May of 2007 and the Ranger's subsequent lack of action, Mike supplied Hunter's cell phone number to Charlie Hury and Héctor Canales, Tony's son, and a lawyer as well.

Both attorneys spoke by telephone with the sergeant. On May 8, Hury emailed Tony Canales that Hunter had informed him he was "ready to move now" but did not.

On the ninth, as Hury recollects, he called the Ranger on his cell at midday, catching him at lunch in Laredo. He says Hunter was displeased to be bothered. Hury, in turn, was upset with Hunter—in part, because of his manner on the phone and, in part, by what Hunter told him: that he'd driven out to the ranch and there interviewed Oscar Ozuna, a gatekeeper, and others, all of whom insisted that Robert was in fine shape. They said there was no need for Hunter to *personally* check on Robert, and so he hadn't. Hury recalls no further contact with Hunter.

Ozuna later claimed not to know Hunter or to ever have seen him at the San Antonio Viejo.

Twelve years later, in August of 2019, Mike telephoned the Ranger, by now retired. East recorded the call. "I just want to see if you can clear up some things for me," he says on it. "You called me from Laredo and then you called me from Hebbronville . . ."

"No, I never went to Hebbronville," Hunter interjects. "I thought that you called me."

"It wasn't me. I got this call from you out of the blue."

"You know, his attorneys started calling me. I called Oscar Ozuna and said, 'Hey Oscar, I want to come down there. I just want to check on him, make sure he's all right.' And my phone started blowing up. I mean, everybody was calling me!

"They said, 'Look, he's okay. No problem with him' and everything.

"I said, 'Okay. You say he's okay?'

"'Yeah, we just talked to him. He's fine,' and just kind of left it at that. I never went to Hebbronville."

"Okay. Wherever you were, you told me that you had talked to Chris Huff, and Chris Huff told you there was no need for you to go out there and make a welfare check, because Robert was fine."

"That might have been what it was."

"I don't know, but we've got some conflicting stories here."

"What can I help you with?"

"I just want to clear this up. You told me there wasn't any need for you to make a welfare check, that you had run into Chris Huff, and Chris Huff said Robert was fine, that they took him in an ambulance and that Robert told the driver not to drive too fast because he'd run over his deer and that he was hungry . . ."

"I don't recall."

"Yeah, well I do."

"I don't recall."

"No, I do! Listen to me. I do."

Hunter laughed. "No, you listen to me!"

"No."

"I don't remember any of that. It's been too long ago. I know that I never went out there. I do recall talking to Chris. I talked to Ozuna . . ."

"I don't believe any of that. You told me you knew it when somebody was lying. This person that had told you this wasn't lying. That you'd been a ranger a long time. And besides, you had a murder to go and investigate somewhere."

"Well, I don't recall."

"Was there a murder you had to go investigate?"

"There might have been. I don't remember."

"Well, I remember."

"You've got a better memory than I do, because I don't. I talked to Chris. Chris said, 'Hey, don't worry about it. I'll take care of it,' or something, I think, to that effect."

"You did talk to Chris, then?"

"Yeah. I believe I talked to Chris."

"So Chris was the one that told you . . ."

"Told me what?"

"That there wasn't anything to worry about."

"I don't recall. I'm not real sure."

"Well, you just told me that Chris said there wasn't anything to worry about."

"Are we being recorded? What's this all about, anyway?"

"We just feel that there was some wrongdoing with my uncle. There was never an inquiry made, to say the least. That's what we're talking about."

"Well, it's something that should have been done way back when."

"Yeah, to a lot of people, it's water under the bridge. But not to me."

"Well, I can't help. I don't recall much about it. Just a bunch of phone calls being made. Attorneys jumping up and down like shortstops . . ."

"What attorneys?"

"I don't remember."

"Did you ever hear the name Price?"

"I don't remember."

"Oh, you don't?"

"I'm sorry. I can't help you. I mean, I just don't know a whole lot about it.

I know there were attorneys. They were calling. They were jumping up and down. 'You don't need to go out there!'"

"Yeah?"

"Yup."

"Why would an attorney call you and tell you that you didn't need to go out there?"

"You got me."

"You don't remember their names?"

"No. I have no idea. Been 12 years ago. Too many years."

"Well, when you're not related, it's been too many years. But when you're related, it isn't."

"I suppose so. No related. I understand there's a lot of money involved there."

"Who cares about the money? We're talking about a life."

"I understand that."

"I don't need any more money. I'm talking about somebody's life. And an injustice."

Pause.

"Yessir."

CHAPTER 48

With three candidates now vying to serve as Robert's guardian, an initial court date was scheduled for Thursday, May 10, 2007, at the two-story Jim Hogg County Courthouse in Hebbronville.

Built in 1913 from a design by San Antonio architect Henry T. Phelps, whose public buildings were then popular, the courthouse is a tan, boxy affair on East Tilley Street. Inside on the first floor hangs a portrait of British-born James R. Hebbron, who founded the town. Upstairs is the district courtroom, where, at 2 p.m. on the appointed day, 279th District Judge Alex W. Gabert, 74, gaveled a status hearing on Cause CC 07-65 to order.

Tony Canales would later report that, on his way to court that day, he received a call from Paul Price on his car phone, proposing that they discuss a deal. Canales says he refused to discuss the offer, explaining that he had no reason to want a deal. The conversation went no further.

Canales also spoke briefly with 279th District Attorney Heriberto Silva, telling him that there was evidence of senior abuse committed against Robert, with whom Silva was personally acquainted. The DA opened a criminal investigation. He recalls receiving investigative input from the Texas Rangers as well, although he did not deal with Ranger Robert Hunter. He personally reviewed evidence such as Robert's videotaped testimony in

Oscar's defamation trial. "That wasn't the man I knew," Silva says. "He was incompetent."

The civil proceedings' ostensible purpose was to determine whether Robert needed a guardian and who that person should be. The discussion would soon move in other directions.

The courtroom teemed with lawyers and litigants, as well as the simply curious and one surprise attendee—Ramiro Palacios—whom Rubén Garza had driven to court for the single purpose of disconcerting the opposition. His appearance suddenly explained to Oscar and his allies how, for weeks, their mystery tormentors had known their every utterance. Ramiro Palacios!

"As soon as they saw him, it scared the shit out of 'em," says Charlie Hury.

Mike East was curious to see Chris Huff there. He wondered what business brought the uniformed game warden to court that day. East soon discovered that Huff, who declined to be interviewed for this book, had aligned himself with Paul Price, along with Ron Davidson.

Jim Robichaux from Branscomb PC, Paul Price's cocounsel, argued to Judge Gabert that the crowd in the courtroom was an invasion of Robert's privacy. Accordingly, Robichaux motioned that everyone except those immediately involved in the proceedings be excluded.

Tony Canales, Robichaux's counterpart as his side's courtroom operator, raised another issue. He informed the court that, when a deputy went to the San Antonio Viejo to serve Robert with his copy of the pleadings, as provided for by law, he was refused admission on Oscar Ozuna's orders. An absolute prohibition on *anyone*, including cops, visiting Robert was being strictly enforced.

Canales offered to send another deputy to the ranch with a copy of the pleadings for Robert. If someone tried to prevent the papers from being delivered, he added, the deputy could arrest that individual, then proceed to serve the documents according to the law.

Paul Price would deliver the papers without reported incident.

Before Judge Gabert took up the day's business, he accepted with apparent relief a suggestion jointly put forward by Tony Canales and Price. They proposed that the herd of attorneys arrayed before His Honor in the court-room roam somewhere neutral, like the jury room, where, in private, they could try to thrash out at least some of their multiple disputes. There is no transcript of the unusual gathering.

"The first thing that happened is that almost everybody savagely attacked Oscar," Charlie Hury writes of the 90-minute conference. "Figuratively speaking, half the people in that jury room wanted to shoot him, and the other half wanted to hang him. Preston Henrichson had to feel like Custer looking at all of the Indians descending upon him.

"Robichaux and his bunch wanted to keep control of Price," Hury surmises. "They probably also wanted and needed to protect Price, the bag of gold they thought came with him, and themselves [as well] from a half-billion dollar or more malpractice suit if everything went badly."

Paul Price declined to be interviewed for this book, citing attorney-client privilege.

The lawyers corralled in the jury room next trained their firepower on Ron Davidson. He appeared with four lawyers of his own, including Donato D. Ramos Jr. of Laredo, a friend of Judge Gabert. "We wanted Ron out to make room for Carlos, who was a possible ally," Hury explained, "and hoped [that he'd] be no more than a second-level problem if he wasn't."

"After a barrage of questions regarding his qualifications," Hury recalled, "he caved in relatively quickly and essentially wanted out." Tom McDade, Ron Davidson's lead lawyer, made it official three days later in a call to Tony Canales, adding that his client expected to be reimbursed for his expenses.

Davidson claims he dropped out because Mike East and others would pressure him to fire Oscar Ozuna the moment he was named guardian. He refused, he says, "because I believed that Oscar was someone Robert knew and trusted, and it would kill him if Oscar had to go." This was Paul Price's position as well.

The assembled attorneys also agreed that Dr. Jetta Brown's services would no longer be needed at the San Antonio Viejo. The following night at the ranch, according to witnesses, the doctor and Carilu Cantú Leal got into a scrape, and Brown then departed.

"Knowing Jetta like I do," Charlie Hury opined the next day in an email, "I strongly suspect that [they] got into accusing each other about whose fault it was that everything was falling apart, and that escalated into the fight. Jetta is a very large woman, and [Carilu] is not, so that may have been a rather one-sided fight."

The jury room combatants also agreed to limit Oscar Ozuna's continued access to Robert's checking accounts. Henceforth, all ranch checks he signed would require Lyndy Hernández's signature as well.

During a recess, Mike East and Letty García approached Paul Price, whom they'd never met. Mike introduced himself and Letty to the attorney and then said with a smile as he nodded at Letty, "This is the shocker. She goes around *shocking* people."

According to Mike, Price said nothing and hurried away.

Charlie Hury writes of later encountering Price on their way out of the courthouse. Price, says Hury, conceded that "Jetta Brown had not been a good idea" and "admitted that he knew we had information from inside the ranch. I told him we not only had past information but also continuing information from multiple sources and that we never would have started a fight like this unless we were sure of what was going on."

One of the contest's key issues was Mike and his sisters' and the Kleberg litigants' demand that their own medical expert examine Robert. The other side stalled until Tony Canales suggested an acceptable compromise, Dr. Antonio Falcón of Rio Grande City—coincidentally, the physician who'd been on duty the night Robert brought his sister Lica's body to the Starr County Memorial Hospital.

"Tony was very concerned that Mr. East was not getting taken care of and was basically neglected," Falcón recalls. "When Tony called me, he was very concerned that they were just letting Roberto die out there. Also that someone who had been taking care of him may not have been giving him the appropriate medications."

Soon after the hearing, Dr. Falcón paid the first of several visits to see Robert at the San Antonio Viejo. On May 17, he sent a typewritten report to Paul Price that strongly contrasted with Mike and Letty's impressions of Robert from April, as well Helenita Grove's recollection of her visit at about the same time as Falcón's report.

The doctor minimized the importance of some medical issues, such as Robert's AFib, and found him to be "comfortable and well taken care of at his home." Nevertheless, Falcón observed, "he is recovering from a pneumonia, and his overall health is fragile at best. He should not travel outside his home unless it is for a major medical event that may cause death or require hospitalization. There are no conditions that require specialty or subspecialty consultation at present."

Falcón also reported that Robert suffered from "mild malnutrition, which has probably resulted from his recent major medical illness, age, and poor intake as a result of mental stressors. Proper nutrition is a critical element in Mr. East's recovery plan. Without it, he will enter a downward spiral that will lead to his death. A low albumin, which he has, is an ominous laboratory finding in elderly patients. Proper nutrition can fix this problem."

Dr. Falcón wrote that he specifically remembered hearing from Lalo Salinas that Robert "gets upset and withdrawn when served legal papers or visited by attorneys. On such days, his caretakers have noticed that he refuses to eat, gets withdrawn, and stops taking fluids. We must find a way for him to rest and remain free of controversy until he has recovered. If not, this will directly lead to his death."

As far as is known, the only lawyers to visit Robert at the ranch in 2007 were Paul O. Price and one or more of his associates.

Dr. Falcón closed with responses to a specific query from Price. No, he wrote, Robert was "not in any physical condition that would allow a psychiatric evaluation to be performed."

The doctor recalls that his report did not please Tony Canales.

"I actually found Roberto to be very well taken care of," Falcón says. "I was expecting to see somebody that was full of ulcers and just neglected. Dirty. He was very well taken care of.

"By the time I saw Roberto, he was already unable to communicate. He was bed bound. I tried several times to get him to respond. But nothing. He may have been aware that I was there, but if there was any communication with him it was just minimal."

Unlike Drs. Brown and Arambula, Falcón hazarded no guesses as to when Robert might regain his cognition.

"I talked to Tony about it, and I think Tony was very disappointed that I was not going to go and testify that he was not being taken [care] of. I think Tony was looking for more than that. He didn't tell me that, but I got the impression. Then I got a call from Price, saying, 'Hey, can you continue taking care of Roberto?' I said 'Sure.' So I continued under Paul Price."

CHAPTER 49

A second court hearing in Cause CC: 07-65 was convened on Monday, May 21, at the Duval County Courthouse in San Diego, about 43 miles northeast of Hebbronville via Texas 359 W. The two-story red brick structure, surrounded on three sides by a dense stand of stout and leafy live oaks, is situated astride the Duval–Jim Wells County line.

Eighteen attorneys representing a dozen clients came to court, along with five financial experts there to advise the Kleberg heirs and their lawyers. Charlie Hury, in a memo to his file, estimated that the legal teams were billing $5,000 an hour in combined attorneys' fees, or about $50,000 a day.

The hearing opened with lawyer Donato Ramos of Laredo withdrawing Ron Davidson's application for temporary guardianship, "for medical and other personal reasons."

Davidson, however, had not dropped out of the game. Mike East recalls that, after the first hearing, Carlos Martínez shared his concern about whether they could prevail in the legal skirmishing and told East that he had been indirectly in touch with Paul Price. Ron Davidson acted as a go-between. Martínez, in time, would also join with Price.

Judge Gabert then heard arguments on Jim Robichaux's motion, first filed at the Hebbronville hearing, to close the proceedings to the public. Robichaux argued that sealing the courtroom was Robert's right under the

Texas probate code. "Mr. East is a very private person," he said. "Issues of his medical health and well-being, issues of his financing will be discussed, and it is not appropriate."

The lawyer did not address an associated possibility that some of the information likely to be aired in the courtroom was potentially damaging to his fellow Branscomber, Paul Price and, therefore, his new law firm's reputation.

Judge Gabert granted Jim Robichaux's motion to close the proceedings to the public. But he seemed defensive about it. "There's no question how I feel about open court proceedings," he said from the bench. "Of course, the fact that Mr. East is not in the courtroom at this time is something that the court, in its ruling, took into consideration. It would have been a lot better if he was to be in the proper physical and mental condition to be here."

The hearing's main event was to be Tony Canales, an aggressive and nimble courtroom presence, versus Paul Price, whom Charlie Hury frequently dismissed in his emails as a "dufus" but who, nonetheless, had one or maybe two dogs in the guardianship fight and fair prospects for carrying the day.

Price contended that Robert was at full capacity—necessary for some of the estate documents he authored to survive a possible challenge, and just as Drs. Brown and Arambula had forecast.

Canales asked Price if he had any medical training.

"No," he replied.

"Do you think you are competent to declare that somebody has mental capacity or not?"

"I don't. I am not a doctor. No, I am not a medical doctor. No."

"So you agree—"

"I have a personal opinion. I am not a medical doctor."

"So if you happen to have a personal opinion, that's just your own personal opinion?"

"Yes, sir."

Canales turned to Drs. Arambula and Brown's roles.

"How many times did Dr. Arambula, as far as you know, sir, examine Mr. Robert East?" he asked.

"Once."

"Sir, did you have any role at all in preparing the affidavit of Dr. Jetta M. Brown, MD?"

"Uh, yes."

"What role did you play, sir?"

"I was involved with other lawyers in our firm drafting the affidavit."

"Do you know, sir, whether or not Dr. Arambula made a conclusion that Robert was going to need the assistance of a guardian to manage more complex decisions?"

"Yes, he did."

"Do you agree with that? At that time, for a temporary period of time?"

"Yes."

"Has something happened since the date of this particular report, April 26th of 2007, that made you change your mind?"

"His condition has improved."

The only other witness who professed to believe Robert could think for himself at that moment was Oscar Ozuna.

"You know this because you have seen him since then?"

"Yes."

"Were you present when Mr. Robert East was served with citation [*sic*]?"

"Yes."

"All right. Did he have a conversation with you at that time?"

"I talked with Robert East that time, yes."

"I know you talked to him, but did he have a conversation with you?"

"Well, Counsel," he said, "I am trying to remember. I don't recall if he had any responses to me."

"Now I just want to know whether or not you had a conversation with him. So, would you agree, sir, with the proposition that whatever conversation you had with him, it [was] a one-way conversation?"

"I do not recall."

"Very well. By the way, tell me how you assisted in the preparation of the Jetta Brown affidavit."

"Well, I think my recollection is another lawyer in our firm drew up a first draft. I reviewed it, made comments, and I was one of the lawyers that looked at it, discussed it. I did discuss with Dr. Brown about it."

"So for sure your office did the actual physical preparation of the document. Correct?"

"We were involved in the word processing of the document."

"And the word processing and the typing out of the document [that] was then forwarded to Dr. Brown for signature?"

"It was discussed with Dr. Brown and given to her for signature. It was revised per her request."

"Now, Dr. Brown makes a conclusion regarding mental capacity of Mr. Robert East, does she not?"

"Yes."

"Do you agree with that conclusion?"

"Let me find the conclusion that you are referring to."

"Let me show you [the exhibit]. Can you read it?"

"'I estimate the incapacity will be temporary and Robert C. East will recover after treatment.'"

"Okay, what's the date of that affidavit?

"April 29, 2007."

"Dr. Brown had an opinion that his mental capacity was impaired at that moment, right?"

"Yes."

"Now, can you tell us whether or not, at the present time, Mr. East is able to write his name?"

"He has great difficulty writing anything. He has great difficulty with fine motor skills, which makes it difficult for him to write anything."

"So what does that mean? Can he write his name?"

"Sometimes, he can scribble his name, yes, sir, most of the time."

"And you would be there to ensure that he would write his name in the most important of the documents that would be placed under him. Correct?"

"I was there to be sure that he placed his mark on the document evidencing his consent to that document."

"His mark meaning his signature?"

"His mark being however he wanted to do it, Counsel."

"In this part of the country, there's a lot of people who still can't write and might put a big X or a little x if he happened to be junior. Does he sign his name with Xs?"

"He would sign sometimes his full name, sometimes with initials, sometimes Robert C. East, sometimes Robert East."

"What would be the difference in his mental capacity when he signed his full name versus when he was signing with his initials?"

"None. That has to do with fine motor skills."

"So you would say that there's no difference when he signs R. E. versus when he signs his full name?"

"Yes, sir. No difference."

"How many documents do you think, sir, he has signed as R. E.?"

"I do not know. I have no idea."

"You don't know. But would you agree, sir, that the signing of R. E. would be an unusual way to sign his name because his name is Robert C. East, correct?"

"No. I don't think it's unusual. It was painful watching him trying to write, Counsel."

"Well, let me back up. You have Dr. Jetta Brown's affidavit there in front of you that says he was temporarily incapacitated, at least. During what month did she see him?"

"I think she started early this year. I do not know. I was not involved. I do not know when she first saw him."

"We know [that], for some time in 2007, she is of the opinion that he was mentally, temporarily incapacitated."

"As of this date, yes, sir."

"We know that Dr. Arambula feels the same way, that, sometime in 2007, he was mentally incapacitated. Correct?"

"He was personally incapacitated, yes."

"Yes, sir. Now, sometime in the year 2006, sir, do you recall whether or not you presented documents for Oscar Ozuna to be holding the power of attorney?"

"I presented the statutory durable power of attorney that named three coagents."

"Did you have anything to do with preparation of that document?"

"Yes, sir, I did."

"What did you have to do with it?"

"Well, I and another lawyer in our firm drafted this document."

"And the date of that document, sir?"

"November 16, 2006."

"Okay. Who are the three people that are supposed to be acting as power of attorney?"

"Oscar Ozuna."

"That's number one. Right?"

"Yes."

"And in the pecking order who would be next?"

"Carilu Cantú Leal."

"All right."

"Celestino Canales. He is a [justice of the peace]."

"You are the lawyer involved with the entire responsibility of the execution of this document?"

"Yes."

"And since the execution of this particular document, sir, can you tell me whether or not this document has come into effect?"

"I think it has come into effect."

"Because?"

"Because of the affidavit of Dr. Brown and the opinion of the psychiatrist."

"The affidavit of Dr. Brown being that he lacks mental capacity?"

"Correct."

"Sir, do you believe that at this moment right now this particular document is effective?"

"Yes, I do."

Canales then explored with Price details of how Robert's business was being operated at the time that Ozuna, Leal, and Canales the gateman became his trustees and directors and each held power of attorney as well.

"Do you know, sir," he asked, "who is the accounting firm for Robert East?"

"Hermelinda Hernández and the firm of Long & Chilton, I believe."

"Where are they at?"

"Brownsville."

"And Ms. Hernández is where?"

"I think she's in Edinburg."

"Is Ms. Hernández a CPA?"

"I don't believe she is."

"So what's Ms. Hernández's role?"

"Outside accountant."

"Do you know, sir, whether or not a tax return for the year 2006 has been prepared and filed?"

"I don't believe so."

"Do you know, sir, who at the present time is handling the month to month reporting of income and expenses for the operation of Robert East?"

"I don't know that the month-to-month reporting is going on, but in the past, since the termination of Carlos Martínez, anything like that would have been done by Hermelinda Hernández."

"So, last month, for example, let's say who took care of the cattle sales at the ranch, or do you know?"

"The ranch foreman would have been in charge of cattle sales."

"All right, and the ranch foreman would be who?"

"Oscar Ozuna."

"Okay. Who would know and take care of the receiving the income from the royalties?"

"Receiving the income from the royalties? Those go directly to banks."

"All right, sir. And who would be involved in informing or telling the banks how to invest that money?"

"Robert East has instructed the banks on how to invest the money."

"And when is the last time that Robert East made such a call to the banks and advised them where to invest the money?"

"I don't know if he's ever made a call to the bank. That's not the way he communicates."

"Do you think today Robert East could call the bank and tell them how to invest the money?"

"He has the ability, sir."

Dr. Falcón had described the old man as "unable to communicate."

"Does he have the capacity to do that, to make that financial decision?"

"Sir, there's not a financial decision to make in terms of how Robert East for years wanted to invest his money."

"Sir, do you believe that Mr. Robert East at the present time, today, has the mental capacity to pick up the phone and know what he's doing to call the bank as to where to invest his money?"

"I think he does know whether he wants to continue doing what he has been doing, investing his money. He has his own unique philosophy, which he understands and knows and wants to continue."

"At the present time, sir, as far as you know, who is taking care of Mr. Robert East at the ranch? I am not asking for any legal conclusions, just who is taking care, as far as you know, that you have seen, who is taking care of Robert C. East at the ranch?"

"There's Oscar Ozuna, Carilu Cantú Leal, Ricky López, and private nurses."

"And at the present time, how is the payroll being handled? How are the operating expenses handled? Who signs the checks?"

"The checks, as of this moment, I understand are now being signed by Oscar Ozuna and Hermelinda Hernández."

"Is there a point in time where that started?"

"Yes."

"When did it start?"

"I think it started today."

"All right, and who was signing before?"

"Oscar Ozuna."

"All right. And for how long had Oscar Ozuna signed those checks before?"

"Since the termination of Carlos."

"All right. So whenever Carlos left, at least over a year—is that correct?"

"Well, it's around a year. I think it was summer of last year, but I don't remember exactly."

"Very well, but whenever Carlos left, from then on, the checks have been signed by Mr. Ozuna by himself. Is that correct? Until this weekend?"

"Sir, I am not a witness to it, but that's my understanding."

"I understand that, but you are the lawyer."

"Yeah. I know, but I have not been engaged in auditing the books and that kind of thing. I'm not out there, but that's my understanding."

"Let's go back a year. Do you know, sir, whether or not there's been any type of audit of the Robert East books within the last 18 months, since Carlos left?"

"Audits and those kinds of things were foreign to Robert C. East. An auditor has now been engaged."

"Oscar Ozuna was able to sign the checks by himself for the last year. What caused that?"

"That's what Robert East directed."

"Robert East said, 'Oscar, from now on, you sign all my checks'?"

"Right."

"And yesterday, did Robert also say, 'Oscar, I need some help. Now you sign and now Ms. [Hernández] can sign too.' Did that also happen yesterday?"

"What happened yesterday is to deal with the concerns that have been raised in this case. Practices were instituted. That is not the way Robert East would like to do things, but they were done in order to provide some safety and address concerns."

"All right. So, you would agree with me that, prior to last Thursday, those security measures were not in place?"

"That's correct."

"All right. And so would you agree with me, sir, that that's not the right way to run things, not having any type of security? Correct?"

"That's not the way I would run things personally, no, sir."

"Who has been running the financial operations of Robert East for the last year? Is this you?"

"No."

"Has Robert been running it?"

"Oscar Ozuna and Hermelinda Hernández."

"They have been running it?"

"Right."

"Okay."

"Under the direction of Robert East."

"These are things that you heard? You heard these directions? Or something that's been told you?"

"Sir, I have not been down to see what Oscar Ozuna has done and what Hermelinda Hernández has done or what Robert East has done."

The uncomfortable truth for Paul Price was that Oscar had been running a huge ranch and cattle operation out of his back pocket at least since the spring of 2006 under no constraints and accountable to no one. Price testified that he had paid no attention to Ozuna's dealings with Robert's funds at the same time he was assiduously revising Robert's estate planning documents, as well as drawing up powers of attorney for Oscar, Carilu, and Tino Canales.

"You told me you haven't audited the books. Have you audited any type of cattle sales for the last year, year and a half?"

"No, sir."

"Do you know if anybody has?"

"I don't think it's ever been done in the lifetime of Robert East."

Judge Gabert finally gaveled the hearing to a close at 5:30.

Mike East thought Paul Price looked relieved to at last vacate the witness stand.

"Tony put Price through the wringer," he says. "Price didn't have any good answers for Tony at all."

"How did you like it?" he asked Price as he left the stand.

Price said nothing as he walked on.

CHAPTER 50

Although Tony Canales had expertly filleted Paul Price on the witness stand, he'd only weakened the lawyer and his faction. He hadn't knocked them out of the game. Since the hearing ran late, Dr. Francisco Peña was prevented from rebutting the medical testimony, particularly Drs. Brown and Arambula's opinion that Robert was only suffering from temporary mental incapacity.

Court was scheduled back into session June 4, provided Robert lived that long. If he didn't, any argument over guardianship would be moot, and Oscar, Carilu, and Tino would assume control of both Robert's estate and the foundation per the legal documents already in place.

On May 24, a disquieted Ned Hartline reported to his client, Tres Kleberg, on the court room impasse. "We seem to be having great difficulty accomplishing some simple, altruistic goals," Hartline wrote.

1. "We want an examination of Robert East by a qualified doctor so we can have some independent evaluation of his current medical condition and whether his current medical maladies are being properly treated.

2. "We want some assurance that he is being provided access to medical care to ensure that any current problems are being treated with a view toward eventual health.

3. "We would like to see that he is not being swindled with the current management of his operations.

"It doesn't seem that anyone would object to these requests," the lawyer continued, "but, at the hearing last Monday, there were approximately 18 lawyers actively arguing."

Another complication, wrote Hartline, was Judge Gabert. "The judge seems like a nice man who is reluctant to make a decision," he informed Kleberg, "because his decision is going to anger one group or another, and each group has sufficient resources to pursue (and appeal) any decision made. I'm sure he will be inclined to make the most popular decision, but with six (at least) competing groups, no decision will be popular."

Hartline's number-one goal seemed to have been met on May 30 when Dr. Mark Burns, a geriatric psychiatrist whom Ed Hennessy had recruited, at last examined Robert at the ranch.

It was at first agreed that Mike East would pick up the doctor in Hebbronville then drive him out to the San Antonio Viejo to see Robert. But after Preston Henrichson objected on the grounds that East might unfairly influence Burns as they drove along together, Vicky Rodríguez, the book-keeper, was assigned to chauffeur the doctor, as if she was a neutral figure in the case.

Besides his clinical examination, Burns conducted interviews with Dr. Falcón, Vicky Rodríguez, Oscar Ozuna, Ricky López, and Carilu Cantú Leal. There's no indication in his reports whether he directly consulted with Dr. Brown or Dr. Arambula, although he read and cited Arambula's report of Robert's forensic psychiatric examination in his own write-up.

None of the doctors who personally examined Robert and produced writ-ten reports of their findings in April and May of 2007 interviewed Ramiro Palacios or either of the López brothers. Although the physicians couldn't know it, they were denied access to those most intimately familiar with nearly every detail of Robert's existence for the past year or longer. They were cer-tainly more knowledgeable than many of the people upon whom the doctors relied for their input. Nor were they ever accused, as was one of the other caregivers, of tossing Robert's uneaten meals in the garbage, then claiming that Robert had consumed the food himself.

Mark Burns was the only doctor to mention Robert's left eye droop (ptosis) or his "left hemifacial droop." He noted possible signs of Bell's palsy, which, in most cases, disappears on its own in a matter of weeks. Robert's did not. Burns also observed in his report that "Mr. East certainly has a number of risk factors for a stroke" and recommended that an imaging study be done. The psychiatrist was as well the only doctor to mention Robert's infected ear, noting that the patient's right eardrum was punctured and discharging pus.

Paul Price's testimony notwithstanding, Dr. Burns found Robert as unresponsive as had Dr. Falcón and ventured no forecast for his mental recovery. "He appeared withdrawn," the doctor wrote, "cachectic, and made eye contact only briefly on approximately two occasions during the physical exam." He added that Robert had never been diagnosed with dementia nor, as far as Dr. Burns was told, ever suffered hallucinations or delusions. Had he spoken with Ramiro Palacios or Eddy López, he would have learned otherwise.

Among his "mental status exam" findings, the psychiatrist wrote that, "Severe psychomotor retardation was present" and that Robert "did appear to briefly attend to instructions given him by Mr. Ozuna or Ms. Cantú but did not open his eyes at one point when he was requested to do so by Mr. Ozuna. On another occasion, he did open his eyes at Mr. Ozuna's request. When asked to point to familiar individuals in the room by Ms. Rodríguez and then Mr. Ozuna, Mr. East did not comply.

"Speech: I did not observe Mr. East speaking at all during the course of the interview.

"Mood: Mr. East did not report his subjective feeling state."

The doctor also recorded a "paucity of thought" and found Robert "severely impaired" in sight and judgment, with his intelligence "severely eroded" as well.

Under "physical diagnosis," he entered "delirium (severe)" with a "guarded" prognosis. Under "mental diagnosis," he wrote "depressive disorder," also "severe" with a "guarded" prognosis.

Robert was not senile, in Dr. Burns's view but suffered from a "severely impaired decision-making capacity," leaving him "totally" incapacitated.

Burns wrote that laboratory tests conducted on May 17 disclosed Robert's total protein was still low, at 5.5, as was his albumin, 2.2, indicating he was still malnourished. His digoxin remained low, at 0.9.

CHAPTER 51

Charlie Hury did not abandon his strategic imperative. "Getting rid of Oscar and his bunch was our first and foremost problem," he wrote. According to Hury, Ozuna's attorney, Preston Henrichson, "indicated it could be done. The best way that I could see to accomplish that was to at least partially abandon the legal procedure and try to form some kind of alliance that would force it or, more precisely, [allow me] to buy it."

The lawyer's plan was to temporarily ally with Paul Price against Oscar "and his bunch." On Monday, March 28, Hury shared his thinking with Mike East, who asked what he intended to do about Paul Price if and when Oscar and his team could be rooted out. According to Mike, Hury told him that he'd deal with Price when the time came.

Unsure exactly what his attorney meant by that, Mike gave him the okay to talk to Price but nothing more. Mike still preferred going to APS, although he now knew from Drs. Falcón and Burns's reports that his uncle might soon be beyond an intervention of any sort.

The next day, Hury met with Price in Kingsville. Hury wrote that he tried to "play Price by scaring him to death" with a look at all the intelligence that Ramiro Palacios and his clandestine network had gathered against Oscar— and Price too—in just three months.

"It was important to show him just how flimsy his claim was about not trusting Oscar but never being able to get any hard evidence on him," he writes. "If we could get that much that quickly with no direct access, there was clearly no excuse for his failure to do so over a period of years when he had unfettered access. That was, of course, unless he was not looking for it because he was part of—or the mastermind behind—the problem."

In what Hury calls the Hebbronville "jury room bloodletting," he says that Price argued that Oscar needed to be kept in place as foreman of the ranch "so as not to shock Robert with the change." Price's plea, he says, "went nowhere. It did not take long in Kingsville for us to agree that Oscar was out."

The mechanism would be a mediation restricted to Hury, Price, Jim Robichaux, Mike East, Carlos Martínez, Preston Henrichson, and allied lawyers representing Oscar, Carilu Cantú Leal, and Tino Canales. Attorneys for Tres Kleberg, Helenita Groves, and her daughter Cina—the "Houston lawyers"—were excluded, as was Tony Canales.

Hury knew that there'd be significant skepticism from this group over any deal with Price, especially from Tony Canales. He therefore hoped to engineer a fait accompli—Oscar off the ranch and Robert's health rescued by first-rate medical care—before the naysayers had a chance to gum it up. Hence the need for speed and secrecy.

It was decided the mediation would take place on Friday, June 1, with the aim of finalizing a settlement for Judge Gabert's consideration at Monday's scheduled hearing in Hebbronville.

Thursday, Price drove to Hury's Edinburg law office to listen to Ramiro Palacios's tapes. They were of uneven quality, but there was no mistaking what the young man had captured on his 26-minute Prayer Tape.

Price, Hury wrote, "got to listen to just how clear his hammering of Robert was to keep Mike out . . . and how clearly Robert did not want him to do so. Those recordings also had Carilu hammering away at Robert about how Mike's girlfriend was trying to kill him, Carilu badgering Robert to try to get him to agree to keep Mike out, Oscar badgering Robert to keep Mike out, Carilu and Oscar lying to Robert about things Mike did or did not do, and many other things."

Hury says Price remained poised and attentive while listening to the recordings. When the session was over, he said he was pleased at what he'd heard, because, at last, he had "the hard evidence he'd always been looking for against Oscar."

CHAPTER 52

riday's mediator would be Reynaldo Ortiz, a former criminal defense attorney who operated out of offices in a McAllen strip mall. In a process that is a bit like an auction, late on the morning of June 1, each of the three contending groups was assigned a room, where Ortiz would keep them apprised of the action and solicit their input as a deal took shape, if it did. It would be a lengthy process.

Mike East was joined in one office by Charlie Hury and Carlos Martínez. Paul Price and Jim Robichaux camped in another. Preston Henrichson, Oscar Ozuna's lawyer, headed the third group. With a couple exceptions, all the teams communicated exclusively through the mediator.

The starting points were the buyout clauses in Oscar and Carilu's employment contracts. The sum in Oscar's case was $50,000. Tino Canales had no contract. Mike made an opening offer to Oscar, Carilu, and Tino Canales of $100,000. It was in part a preliminary probe to help gauge what sort of money they were looking for, but as Hury writes, "also intended as a clear sign to Price [and Robichaux] that, since Price hired those people, it was going to be their problem to get rid of them."

Early in the mediation, Price and Robichaux approached East and Hury with a proposal. If Oscar was stripped of all his authority, could he be allowed to remain at the ranch as a vaquero? Mike guessed that Price was worried about dipping in Robert's money to pay for any buy-out.

Hury said, "All right. I'm listening. I'm listening."

East wasn't. "Jim," he said, "see how my arms are crossed? I'm not going to agree to that."

Next came a bid via Rey Ortiz from Henrichson's team: $12.5 million to get rid of Oscar, Carilu, and Tino Canales. Mike instructed his attorney to reply that if they wanted that much money, they were going to have to get it out of Price.

"We were, therefore, fighting a battle on two levels," Hury writes. "One was to get rid of the obvious devils in Oscar and his little bunch of thieves. The other was to get rid of Price and his pirates. Doing both in one big swing of the ax, however, was just not practically viable. Just getting rid of the first level of devils was going to be hard enough."

Mike differed with his lawyer. He felt that Paul Price was weakened after Tony Canales savaged him in San Diego, put off his game and left with little room to demand much of anything. East urged Hury to press the advantage. It was not to be.

"Rey would come in from time to time to try to see if he could get more money from us," Hury remembers, "but he knew that was unlikely. Mostly, his visits were to reassure us that something was getting done, but it was taking a long, long time."

The needle finally moved, however. By nine o'clock that night, Mike sensed there had been sufficient progress toward a deal to direct Hury to call Rogelio Garza, the acting San Antonio Viejo foreman, and instruct him to have Lalo Salinas immediately put someone at the front gate with orders not to let Oscar, Carilu, or Tino Canales onto the ranch without an escort. The three of them were to be given 10 days to clear out their belongings and gear. In Oscar's case, some livestock, as well.

On Saturday morning, Garza called a meeting at the ranch to announce, without explanation, their permanent departure and his interim appointment as boss, details to follow. Chris Huff, the onetime game warden, would be the ranch's general manager, responsible, in the main, for security.

Not until midnight was a tentative mediation agreement signed by the principals. Mike and his family's access to Robert was restored. His uncle's health would immediately be entrusted to Drs. Falcón and Burns.

In return, Lyndy Hernández, with Oscar Ozuna, would hit Robert's accounts for the nearly $2 million that Preston Henrichson accepted to make Oscar and Carilu go away. Mike would contribute another $125,000, earmarked for Tino Canales. The amount was a comparative steal, given the size of the fortune they would be signing away.

Oscar and Carilu and Tino Canales were then to resign both their management trust and foundation board positions, to be replaced by Paul Price, Carlos Martínez, and Ron Davidson.

The expected incredulity arrived at once.

Houston lawyer Sharon Gardner responded with a number of questions, and a statement: "We need a lot more detail," she declared.

"Charles, my friend," wrote Tony Canales, "I know you have good intentions, but let this old friend tell you that you are playing with fire. There is only one way out of this mess, and that is to get rid of Paul and Ron. Why in the world are you bringing Ron back? Mike East and his sisters are the only real relatives of Robert East, and they should be in control without any interference from Paul. Get rid of Paul."

Canales repeated himself in another email a few days later. "You really need to get Paul out of the equation," he admonished Hury once more, "as a lawyer and a future trustee."

Instead, there would be what Hury called "a necessary, albeit somewhat factually questionable, agreement" that would expedite the flow of Robert's estate into his management trust—and, ultimately, the foundation—just as Paul Price had urged Robert to do on the Prayer Tape of April 21. The game was over.

In the agreement, Mike and his sisters swallowed hard and dropped their assertion that Robert lacked the capacity to execute the documents of November 16, 2006. In the consensus view, it was among their strongest contentions. This cleared the way for the transfer of Robert's estate into his management trust under Oscar, Carilu, and Tino's control, leaving little for a guardian to guard and no reason for the original litigation to continue.

Mike was especially unhappy with the concession and says he warned Robichaux and Hury that he should not be asked to affirm the agreement under oath.

At Monday's scheduled hearing in Hebbronville, Letty García noticed that Tony Canales was audiotaping the proceedings. Mike recalls the attorney was clearly unhappy when Judge Gabert announced that a deal had been cut. Tony's son, Héctor, later said that he had to persuade his father not to stand up and leave. He told Tony not to abandon Mike at this key moment.

Ed Hennessy came to court with Dr. Burns's report, which he politely but persistently urged the judge to place on the record. "He pleaded with him," Mike says. "'Take this. Please take this and file it, so it's on the record.' Finally, the judge took it."

After court, Mike and Letty headed to the San Antonio Viejo to be with Robert for the first time in six weeks.

Ramiro Palacios had already moved back to the ranch. Robert, in his lucid moments, asked where he'd been. Ramiro was shocked at how much weight *el patrón* had lost in the month since they'd last seen one another.

According to Palacios, Chris Huff became a daily annoyance. "He really didn't do anything when he came there," Ramiro remembers. "He'd eat breakfast then get out his little laptop and start reading emails on the bench in front of the walk-in cooler, whining about how many thousands of emails he got and how he was looking forward to his retirement. He said he was there to help.

"Do what? I wondered. *Who the hell is this guy?"*

Johnny East also traveled to the San Antonio Viejo to visit his great uncle. When Ramiro walked into the kitchen after spoon-feeding Robert some Ensure, he found Huff interrogating Mike's son.

"Who are you?" he asked Johnny. "What are you doing here? What do you want to discuss with Robert?" Ignoring Huff, Palacios invited Johnny to go say hello to Robert. "I told him, 'Yeah! Yeah! C'mon in.'"

The visit was brief. "Robert was kinda sleepy," Palacios remembers. "He wasn't very vocal anymore. But he could recognize people.

"When I walked back to the kitchen, Chris Huff was there, pretty pissed off at me. I didn't know exactly what was going on. He said, 'Don't do that ever again. I'm here for a reason. I'm doing a job.'

"I guess he didn't know who Johnny was."

Ramiro briefly contemplated punching Huff in the nose for his impertinence, then thought, *Not right now, another time,* and looked forward to the opportunity. Instead, he reminded the security man that the East family had just spent a fortune just to see Robert. He should know his place. Then Palacios walked away.

When Mike walked through Robert's bedroom door after court that afternoon, he understood at once why Robert's attorneys had not wanted Ranger Hunter conducting a welfare check and why Oscar Ozuna had blocked even a citation server from seeing *el patrón*. He found the old man lying still and shrunken in his bed. His breath was labored. Ramiro, who walked in the room behind Mike, thought he saw a flicker of recognition in Robert's eyes. Mike did not.

He realized there would be no heroic medical intervention to snatch his uncle back to life. Robert was lost, and so was his estate, which, in the East family's view, had just been stolen. "All we had left was to plan the funeral," Mike later said.

He sternly berated himself yet again for okaying Charlie Hury's doomed strategy. *It would have been better to keep fighting,* Mike thought as he walked from Robert's bedroom toward the living room, determined somehow to keep the cause alive, find some note of redemption in Robert's story.

He picked up a pair of Old Mama's spurs, a coveted link to the family's past, resting on the dining room table. Robert had already made gifts of important family heirlooms to family namesakes. Mike's son, Thomas, for example, who was named for his great grandfather, received from his great uncle a ring that once belonged to Tom T. East Sr. Alice, named for Old Mama, was given her grandmother's wedding ring. Robert had told Lica Elena she would have her Aunt Lica's silverware.

Although Alice East's spurs legally belonged to Robert's estate and, therefore, eventually, the foundation, Paul Price had told Mike to take them if he liked, although he might at some point have to give them back.

As he stood with them in the dining room, Chris Huff produced a still camera and told East that he wanted to make a photographic record of his grandmother's spurs. Mike placed the spurs on the table for him. But Huff said no. He wanted a picture of Mike holding the spurs—evidence. East bristled. It was the second time in less than an hour that Chris Huff had risked a bloody nose.

Drs. Falcón and Burns, Robert's new medical team, came to the house. As they discussed steps ahead for his care, they referred to their patient's health directive of two years before.

"If I am unable to swallow," it said, "*artificial* nutrition and hydration must be administered even when other interventions are withheld or withdrawn."

So, contrary to what Dr. Brown had claimed to Mike and Letty, the directive made clear that Robert wanted to be placed on a feeding tube should that someday become a health care option. Both doctors took note.

Standing in the kitchen as the directive was being discussed, Mike overheard Burns say that Jetta Brown's medical license should be lifted. He also heard the psychiatrist ask Paul Price how recently he'd had an intelligent conversation with Robert. He did not catch the lawyer's answer.

The next day, Charlie Hury emailed Paul Price. "BIG PROBLEM," he wrote. "In a period of about six hours yesterday afternoon, Chris Huff managed to infuriate Mike East, Alice G. East, Lica Elena East Pinkston, Johnny East, Ramiro Palacios, and Rogelio Garza.

"He has told the family and employees, including Rogelio, that he and Paul Price are in charge, and the family and employees must clear everything through him, and him alone. He also feels that it is his duty to interrogate family members regarding their presence and their motives for being there.

"IF YOU DO NOT GET CONTROL OF THIS CLOWN, THIS WHOLE THING IS ABOUT TO BLOW UP, IF IT HAS NOT DONE SO ALREADY."

"I have talked to Chris Huff," wrote Price in response. "I believe he will show better 'bedside manners' with the family in the future. He told me that he thought he knew Mike well enough to joke around with him, and he was just kidding around when he asked to take a photo of Mike with the spurs."

CHAPTER 53

Recognizing that the settlement left him no leverage with Price, Martínez, and Davidson, Mike nonetheless called them to the San Antonio Viejo to discuss issues going forward and to share some thoughts. His son, Thomas, sat in on the meeting.

"I expressed to them that I knew I didn't have any power," he remembers, "but since I had a lot to do with them being in the position they were in, I said they should run things by me before they made any major policy changes."

He sat them down at the dining room table, where his father once presided over Thanksgiving and Christmas and all other East family meals. While the family was intact, Robert always sat at one end of the table, his back to the kitchen. Everyone else knew their usual places as well. Alice, Lica Elena, and Evelyn all sat to Robert's left. Alice, Old Mama, and Mike sat to his right. Tom oversaw the meal from the opposite end. Only death had ever altered the holiday ritual, now nothing more than a memory.

Searching for some sort of common ground, Mike told his visitors that he was conditionally satisfied with the settlement and might remain so if they managed his uncle's ranches according to Robert's wishes—a vain expectation, he knew.

First of all, he said, there should be no game hunting of any sort—anywhere. Mike was particularly concerned lest Ron Davidson treat the settlement as an invitation to resume stalking the ranch's trophy white-tails. The two exceptions to the rule were the nilgai that competed for grass with the cattle at the Sauz pasture. They needed to be thinned from time to time. Robert had also told Mike to take the very occasional trophy buck white-tail to buy feed corn for the other game animals.

Mike advised Price and the others to promptly add East family relatives such as Tres Kleberg and Helenita Groves as foundation directors. He repeated that he had no interest in joining the board himself or accepting an advisory board position as Ron Davidson, in particular, had urged him to do. East realized he'd be outgunned on any future foundation board, tolerated by the majority as window dressing. He suggested that, in the interest of transparency, there should be a written job description for every seat on the board, and there could not be any self-dealing, no conflicts of interest.

He reminded them that one of Robert's major concerns, which he mentioned often to various people, was whether Mike and his sisters might have to sell land to pay the inheritance taxes if he left them all or any part of his ranches. The foundation was supposed to be an answer to this potential problem, which, in any event, should have vanished with the windfall royalties Robert received when the Tom East gas field began its prodigious production in the early 2000s. Had Robert known how rich he had become, he would have had no need for the foundation. In every way possible, he went on, the directors should respect Robert's desire that the ranch be preserved as he left it.

As extensively as Paul Pearson and Paul Price had recast and discarded codicils to Robert's will—of the seven, only the sixth and seventh survived— as well as amendments to his management trust—of the 10, only three are extant, the sixth, ninth, and tenth—one phrase survived, that it was Robert's "primary desire that my overall ranching operations and business affairs be conducted in the way I have always conducted same."

Mike advised the group that integral to Robert's primary desire was care for all the ranch animals, from goats to dogs, chickens, ducks, peacocks and hens, macaws and all the rest—most especially his horses.

He further explained that Robert wanted many of the ranch residences and other structures, each with its own important place and role in San Antonio Viejo history, to be maintained and preserved as Old Mama and Lica had done. Chief among them was the barn where Old Mama had been surrounded at gunpoint by the bandits 90 years earlier. He also wanted the large Quonset hut on the property to be maintained in place, along with some very old residential structures, such as Casa Verde and La Perla, Tom and Alice's first house on the ranch.

Rogelio Garza was a good choice to oversee the cattle operations, he said. In Mike's view, Garza's major asset was that he'd run the operation as Robert would have liked, including the imperative—passed along by his brother Tom—that the cattle operation should pay its own way. He added that Rogelio knew the ranch vaqueros and their families well and was aware of those who had earned Robert's trust and respect, as well as those who had not.

There was more.

"I said, 'I think Robert wants this house left like it is, and I would like it left like it is because I want to be able to come here and remember where everybody sat when we got together and remember what we all said, and I want to show it to my grandkids.'"

East told his visitors that he had moved Martín and Iza Palacios, as well as their two children, Ramiro and his little sister, Judy, into the unoccupied west wing of the main house.

"They're trustworthy," he said. "They could live in the west wing because nobody uses it. It has no sentimental value. They can live there and take care of the house, as caretakers."

He concluded with a long look at Price. He said that he didn't yet know if the lawyer was evil or simply dishonest. Now, with Oscar Ozuna gone, he expected to learn the truth.

Price made no response, nor had he or Ron Davidson said anything at the meeting. Carlos Martínez spoke up though. He guaranteed Mike that he would always have his vote.

"The ruling group" as Hury called them, was civil, if unforthcoming. Mike's relationship with them soon soured, however, a process exacerbated by the omnipresent Chris Huff. When, for example, at Paul Price's invitation, Lica Elena and Alice undertook to inventory, sort, and clean the main house's heirlooms, they complained that Huff treated them like shoplifters.

"He bird-dogged them," Mike recalls. "Huff was right there. They couldn't go out to Robert's ranch without him waiting for them at the door."

All the while, Robert's health continued to worsen.

On June 10, a Sunday, Dr. Falcón examined *el patrón* at the ranch. According to the physician's notes, he found his patient "quite ill, with a little bit of fever, cough, and tachypnea," or hyperventilation, a symptom of pneumonia. Robert needed to go to the hospital.

Mike and Letty's friends, Lannie Mecom and Polly Hollar, were at the ranch. Dr. Falcón had brought along his brother, Gene, the former Starr County sheriff. Dr. Francisco Cigarroa, a renowned transplant surgeon, together with his brother, Dr. Richard Cigarroa, an interventional cardiologist who practices in Laredo, were on hand as well. The Cigarroas were looking in on Robert as a favor to Helenita Groves.

An ambulance would carry Robert to Starr County Memorial Hospital, the same route he'd taken 14 years earlier with his stricken sister Lica. Falcón's office nurse, Gracie Guerra, fit Robert with a condom catheter. She would follow the ambulance to the hospital in her red Dodge.

Melva Elizondo, Robert's day nurse, climbed into the back of the ambulance, where she and a medic would tend to Robert on the trip. After grabbing *el patrón's* wallet, a blanket, and a couple of pillows from Old Mama's room—where he also stopped to say a short prayer—Ramiro Palacios drove to the hospital in Melva's green Ford Expedition. Chris Huff followed in his own vehicle.

Robert was admitted to the 45-bed medical facility at 4:45 that afternoon. He was given patient number 86739 and taken to room 120. According to Palacios, who would stay with Robert throughout his hospitalization, the accommodations were pleasant. The room featured a shower and a small patio reachable via a sliding glass door. There was also a comfortable ottoman where Ramiro would sleep.

The bed scale indicated Robert weighed 128 pounds on admission. Nurses started an IV in the back of his left hand at once, dripping 50 cc, or about three and a half tablespoons, of saline solution into his blood stream every hour.

This typewritten statement was included among his hospital papers:

> "I understand that Texas law allows me to designate a spokesperson to make a treatment decision for me if I should become comatose, incompetent or otherwise mentally or physically incapable of communication. I hereby designate OSCAR OZUNA, 6349 North FM Road 755, Rio Grande City, Texas, 78582, (956) 500-3202, if he is then able and willing to act, to make such a treatment decision for me if I should become incapable of communicating with my physician. If OSCAR OZUNA is not able or willing to act, I designate the person named immediately hereinafter, as long as said person is able and willing to act, to make such a treatment decision for me if I should become incapable of communicating with my physician: PAUL O. PRICE, Suite 1700 South, 800 North Shoreline Boulevard, Corpus Christi, Texas, 78401, (361) 549-3293. I have discussed my wishes with those persons named hereinbefore in this paragraph and trust their judgment."

Dr. Falcón's admitting diagnosis was pneumonia in Robert's left lower lung and sepsis, or blood poisoning, caused by a staph infection in his lungs. He was anemic. His blood sodium was elevated, and his potassium was low.

Robert could not chew or swallow. His diet prior to admission had consisted of baby food and Ensure. The admitting document incorrectly indicated that his weight had been stable over the previous three months.

Rocephin, a powerful broad-spectrum antibiotic, was added to his IV drip to fight the staph infection. The condom catheter was removed in favor of a Foley catheter, and he was given a bolus of potassium. His temperature at nine o'clock that first night was 102 degrees.

Iza Palacios would send her son a change of clothing each morning by Lalo Salinas, who stopped at the hospital on his way to work. Although Robert could not eat, the nurses brought him trays of soft food on schedule anyway and left them for Ramiro to consume.

He recalls that Robert was disoriented, but he seemed to know where he was. Pain did not appear to be a problem. According to his chart, Robert was given no analgesics, save for a single dose of Tylenol. But he'd frown at a nurse's touch or when his IV was changed.

He slept and awakened in roughly four-hour cycles, about the same as at home on the ranch. Although Robert never spoke during his hospital stay and evinced a limited range of responses, Ramiro believes *el patrón* recognized him at some level and knew when Mike was in the room as well.

On June 11, Robert was taken across the street by ambulance to undergo an MRI. The next day, the results showed "a vascular lacuna," or a gap about one eighth of an inch across, in Robert's basal ganglia, at the base of his forebrain. Dr. Falcón believes the lesion could have been an artifact of the suspected stroke Ramiro first detected on the left side of Robert's face back in April. The scan also indicated that Robert had suffered generalized brain atrophy, not unusual among the elderly. It revealed mastoiditis and vascular ischemia, or localized anemia caused by blockage of blood flow, not necessarily a serious problem.

Robert's old friend James King learned of his hospitalization and went to Starr County Memorial to see him.

King's recollections: "I was surprised that Robert was in Starr County and not in San Antonio, as I knew he had a long relationship with Dr. Nixon in San Antonio and, for sure, if he needed serious care, San Antonio would have been a more obvious choice.

"So I walked in, found his room and went to see Robert. I was astonished at his condition. He looked to me like a dying man, so skinny and drawn. He was not conscious, so I went over to him and held his hand and said a few words about the weather and rainfall in Hebbronville. I was really shaken, as I had never seen Robert in such bad shape. He was always so physically strong, even for an elderly man.

"Sure, he'd had some tough miles, but this was like 'Damn!' I was too late and was not able to say good-bye.

"I saw Mike in the room, and I think his sister and several other folks I did not know. Mike and I walked into the hall, and I said, 'What happened?' I was glad that Mike was there for Robert. Without knowing at the time any of the backstory, I assumed that Robert was dying from something that just could not be addressed.

"It was sad for me to see him that way in a South Texas hospital, away from his familiar ranch surroundings. It was at that time [that] I learned that he was potentially not cared for by his handlers, which made me very angry and sad. He should have had, and could afford, the best care possible.

"After visiting with Mike and a few others, I simply left and drove away, astonished that there it was, the end for Robert."

Robert's chart characterized his condition as guarded.

On June 14, Ramiro Palacios was surprised by the unexpected arrival in Robert's room of Chris Huff, accompanied by Oscar Ozuna and a woman Ramiro did not recognize. Chris Huff later identified her as a nurse. They had come with instruments to harvest tissue samples from Robert.

According to hospital records, at 10:40 that morning, Dr. Falcón ordered by telephone a blood transfusion for Robert, placement of a "peg" to accommodate a feeding tube, and a DNA analysis. The physician later signed orders at the hospital. Oscar was called because he held Robert's power of attorney, so his approval was necessary as well.

Palacios remembers that, when he returned to the room, the nurse was taking a photo of Oscar and Robert together with a digital camera. Ramiro had his recorder with him that morning and turned it on as he and Chris Huff spoke together in the room. The television can be heard in the background of the recording, as well as Robert's IV pump.

Huff told Ramiro, "Don't tell anybody about this," and added, "Paul Price and them had nothing to do with this. Mike didn't have anything to do with it. Nobody except Dr. Falcón made the decision to do this for his patient. He is concerned about Robert.

"So he just called Oscar to come sign those papers so he could get this done. This procedure they just did right now is a DNA procedure. The idea of that is so somebody doesn't come later and say, 'You know what? I'm Robert's son.'"

Palacios asked about the DNA procedure.

"It can be done," said Huff, "but [Oscar] has to be there. By medical regulation, he has to witness that. That's why he took a picture of him with Robert."

"What about the family?" Ramiro asked.

"What about the family? Like what?" Huff replies.

"Like Mike and his sisters."

"What about them?"

"That's what I'm asking."

"Am I concerned about them? Is that what you are asking?"

"No," Ramiro answered. "I'm asking [about them] because, [with] all this is happening, I need to tell them what's going to be happening with Robert."

"I don't have a problem with you calling," Huff said. "Don't get me wrong. Just somehow, it got turned that I was the bad guy here. When I went in there, [it] was to make sure Oscar [was] not doing something wrong."

Huff hadn't behaved in Robert's room like a watchful observer, Palacios thought, more like Oscar's associate or helper.

"How come you didn't tell the family?" he asked.

"Well, Oscar was already in the room when I walked in," Huff said, which contradicted Ramiro's recollection that the two walked in together. "I went over there and told the nurse, 'Hey, what kind of procedure is going on?'

"The nurse said, 'I can't tell you.'

"I said, 'Well, I'm working straight with Dr. Falcón. Let's get him on the phone, and let's talk to him.'

"So she got him on the phone, and I told Dr. Falcón that I would like to be in the room when Oscar is in there. I don't know what Oscar is doing in there by himself. Y'know what I'm saying? So that's why I want to be there, to see. If I'm the security guy for Robert, I need to see that he is taken care of.'"

Huff then spoke to Palacios of his goodwill toward Robert's family and complained again that he was regarded as an enemy. He told Ramiro that he did not care about his job and hoped the family would win their legal battle with Paul Price and his allies.

"Don't let the devil lie to you about me, about what I'm doing," he said. "Right now, Oscar, I would say, cares for Robert."

"Well," Ramiro replied, "if he cared, he would have done this a long time ago. If he cared, he would have done this in March when I was still there [taking care of East at his ranch]. He was blowing Robert's medical health. He wasn't keeping Robert's appointments."

"Well," said Huff, "he still wants to do that."

Palacios was unmoved. "Because they're after him," he answered.

"You can't hold something forever, you know," Huff advised him, "like hold something against somebody. Uh, you do that, [and] you're tying yourself up with God.

"You know what I'm saying? 'Our Father, God, forgive those who trespass against me,' and all you have to do is ask God to forgive you. That's what we've got to do. I'm not saying that Oscar was right, but this is kind of a spiritual thing we are talking about here. Sometimes, you just got to let those things go."

When Charlie Hury learned that Oscar and the nurse had visited Robert's room to harvest DNA, he emailed Jim Robichaux. "If that occurred, it is pure BULLSHIT, and it MUST be stopped now," he wrote. Robichaux emailed in reply that it was an innocent errand on behalf of Dr. Falcón, who "needed Oscar as attorney in fact under the medical power of attorney to sign authorization to allow DNA testing of some type to facilitate a blood transfusion . . . Chris cleared it with Carlos first . . . [Chris] is observing to ensure nothing improper happens."

Not so, says Falcón, who insists he had not authorized Huff and Ozuna to harvest Robert's DNA and was dismayed to learn of it.

"Chris did that without me knowing about it," he says. "I don't appreciate that. That's pretty crappy. I thought that I had a good relationship with Chris. I never had any problems with him. He wouldn't be happy if I went over there to shoot a deer without his permission.

"You know, I worried a lot about Robert's DNA. Not so much about him fathering somebody but about somebody trying to poison him. I'm shaking inside I'm so pissed off. He had no right to do that. To go into the hospital without permission? He had no right whatsoever to go in there. Damn!"

It was also decided on June 14 to attempt a transfusion of two units of packed red blood cells, "to perk Robert up a little bit," as Dr. Falcón explained it. "His oxygen levels would be a little bit better. Circulation better. It won't do anything for dementia or overall status. But he'd feel better for a while."

The procedure was started at 8:00 that night, but Robert could not tolerate it. His blood pressure plummeted to 60/40 and then 50/30. The transfusion was halted. A Catholic nun administered the last rites.

Ramiro telephoned Mike and Letty at home with a warning that Robert was in grave shape. When the immediate danger passed, he called again not long thereafter to report Robert had been stabilized and should make it through the night. Mike once more headed for Starr County Memorial Hospital early in the morning, as he had when his Aunt Lica died. It was Friday, June 15, 2007.

Had the transfusion not gone awry, Robert was scheduled to be taken to McAllen on Friday to have his feeding tube installed. As it was, there was nothing more to be done. He was sent back to the ranch instead. His "discharge assessment/instructions" document, dated 12:55 p.m., June 15, 2007, read, "To home to die there."

Gracie Guerra and Ramiro Palacios, who would accompany Robert in the ambulance, were told there was a chance he wouldn't survive the trip. Guerra, who monitored Robert's vital signs as they sped *el patrón* along on his last journey home, twice saw that they almost lost him.

"Robert *cannot die* in this ambulance!" Ramiro remembers her calling to the driver, who responded accordingly. The vehicle roared ahead, and Robert made it back to the San Antonio Viejo one last time.

"We were really hauling ass," Palacios remembers.

CHAPTER 54

As Robert rolled home that afternoon, 30 miles away, in Judge Gabert's Rio Grande City office, the comprehensive settlement agreement was finalized, a triumph of folly, duplicity, and greed.

Judge Gabert wore blue jeans that day, as reporter John MacCormack noted a month later in an enterprising article for the *San Antonio Express-News*. MacCormack was the first journalist to lift the curtain on the cutthroat scheming for Robert's immense estate. Mike East attended the hearing. His sisters did not. Both of them were unhappy about the settlement deal.

"I always felt like Alice and I were left out," Lica Elena says. "We didn't know what was going on. Alice and I weren't happy about Hury, and we kept telling Mike that."

Nor were any of the Easts happy with the settlement terms that "released, acquitted, and forever discharged" Price, Martínez, and Davidson from "all claims of any kind."

In Hebbronville, Oscar Ozuna and Lyndy Hernández had already cashed a check for $1,928,319.49 on Robert's National Bank of Hebbronville account.

Oscar Ozuna was the single witness called to testify at Gabert's office hearing that day. Under questioning by his own lawyer, Preston Henrichson, he testified that Robert was in full command of his wits when he signed all those estate-planning documents drawn up by the two.

"Did Robert, with the assistance of Paul Price, develop an estate plan that included a last will and testament, a management trust, a declaration of guardian, a statutory durable power of attorney, and a medical power of attorney?" Henrichson asked.

"Yes," Ozuna replied.

"And did he sign these documents at various times throughout the period from November of 2002 through November of 2006?"

"Yes."

"Do you have an opinion as to whether or not he understood the nature and extent of his property and who his heirs were?"

"He was in his five senses. He knew everything about that, and he knew everything he did."

"And he was familiar with who his heirs were?"

"Yes."

"And was he under any undue influence by anyone during that time as regarding his decision related to his estate planning?"

"No."

"Did he make those decisions on his own, unencumbered by the influence of others?"

"He made his own decisions, on his own."

"That's all I have at this time," Henrichson finished and took a seat.

Jim Robichaux asked one question over the telephone, which Hury repeated to Ozuna.

"Mr. Robichaux asked," the attorney said, "if it was correct on November 16, 2006, before he signed the document, that Robert was examined by a psychologist who said that he had capacity." Mr. Ozuna's answer was yes.

Then Henrichson posed his own additional query.

"Was the signature of that done outside of your presence and outside the presence of Carilu Cantú Leal and Celestino Canales?"

"Yes."

With that, Judge Gabert signed the agreement. Former district attorney Heriberto Silva says that, as soon as he heard of the deal exonerating Oscar Ozuna, he closed his investigation.

Sharon Gardner was deeply dismayed. "I want to make it clear where I stand personally on this matter," she emailed Charlie Hury, Ned Hartline, Ed Hennessy, Jim Robichaux, Preston Henrichson, Paul Price, Scott Morrison, Tony Canales, his son Hector, and others. "In my entire career, I have never witnessed such conduct by lawyers. I am appalled at what has transpired, and there is no legitimate way to justify the manner in which this hearing was held.

"I will be interested to hear who got money as a result of this order and the total dollars that have flowed out of Mr. East's estate while he lay on his deathbed and to whom money was paid while Mr. East was clearly incapacitated. Somebody is going to have a lot of explaining to do."

The money was distributed as follows: $868,823 to Oscar's IRA account at A. G. Edwards & Sons and $336,177 to his attorney, Preston Henrichson, plus another check to Henrichson for $125,000; $200,000 to Carilu Cantú Leal "for the settlement of disputed claims" and $208,713 to her IRA, also at A. G. Edwards & Sons; $159,356.49 to her lawyer, Frank Enriques, and $125,000 apiece to assorted other attorneys. Celestino Canales, who had already been given $125,000 by Mike East, received another $250 in back wages.

For a little more than $2 million, Oscar, Carilu, and Tino had signed away control of an estate worth at least a hundred times that amount and, eventually, hundreds of millions more.

An hour later, Charlie Hury returned Gardner's fire. "I am equally appalled," he wrote, "that out-of-the-area lawyers like you, with little or no knowledge of either the facts or the people involved, have ignored the imminently terminal condition of a proposed ward by seeking continued delays that could only have the effect of having his entire estate hijacked by the very people who are alleged to be responsible for his condition.

"Had your proposed actions been pursued, Oscar Ozuna; his girlfriend, Carilu Cantú Leal; and their partner in crime, Celestino 'Tino' Canales, would still be in charge, the bulk of Robert's estate would not have been transferred to his management trust, and his estate would be wide open to every two-bit huckster who wants to claim he or she is the illegitimate child of Robert East.

"For the benefit of those of us who are less enlightened, would you please be so kind as to share your vast knowledge with us and explain how that would have been a good thing?"

Gardner replied a half-hour later, "I stand by what I wrote, and I do not apologize for any action taken to get Mr. East outside medical treatment and to express concern over who was controlling his pocketbook.

"I fought for Mr. East to have an independent attorney, someone who was truly looking after his interest with no conflict of interest.

"Mr. Hury, out-of-town lawyers are governed by the same rules as in-town lawyers. All I have are my ethics and reputation. Without that, I am not much of a lawyer."

CHAPTER 55

Robert fought off death for three more days. Then, just before one o'clock on Monday morning, June 18, Ramiro Palacios heard the old man breathing rapidly. He walked over to his bedside, where he saw *el patrón*'s face contorted into a scowl. The young man, who had never before seen anyone die, watched as Robert took a long deep breath, exhaled, and went still. Then Palacios rushed to Old Mama's room, where Mike and Letty slept, and pounded on the door.

"Robert's dead!" he called out.

Nurse Gracie Guerra, who had been staying in the west wing of the house, was awakened by Palacios's call. She came into Robert's room, saw him motionless, his mouth open, and confirmed he had expired. The nurse pulled Robert's mouth shut with a bandana, which she tied over his head.

Mike came into the room, walked over to Robert's bed, and closed his uncle's eyes.

Almost at once, a line of ranch hands appeared in the dark at the kitchen door. "Let 'em in," Mike said, and the men silently filed past Robert's bed, making their farewells. The line lasted for hours. Sometime before dawn, Chris Huff's wife, Julia, a justice of the peace, arrived to officially confirm Robert's demise.

Later in the day, Charlie Hury circulated an email among the attorneys, informing them that "unless I hear objection from someone this morning, I am going to contact the court and request that the status hearing set for this Wednesday in Duval County be removed from the docket, all pending matters classified as moot and the court's file be closed."

Ed Hennessy demurred in a return email that he also sent to all the lawyers. "I object to your asking the court to close this file," he wrote Hury. Hennessy complained that his client, Mrs. Groves, should be reimbursed for her costs, which came to $70,000 or more. Like Sharon Gardner, Hennessy was uneasy over the final settlement and added that "the attorney general probably will be interested in the last will and testament approval process as well!"

"Dear Ed," Hury replied, "if we had not done [what] we did, the entire estate of Robert East would have been subject to every two-bit huckster who wants a piece of it. Accordingly, the only effective alternatives available to us were considered to be (1) [to] risk the entire thing and control over it by that thief Oscar Ozuna and his cohorts in crime or (2) [to] spend some of Robert's money to get rid of them.

"I know you keep asking what makes Branscomb PC think they have the right to do that, even if it is a good idea. I told them repeatedly that you were questioning that authority, and they kept telling me repeatedly that they had it covered. Whether they do or not, the short answer is *Why should we care?*

"If the attorney general's office gets greedy and takes the position that Robert's estate should have the entire amount available for charities and if they can show that Branscomb PC did not have authority and if they can show causation of any damages in light of combined attorneys' fees and expenses that could easily have surpassed that amount and if they can get past the exposure of the entire estate to potential illegitimate heirs of Robert, their relief would be to get that $1.9 million dollars back, if they can.

"That would mean that either the AG or Oscar, Carilu, Preston, and that bunch would probably get a wee bit miffed at Branscomb PC. If Oscar and his bunch lose their money, and either they or the AG tries to get it back from Branscomb PC and Branscomb goes down because of that, oh gosh, what a shame.

"Oscar and his bunch will still be gone. Robert's estate will still be protected, and the attorney general and the charities that he has the duty to protect will still be protected.

"I would have preferred to see Robert leave everything to his nieces and nephew and to have kept everything in the family. Robert told Mike on several occasions, however, that he did not want to do that because Mike and his sisters would never be able to pay the taxes on it without breaking it up.

"Robert also told Mike that, because he could not give it all to them, he would like to see the ranch kept together and its profits be used for both a wildlife foundation and other charities. If there ever was a contest, Mike would have no choice but to testify to that.

"Robert probably would have changed his mind and given it all to Mike and his sisters after the big gas find in the Tom East oil field. That is because there was plenty of money after that to pay taxes. Paul Pearson, Paul Price, and Ron Davidson, however, kept talking him out of that. That was probably partially due to what they thought was a legitimate effort to protect what Robert really wanted, probably partially to feather their own nests, and probably partially because they were too devious, stupid, or both to either know or care what Robert's real wishes were."

Control of financial assets. There were changes to Robert's estate plan that could not reasonably have been anticipated by those who knew Robert and his family's deep connection to their land.

Charlie Hury wrote, "The continued influence of Oscar Ozuna and Carilu Cantú Leal on Robert to the effect that Mike wanted to do bad things to Robert probably helped keep him from doing that, but there is no way to really know that or to prove it. Even if we could, leaving Robert intestate would leave the whole thing subject to so many claims from others that [it] was considered to be way too big of a risk. Accordingly, as distasteful as it was, Mike and his sisters made peace with that issue a long time ago."

Hury had limited success with the rest of his strategy, which was to apply indirect pressure on Price, Martínez, and Davidson to either abandon their grip on Robert's estate or at least to loosen it. As part of this campaign, he emailed Preston Henrichson: "I have received some information that nurses for Robert may have been either improperly interfered with or pulled off from his care. That information also indicates that Oscar Ozuna may have been involved. I am developing this information not to incriminate Oscar but to develop potential evidence, claims, and causes of action against any physicians that may have been involved and to explore the acts or omissions of the current Trustees of the Management Trust as they may relate to independent causes of action [involving] their qualifications to continue as trustees or both."

Hury got just the response he hoped to receive. The lawyer Jorge Rangel, Carlos Martínez's brother-in-law, filed a petition on behalf of the ruling group alleging that Hury's actions "constitute a clear and unequivocal violation of [the 1995 agreement] and covenant 'not to challenge or contest' Robert C. East's 'fiduciary appointments,' which include the plaintiffs herein."

Rangel also threatened to hold up conveyance of La Mula, as well as the mineral rights from Robert's estate to Mike, Alice, and Lica Elena as provided for in the 1995 settlement of the disclaimer suit.

Tony Canales, who represented the Easts in the petition case, then threatened to file a countersuit in which he could compel depositions. Perhaps recollecting how the attorney had shredded Paul Price on the witness stand in San Diego, he, Martínez, and Davidson consented to a mediation, which resulted in a minor victory.

In the resulting settlement, the ruling group agreed that "the expression of personal opinions or criticism [of the group] by the Easts and the investigation or discussion of the acts, errors, omissions, motives, qualifications, abilities, competence, or background of the Trustees or Directors of the Trust or the foundation shall in no way constitute interference, harassment, or any challenge or contest."

It was also agreed that the management trust and foundation would expand their boards to five members each, allowing for the possible dilution of the ruling group's power.

CHAPTER 56

R obert was buried at the San Antonio Viejo on Thursday morning, June 21. Before then, at Dr. Falcón's direction, he was autopsied by Dr. Ray Fernandez, the Nueces County medical examiner. A full toxicology panel was ordered as well, to address persistent rumors that Robert had been poisoned. No evidence of poisoning was found. Dr. Burns asked that a special test be conducted in an effort to pinpoint when Robert lost capacity to control his own affairs. The test proved inconclusive.

There was no public announcement of the funeral's time and place, and a list was made up of those whom the Easts specifically wanted to exclude from the ceremony. They included Oscar, Tino, and Carilu, as well as Jesús Ochoa; Jetta Brown; her husband, Jack; and Mike's ex-wife, Kathryn. No reporters were allowed.

An estimated 150 people attended Robert's funeral. Chris Huff arranged for the Franciscans of Our Lady of Guadalupe Church in Hebbronville to conduct the rites. Although Robert was not known to be a practicing Catholic, he did, on occasion, stop to pray at Catholic churches. In particular, he was known to frequent St. Joseph's Catholic Church on South Closner Boulevard in Edinburg, near Dr. Ochoa's dental office.

Robert's six pall bearers were Juan López, Rogelio Garza, Lalo Salinas, Edilberto López, Ramiro Palacios, and his father, Martín. All were dressed in white shirts, work gloves, and custom-tailored brush jackets. Tom Sr., Old Mama, and Lica already lay side-by-side, south to north, in a row in the ranch cemetery. Robert's would be the fourth grave, next to Lica's.

A vaquero stood with a saddled horse near Robert's grave, just as one of his brother Tom's hands had stood with Shanghai, his favorite line back dun, at his internment 23 years earlier.

Mike hired a mariachi band to come play.

Tres Kleberg eulogized his cousin in a dignified and heartfelt farewell. "I always admired Robert for his dedication to his work, devotion to his family, to the employees of the ranch, and to his way of life, which he loved," Kleberg said. "I got to share many times earlier on with him, talking about family, ranching, wildlife, friends, and what was going on around us. He was a very caring person and someone who shared what he loved with others. He also had a mischievous side to him and a good sense of humor.

"He was a vaquero, a Kineño, who loved the land and that way of life," Kleberg said in conclusion. "He was a steward of his land, San Antonio Viejo, helping to preserve the traditions, history, and heritage of what was left to him by those before him, for those who follow.

"Well done, good and faithful servant.

"*Adios, amigo mio.*"

Although Mike and his sisters issued a written request "that lawyers involved in the recent litigation exercise discretion in keeping their attendance to a minimum," Paul Price hurried home from a vacation in Wyoming to appear. He chose the occasion to direct Chris Huff to fire Robert's Mexican ranch hands.

"The service was a wonderful tribute to Robert," Price later emailed Charlie Hury, "and I am grateful to be there to pay my last respects to Don Roberto."

Helenita Groves also attended the funeral. She recalls being approached by Price. "That lawyer, Price, told me that I was not on that foundation," she says, "that Robert had told him he didn't want any family on the foundation. Robert knew what he wanted, but those lawyers destroyed it."

CHAPTER 57

It was stormy the next morning as Mike and Letty awakened. The sky was dark, with high winds, lightning, heavy rain, and also a surprise visit from Chris Huff. He appeared in the company of Reid M. Harrell and James M. Pettus III, respectively the president and a trust officer of The Trust Company of San Antonio.

Under the terms of the June 15 settlement agreement, The Trust Company was, for the time being, the independent executor of Robert's trust, which then controlled Robert's estate, including the main ranch house and its contents. Lica Elena and Alice had already sorted the heirlooms and other valuables. Now, Harrell and Pettus had come in search of *all* Robert's documents, professional or private, and had brought with them an ample supply of black plastic garbage bags into which they meant to stuff every sheet of paper they could find. A videographer came with them to record the search.

Mike asked the men to hold off their search as he directed Chris Huff out of the house to the cowboy camp and telephoned Charlie Hury. During the wait for the lawyer to arrive, East offered Harrell and Pettus some lunch, prepared and served by Iza Palacios. Hury finally appeared with the bad news: The two executives were within their rights. The lawyer counseled Mike to cooperate. "They know what they're doing," he said.

Letty, already aggrieved at the abrupt intrusion one day after burying Robert, retired to another room, fighting back tears of rage at Huff's presumptuousness.

In truth, there was a logic to the search team's unannounced arrival. Should there be a single stray marriage license or birth certificate lurking in the stacks of papers Robert kept on shelves and desktops, in drawers, and everywhere else around the house in cardboard boxes, control of his fortune could fall into instant jeopardy.

As it was, the search did turn up Tom and Alice East's marriage certificate from 1915, which was never returned to the Easts.

Robert's locked safe, where he was known to keep considerable sums of cash, seemed a likely place for him to have stored important papers as well. Lica Elena's husband, John, located a locksmith, who opened it for the search team. Inside was found only a .22 pistol, suggesting that someone with a key had been there before them.

Mike was later told that some of the letters and papers gathered by the search team were sent into storage in the old ranch commissary, which had a leaky roof. An unspecified number of pages are thought to have been ruined as a consequence.

CHAPTER 58

Carlos Martínez says that Chris Huff's job description included making regular intelligence reports to the ruling group. "He was," according to Martínez, "our eyes and ears." For example, after appearing at the main house on June 28, one week after Robert's funeral, Huff emailed the following report to Price and the others:

"I arrived at the main ranch house at approximately 6:30 p.m. When I entered the house, I encountered Mike, Letty, Ramiro, and Rogelio sitting in the back living room area. I greeted them, and Mike was about the only one that said hello.

"As I greeted them, I noticed that Rogelio and Ramiro began working with their cell phones. It seemed a little odd that they would both be working with their phones and then placing them back in their pockets. I hope Ramiro is not continuing to record conversations.

"I felt very uncomfortable, as no one would carry on a conversation. I mentioned that we had a possibility of rain. I got a few nods out of that statement.

"I then stood around there for a few seconds, and then, after no one saying anything, I told them I was going to make a round around the ranch, and they could call me if they needed anything.

"As I was leaving, Mike said, 'I haven't seen you around.'

"I told him I was taking care of some personal business, such as getting my driver's license renewed.

"Mike then said, 'Do you ever talk to your people in Corpus?'"

"I didn't understand what he said, and I [replied], 'I didn't hear you. What did you say?'"

"He said, 'Do you ever talk to your people in Corpus?'"

"I said, 'Do you mean the board members?'"

"He said, 'Yes.'"

"I told him that I did keep in contact with them.

"He said, in a very angry voice, 'Tell them that I am not finished.'"

"I said, 'Mike, I am only an employee trying to do a job.'"

"He said, 'I don't care who you are. You tell them that I am not finished.'"

"Then he said, 'I want you to call them as soon as you walk out of that door.'"

"I told him that I would relay the message."

Carlos Martínez argues that Chris Huff was not a villain. "It was a very precarious time when we hired him to hold down the fort at the house," he says. "There were a lot of forces involved, especially Mike. Chris's job was to control things. However, we did get after him. We said, 'You need to back off. This is family. They're welcome to come here.' In hindsight, we should have been a little more careful in how [we] explained the job to him."

CHAPTER 59

The ruling group assigned Chris Huff to accompany Rogelio Garza to the San Antonio Viejo cowboy camp for the purpose of informing Robert's Mexican national vaqueros that they'd been fired. Huff and Garza were also directed to tell the men that they would not be paid for the two weeks they'd worked since Robert's death. Thus did the new regime introduce itself to Robert's employees.

Garza arrived first at the gathering, accompanied by Ramiro Palacios with his tape recorder. "The orders that I have from the board," Rogelio announced in Spanish, "are that there will be no more work for you. There's no more work here at the ranch. They will not pay you for the last 15 days of work that you did. That's the decision of Price, Carlos, and Ron. I asked them for a document to read to you, but they said no."

Rogelio disliked this chore. "I should have told Price to do it himself," he says.

"I know you all have worked hard as hell these last 15 days," Garza continued. "I know because I was with you. I know the beating you all have taken, working hard as hell, and I know you do not have money to go home.

"You don't have money to say, 'Okay, *patrón*, thank you much. I am going home.' Right? No, and most of you have families. The other question is I don't know how much time they are going to allow you to stay. I told them we could not run you off until they have made arrangements.

"Y'all don't have any money, and all of you are not going to get paid. Carlos doesn't care."

Rogelio asked them all for their addresses. "I can give them to *el gringuito* if one day there will be a chance you might be able to come back," he said.

Chris Huff, known to some of the hands as *el gringuito*, the little gringo, arrived and addressed the group in a mixture of English and Spanish. "The problem," Huff told them, "is that Robert left the ranch to a company. [He] didn't leave it to Mike or anything like that. It belongs now to a company.

"The company has to follow the law, and it says that I cannot employ people that don't have papers. They are not from the USA: It's the law. Robert could go around the law, but this company cannot. Rogelio and I are working for this company, and yesterday, the lawyer called and said they cannot employ or pay the people who do not have papers."

"We need money to go home," said Eddy López.

"I cannot help you," Huff replied.

As it turned out, Garza had discussed with Mike East the board's refusal to pay Robert's 16 illegals the wages they were owed. Mike wrote a check for the total amount due the men and asked Rogelio to distribute the money after the cow camp meeting.

Garza says he met with the hands in groups of three or four at The Pump, the ranch's main water well. He gave each of them his back wages and collected a receipt from each in return. The money would get these broke and suddenly jobless cowhands, few of whom spoke much English, back across the border to their homes in Mexico if that was where they were going.

Mike offered those who decided to stay work in La Mula pasture, which was in an advanced state of neglect. Some of them showed up, glad for the jobs. Others were arrested on their way to the Santa Fe by the border patrol and were deported. Most of the rest appear to have successfully returned to Mexico on their own.

Other ranch employees accused the new management of ignoring Robert's oral promises to them of lifelong pensions once they retired. Josie Aldaco Day says that, when Robert died, the monthly payments to these employees, including her father, Guadalupe Aldaco, abruptly stopped. When the men protested, she says, they were offered one of the old trucks on the ranch and $600 cash to settle their claims.

Guadalupe Aldaco, who had mainly worked fences in his years at the San Antonio Viejo, refused the offer and went to Aída Garza for help. The former bookkeeper remembered the monthly payments while Robert lived and gave Aldaco a signed letter to that effect.

He took the letter to one of the new managers—his daughter does not recall whom—and was rebuffed. She says Aldaco then hired an attorney, Doan T. Nguyen of Laredo, who took the matter to court and secured for Guadalupe Aldaco an acceptable lump sum settlement. It is not known how many other ranch retirees followed Aldaco's example.

CHAPTER 60

James King was among those approached by the ruling group about joining a foundation advisory board. King had long experience leading the Texas arm of The Nature Conservancy, the international organization devoted to protecting and preserving ecologically important sites. He was therefore a logical choice, given his familiarity with land-use issues. If he joined the advisory board, his name also would lend considerable legitimacy to an already troubled organization.

Following Robert's funeral, James visited Paul Price at the lawyer's Corpus Christi office. "I was trying to feel and understand what was being put in place as per Robert's wishes," King writes. "Price always assured me that he was Robert's confidant and that he designed what Robert wished.

"When I learned about the gate guard being named a trustee and the others, I almost lost it. So, at the meeting, I sat down in the conference room and told Paul that I worked for 20 years with The Nature Conservancy, and I wanted to help the trustees to carry out Robert's wishes.

"That is when he said, 'James, have you ever read J. R. R. Tolkien? And have you ever heard about Frodo the hobbit?'

"I said, 'Sure, I read those books in high school.'

"Paul said, 'Do you remember the ring?'

"I said, 'Of course.'

"Then he goes into this description that being Robert's trustee is like wearing the ring, balancing responsibility with power. I looked at Paul and thought *This guy is an ego maniac and really thinks of himself as trying to save the world!*"

King later received a typescript letter on foundation stationery from Carlos Martínez, identifying himself as the foundation president, as well as a trustee of Robert's management trust. In the letter, Martínez raised the old prohibition Paul Pearson had inserted into Robert's estate-planning documents against any of his parents' descendants "or anyone related to such a descendant by blood or marriage" becoming a director of the foundation. "You fall within the category of individuals that Robert intended to exclude from the operation, management, and governance of the foundation," Martínez wrote.

In other words, as King read the message, any King, Kleberg, or East associated with the foundation would be regarded as an untenable risk to Price's control and must therefore be excluded from managing a foundation named for Robert—himself descended from the Kings and a Kleberg, as well as being an East.

Tres Kleberg does not recall being formally advised that he was also disqualified due to birth but had learned indirectly that he was no longer under consideration.

Still later that year, Mike telephoned Carlos Martínez to say he wished to lease grazing pasturage from the foundation, as Paul Pearson had mentioned in his 1990 letter to Robert and as was explicitly provided for in the original trust agreement that he drafted in 1995. Martínez replied that, in his view, it was Mike's prerogative to do so.

Of all the estate documents Robert signed, he is known to have read only one, the original 1995 trust agreement, which lawyer Tom Wheat remembers reviewing page by page with East. It was in this document that Mike and his sisters and their descendants were granted the right of first refusal to lease Robert's surface estate for grazing. This provision vanished from subsequent iterations of the agreement. Carlos Martínez obviously did not think this was an obstacle.

In keeping with his search for a kernel of redemption, hoping to ful-
fill as much as possible of Robert's intentions for his land, Mike decided to
approach the ruling group with a surface lease offer.

Price's pirates, as Charlie Hury called them, met in Corpus Christi with
Mike in the autumn of 2007. They also listened that day to a proposal from
Rogelio Garza, who wanted, with Mike's blessing, to be named the San
Antonio Viejo's permanent foreman. Both Mike and Rogelio stressed Garza'a
familiarity with how Robert raised cattle, believing that should have been
decisive for Garza's bid.

Rogelio recalls that one of the ruling three told him, "Whatever Robert
wanted, he isn't here anymore, and we are." They refused him in favor of
Vincent "Fritz" Linney, a veteran cattleman, who had been suggested for the
position by Dan Kinsel III, a ranch broker from Cotulla, Texas. Linney was
most recently employed at the Rockefeller Ranch in Raymondville.

Neither Rogelio nor Mike found fault with Linney as the choice for foreman, but Price and the ruling group did raise Mike's ire when they ignored
Robert's explicit wish that the main house at the San Antonio Viejo be
reserved for the East family and as a museum and instead installed Linney
and his family there. The Easts took the move as an unnecessary and calcu-
lated provocation.

When it came to a grazing lease at the ranch, Mike had reason to expect
that he'd receive a more positive and respectful response. Back in June, Paul
Price wrote Charlie Hury that "on an ongoing basis, we would like to maintain a relationship of friendship with [the Easts] so they can assist us in
honoring the East family history."

Price nonetheless vetoed Mike's lease proposal, explaining that it had been
Robert's wish to protect what the lawyer called his "foundation herd," by
sequestering the animals from all other cattle. Mike could not remember ever
hearing the term *foundation herd* in his career as a cattleman and certainly not
from his Uncle Robert.

CHAPTER 61

Judge Gabert was miffed by John MacCormack's newspaper article, provocatively titled "Ranch foreman is inheriting legal fight" and subheadlined "Millionaire's kin claim he manipulated control of considerable assets." It appeared Sunday, July 22, 2007, on the front page of the *San Antonio Express-News* Metro section. The piece discussed at length the June 15 meeting in Gabert's Rio Grande City office, where the guardianship case was concluded with the settlement that installed Paul Price, Carlos Martínez, and Ron Davidson as trustees of Robert's estate, as well as directors of his foundation at its establishment.

MacCormack's mention that the judge wore blue jeans that day didn't seem to bother Gabert. However, in an order he issued on August 22, the judge hammered the newspaper for its "callous, conscious, willful, and deliberate disregard" for his acceptance of Jim Robichaux's motion to seal court documents and close the court proceedings to the public, both measures allegedly necessary to protect Robert's privacy.

In his new order, Gabert forbade the *Express-News* to publish anything touching on East Foundation matters that was addressed in the court records, no matter how the information was obtained. He gave the newspaper five days to surrender all its hard copies of court documents related to the case and to destroy any electronic records it might have retained.

The *Express-News* responded with a terse rebuttal from Robert Rivard, the paper's editor. "[We] published a story that we believe was of significant public interest," wrote Rivard, "based on documents we obtained legally."

Lawyers for the Hearst Corp., the newspaper's owners, were already preparing the corporation's official reaction to Gabert's order, which they would attack as unconstitutional. "Our system," they wrote, "depends on the judgment of the independent press and does not permit judges the option of regulating the content of news . . . any more than it tolerates legislative or executive branch control over news content."

Thus chastened, on September 1, Judge Gabert amended his order, upholding his June decision to seal the record but placing no judicial demands or restraints on the *Express-News*.

Jim Robichaux's attempt to keep the hearings out of public view had boomeranged into a string of unflattering news stories, with each article prominently featured in the region's largest paper.

One reader, Professor Gerry W. Beyer at Texas Tech University, found the story so fascinating that he devoted to it his regular blog post, entitled "The Robert C. East Estate Battle Continues," which recounted much of the saga at length and in graphic detail for the edification of Beyer's readers.

Juan Molina, the San Antonio Viejo ranch gateman, later added his voice in the blog's comments section. "It is what they did to Mr. East and his family," Molina wrote. "But the truth should come out, and only the persons that work for them [know] what the truth is. We lived there since the late 1970s."

CHAPTER 62

The Tom T. East Sr. and Alice K. East and Alice H. East and Robert C. East Wildlife Foundation filed its first form 990-PF federal tax return for the 2008 fiscal year, beginning October 2007. The 13-page document identified Carlos Martínez as foundation president, Ron Davidson as vice president, and Paul Price as secretary treasurer, all three at no compensation. The return also reported, "No assets received to date." The foundation's address was Martínez's accounting office in Everhart Road in Corpus Christi.

Amity did not reign within the ruling group. "Paul Price kinda thought of himself as the top dog, because he's an estate lawyer, and he knew more than us," Martínez says. "He really got upset when Ron and I put him in his place, when we said that I was going to be president of the foundation at the very start."

The foundation reported its first funding from Robert's estate in fiscal 2009, $9,590,450, that the ruling group transferred from his management trust. Martínez, Davidson, and Price remained in their unpaid foundation positions. No employees were reported. The summary of direct charitable activities listed $344,605 in expenses.

The following year, the foundation listed another $16,993,049 of Robert's estate received from the trust. The 990-PF indicated no changes among the three directors, and once again, no employees were listed. Its expenses for direct charitable activities came to $624,207. A highlight of the year's scientific activity was "planning for a project for the management and monitoring of an endangered species, ocelots" living in deep brush on the foundation land.

The Texas Office of the Attorney General (OAG), having previously received critical comment on the June 15 settlement agreement from attorney Sharon Gardner, as well as copies of the *Express-News* articles, now heard from Helenita Groves. On November 18, 2010, she faxed a one-page, handwritten note to Daniel T. Hodge, Attorney General Greg Abbott's chief of staff, reporting that Paul Price had told both James King and Tres Kleberg that Robert didn't want family involved with his foundation. "NOT TRUE," she informed Hodge.

"I would like to talk to you about conversations with Robert [about] making a foundation to see that his ranches *would continue 'as they are' after his death*," she continued. "I suggested that it was important to have a family member, one at least, on the board. He chose a cousin, Tres Kleberg of San Antonio. On the day of Robert's funeral, Tres told me that he was told that he was no longer to be on the board as *Robert wanted no family involved.*

"Some months later, James King, a friend of Robert and a distant cousin, was asked by Paul Price to be an advisor. Some months later, he was 'dismissed.' He told me Price told him Robert wanted no family involved—NOT TRUE."

On May 6, 2022, Mrs. Groves passed away at her residence in San Antonio. She was 94.

Greg Abbott, later the Texas governor, also heard about the foundation directly from Frank Yturria, an old friend of Mike's father. Yturria's daughter, Dorothy, had once received a marriage proposal from Robert.

Many years in the past, Yturria and Tom East Jr. had pledged to one another that if either died or was incapacitated, the other would see to his widow and family's welfare. Yturria therefore felt duty bound to inform Abbott of several irregularities he'd spotted in the creation of the East Foundation. At the time, he also was arguing with the foundation over some disputed mineral rights he claimed under the San Antonio Viejo.

Since Yturria had been active for decades in Texas Republican politics and was a generous supporter of GOP candidates, it was a given that Abbott would see him personally. Mike East accompanied Yturria to the meeting in Abbott's Austin office, along with Letty García. Daniel Hodge attended as well.

Yturria dramatically laid out everything he knew or suspected about the foundation saga for the attorney general. He shared evidence as well, including an audio copy of the Prayer Tape and a transcript of the session. He also left copies of Robert's sixth and seventh codicils, dated September 8 and November 16, 2006, each naming a different set of trustees. "When," he asked Abbott, "have you witnessed a dying man change trustees two months apart?"

When Yturria finished his presentation, Mike remembers, "Abbott said, 'Well, we have no jurisdiction on the criminal side. The best we can do is just follow the money.'"

East later paid a second call at the AG's office, this time without Frank. Abbott was unavailable, he says. Likewise for Hodge. He met with senior staffers Bill Cobb and Marsha L. Acock.

"Right away," Mike recalls, "Cobb said, 'Now, y'all can't bring up anything prior to 2008.' So right there, he chopped us off at the knees."

East had all but given up on the OAG's willingness to intervene when, in early June of 2011, the agency issued a press release. "Executor returns $800,000 to charitable foundation created by South Texas rancher Robert C. East," read the headline. "Under agreement with Attorney General's Office, The Trust Company repays a portion of its executor fee."

The amount of The Trust Company's executor fee was not disclosed, although the company had originally proposed to charge Robert's estate $2.5 million, which included filing Robert's form 706 decedent federal estate tax return. Besides the $800,000 the OAG wanted returned, it also billed The Trust Company $50,000 to recover attorneys' fees and expenses, which were not mentioned in the release. There was no admission of liability.

The AG's office had been busy on another front as well. A few weeks later, on July 12, 2011, Marsha Acock of the charitable trusts section sent a five-page, single-spaced letter to Shane Hudson, an East Foundation attorney, that was critical of the directors' behavior.

Acock reviewed the foundation's brief history in the letter, noting to Hudson that, in the period that Martínez, Davidson, and Price served as successor trustees of Robert's estate, they had paid themselves about $417,000 apiece per year. She further noted that, in the autumn of 2010, when they would become active directors of the foundation, they also proposed to serve as senior executives—chief financial officer, chief operating officer, and chief executive officer, respectively—of the new foundation, again at $417,000 each per year.

The OAG looked upon the management plan with displeasure. Undeterred, in March of 2011, the ruling group notified Acock via Shane Hudson of their intention to implement the plan, which earned them a stiff rebuke from the attorney in her July letter.

"In addition to the conflicts of interest that are inherent when a charitable foundation's three most senior executives also serve on its board of directors," she scolded Price, Martínez, and Davidson, "we continue to be concerned that the executive salaries and organizational structure reflect the best interests of the executives, not the Foundation or the public's interest in preserving charitable assets. Indeed, the very management structure proposed by the Foundation was apparently crafted not to fit the Foundation's particularized needs but, rather, to ensure that the three original directors were also guaranteed high-paying employment opportunities as executive officers."

She continued.

"The proposed management structure you submitted to this office reflects a breach of the original three directors' duty of loyalty to the Foundation. Further, your proposal is inconsistent with a reasonable reading of Mr. East's intentions as stated in the Management Trust. Such an analysis indicates that Mr. East approved of the directors being employed by the Foundation in the professional capacities exercised by those individuals during Mr. East's lifetime.

"Thus, directors receiving compensation for their work on the Foundation's behalf should be limited to the professional roles they fulfilled for Mr. East, and their compensation should be determined with reference to the rates Mr.

East was willing to pay for those services. The compensation levels acceptable to Mr. East, who did not employ any of the three directors on a full-time basis at an annual salary exceeding $400,000 per year, are entirely inconsistent with the compensation proposed by the Foundation today.

"The ostensible basis for this argument is the incorrect suggestion that Mr. East himself named these three individuals as directors on the Foundation's board. However, your reliance upon the trust documentation is misplaced, because the three original directors were named to their positions under the terms of a settlement agreement—not a final estate document executed by Mr. East, and that agreement was never actually approved by Mr. East.

"The paramount duty of a charitable foundation's board of directors is to select the best possible chief executive officer and to provide independent oversight that ensures the most senior executive, and his or her leadership team, is consistently acting in the foundation's best interest."

According to Martínez and Davidson, they hired Greg Abbott's former solicitor general, Ted Cruz, then in private law practice in advance of his successful 2012 run for the US Senate, to consult on the salary issue.

"We met him," says Martínez. "We gave him a tour of the ranches. He goes about $100,000 (for the consultation fee). Then he didn't show up at the meeting because, at that time, he didn't want to piss off the AG. I don't like that guy for that reason. I think he's a lowlife."

CHAPTER 63

As a consequence of the mediation and responding to the OAG's directives, the ruling group added two directors to the foundation in 2011. One was Dan Kinsel III, the ranch broker, who, according to the foundation's 990-PF, was hired to work five hours a week at an annual compensation of $24,500.

The other new director was Bryan Wagner, founder, owner, and president of the Wagner Oil Co. of Fort Worth. Wagner was recruited to the foundation's board by Dan Kinsel. Carlos Martínez was told at the time that Wagner had close ties with Greg Abbott. The oilman, at this writing, is chairman of the foundation board.

Other hires included Chris Huff, the general manager in charge of security at the San Antonio Viejo following Robert's death, who became the foundation's operations manager, with $64,463 per year in compensation.

Verónica Paradez, who, as Verónica Loa, had been Paul Price's assistant, joined the foundation as investments manager at $64,123. The following year, Paradez was raised to $83,239.

Verónica "Vicky" Rodríguez, who served as the ranch bookkeeper after Aída Garza was fired, was hired by the foundation, where, at this writing, she also works as a bookkeeper.

Both Paradez and Rodríguez declined through the foundation to be interviewed for this book.

The OAG had urged the ruling group to hire a competent foundation CEO. In fiscal year 2011, the board went shopping for a wildlife biologist to fill the position. They paid Dorothy Drummer & Associates, an executive recruiter in Austin, Texas, $96,815 to conduct the search.

Drummer didn't have far to look. At the suggestion of Fred Bryant, the director of Texas A&M's Caesar Kleberg Wildlife Research Institute in Kingsville, she interviewed 50-year-old Robert Neal Wilkins, known as Neal, then on the faculty at A&M's Kingsville campus and also Bryant's friend. The board quickly hired Wilkins.

Wilkins, from Irving, Texas, describes himself as a poor student in his youth, bored by his studies, until he got excited about forestry. "I just wanted a job where I didn't have to mess with people and I could work outside," he explains. "It turned out that I also have a passion for wildlife."

He graduated from Stephen F. Austin State University in 1984 with a bachelor of science degree in forestry. Then Wilkins moved to Texas A&M, where, in 1987, he earned his master's degree in wildlife and fisheries science. He completed his doctorate in wildlife ecology at the University of Florida, at Gainesville, in 1992.

Neal Wilkins headed to Olympia, Washington, in 1998 to work as a wildlife biologist for Port Blakely Companies, one of the largest family timber operations in the United States. In 2005, he returned to Texas, where he took a position as an extension wildlife specialist at A&M and then became both a department head and leader of the extension program. At A&M, he also took part in a range of applied research projects, many that looked into avian wildlife management issues. Among them were studies of golden-winged warblers and black-capped vireos.

Wilkins also joined A&M's Institute of Renewable Natural Resources as a professor and then became the institute's director. In August of 2012, after interviewing with Dan Kinsel and Bryan Wagner, he was hired as president and CEO of the East Foundation at approximately $310,000 a year. Paul Price was then the foundation's chief investment officer and general counsel. He received $341,000 a year.

In one of his earliest moves, the new CEO discharged Carlos Martínez and Ron Davidson, who, at the time, were employees but not officials of the foundation. "I fired them both for generally the same reason, which was non-performance," he says. "They had different jobs, so they were nonperforming at different things."

Paul Price would continue on at the foundation in several alternating capacities. According to the foundation's website, which memorializes Price, along with Martínez and Davidson, as the foundation's first board of directors, he spent 10 years as general counsel before leaving.

Mike East and his sister Lica Elena Pinkston remember that Neal Wilkins made a positive first impression as the new East Foundation's chief executive, and they were both eager to meet him. Neither was happy, however, that Paul Price remained on the payroll. Brother and sister were also troubled by a foundation message, posted on its website, celebrating the good news that Robert and Lica East's dream had been realized.

What dream? their niece and nephew wondered. As ever, the East family charges that the foundation twists their narrative to advance its corporate objectives, not the truth. They also object to an assertion on the East Foundation website that the "East Foundation was created through the generous gift of the East family in 2007." Neither can see how Robert's estate—taken from him via machinations, subterfuges, and lies—can be characterized as a generous gift from his family to the foundation.

Mike invited Wilkins to the Santa Fe ranch soon after he was hired. "I hadn't met him," East recalls. "I didn't even know what he looked like."

He prepared materials in advance to share with Wilkins. These included excerpts from Robert's deposition in the disclaimer case, in which he discussed his desire for Mike and his sisters to operate his proposed foundation and lease pasturage from it. Robert also said in his testimony—as he had elsewhere—that he wanted such a foundation, should it ever come to pass, to honor his parents, just as his Aunt Sarita's foundation had honored hers, and to materially support cancer research in honor of his late sister.

Mike called Wilkins's attention to the first page of the seventh codicil to Robert's will, written by Paul Price and signed by Robert on November 16, 2006, at the San Antonio Viejo ranch, in which Robert's executors are directed "to retain the services of legal counsel representing me personally at the date of my death to represent the Executor(s) of my estate."

East also pointed out to Wilkins that Robert had been unable to decipher a copy of Oscar Ozuna's employment contract, with or without his reading glasses, during his videotaped testimony at Rubén Garza's defamation trial in February of 2006. Therefore, he said, it was unlikely that, nine months later, his uncle could have read the smaller, single-spaced type of the seventh codicil, in which he guaranteed Price's future employment.

"I had all the stuff highlighted," Mike says, "and I pointed it out to Neal. Then I basically told him the story, all that happened to Robert." Mike talked about Robert's questioned signatures, his lack of medical care, the constant revisions of his estate documents, his isolation—everything. "Neal never said anything. He didn't agree, and he didn't disagree. He sat there with a blank look on his face."

Disappointed though he was with Wilkins's evident lack of interest in the foundation's tainted past, Mike remembers, "we got along pretty well for a while," as did his sisters. All three siblings believed that the East Foundation might eventually redeem itself by acknowledging the less savory aspects of its beginnings, respecting Robert's wishes instead of inventing them, and relieving Paul Price of his executive positions.

In that spirit, Mike made a gift to the foundation of an extensive family legal archive created and maintained for decades at the old Perkins law firm in Alice. "My thought," he says, "was that a future generation of Easts might not preserve all that material, so maybe the foundation should have it. I talked it over with my sisters, and they thought it was a good idea. Neal came down to the ranch with a U-Haul truck, and we loaded him up."

Lica Elena and her husband, John, donated a collection of detailed San Antonio Viejo mineral maps to the foundation. Alice shared a large portion of her extensive photograph collection and also supported Wilkins's membership on the South Texans' Property Rights Association board of directors, of which Alice is also a member. The Pinkstons similarly backed Wilkins for a seat on the Texas Land & Mineral Owners Association board of directors.

Mike did not reengage with the foundation for a couple years, "but then I started getting more and more disappointed with Neal," he says. One irritation was the foundation's move to register all the East cattle brands so that Mike could no longer use them on either side of his animals. He thought it a pointless provocation, belying foundation statements of friendship and respect for Robert's surviving family members. They are also affronted by the foundation's requirement that they call ahead when visiting the family graveyard.

The slights began to feel deliberate. Although Robert's special affinity for the ranch's collection of old wagons dating from his boyhood was common knowledge, when Letty East initiated a project to restore some of the treasured antiques, she found them in broken pieces in the ranch garbage pit. At this writing, she has fully restored two of them.

In 2021, vaqueros found Robert's collection of old East family branding irons in the ranch dump and retrieved them as the wagon wreckage had been saved.

A number of old ranch structures had already been destroyed; a process begun while the ruling group still ruled. The lost buildings include the iconic barn, built in the style of a Quonset hut, which Mike mentioned at his meeting with Price, Martínez, and Davidson before Robert's demise. The building, which dated to the 1950s, was commonly featured in old ranch photos. Neal Wilkins ordered its removal.

Among the earliest structures to be demolished, at Ron Davidson's order, was the shed where Old Mama was temporarily detained by the Mexican bandits. Several ranch residences have been razed, including the wooden one-time headquarters.

Robert was adamant, as Mike had told the ruling group, that he wanted the ranch left as it was. Ironically, if he had not become so extraordinarily wealthy, his wishes might well have been respected.

"All of these old structures over time deteriorate," say Wilkins, who offers Casa Verde, Rogelio Garza, and Jesús Sifuentes's former abode as an example. "There's a likelihood we may do some stabilization of that.

It is not a serviceable structure, and it probably has not been a serviceable structure for decades.

"There's deep, deep, deep history in that entire country, in all of those structures, not just Casa Verde. There are structures all *over* the San Antonio Viejo. They're not necessarily deteriorating very fast. But the ability to recondition those into any kind of serviceable structure, beyond just the historic structures that they are now, is pretty limited."

Wilkins says the same holds for old stone buildings from the nineteenth century, such as La Perla, Tom Sr. and Alice East's first domicile on the ranch. "Those are relatively stable," he says. "They've been ruins at least since the turn of the last century, and they are ruins now.

"I've had historic architects look at them. Do you take something and rebuild it and kind of Disneyfy it and essentially make it more artificial? Or do you leave the historical context intact? Thus far, we've chosen to leave the historical context intact."

Mike East set a second grievance meeting with Neal Wilkins at his feed yard office. He brought with him a special signed edition of *Horses to Ride, Cattle to Cut*, a coffee table book written by Henry Chappell, with photography by Wyman Meinzer, about the San Antonio Viejo. Wilkins had sent him the book, which was published by the foundation, which East now returned as a gesture of annoyance at what he and his sisters call the foundation's misrepresentation of their family history and their uncle's intentions for his estate.

"I told Neal about going out to the San Antonio Viejo on Thanksgiving, and Robert was crying and all that, because people treated him like he was crazy." According to Mike, Wilkins again asked no questions and said very little.

He recollects his message at the feed yard meeting was "you gotta get rid of Price, and you gotta give money for cancer research."

Wilkins at first seemed open to discussing cancer contributions. "There are a lot of different organizations," he said. "Which one would you prefer?" Mike replied that he had no particular program in mind at the time. Today, however, he thinks the Vannie E. Cook Jr. Cancer Foundation in McAllen, which specializes in pediatric cancer care and research, would be an appropriate choice, particularly since it is a Rio Grande Valley institution.

"My sister Lica," he continues, "told me two or three weeks later that she had run into Neal somewhere, and he told her Price was going to retire. He also asked her to be thinking about the cancer funding and all that. She kinda told me to back off and let all this happen. Well, it never did."

Lica did not let the matter drop. In 2018, she sent Wilkins a *Wired* magazine adaptation of Charles Graeber's book, *The Breakthrough: Immunology and the Race to Cure Cancer*, in which Alice native Jim Allison, that year's Nobel laureate in medicine, is discussed at length.

"Neal," she emailed him. "You and I talked sometime back about the East Foundation doing something in regards to cancer research. It was something my aunt Lica talked about and something I know she wanted to do. Jim Allison is a South Texas boy, born and raised in Alice. His family still lives there. I think some sort of funding by the East Foundation would be a way of honoring something Lica felt very strongly about. Please give it some thought. I feel certain I can put you in touch with Dr. Allison."

"Lica," Wilkins responded three days later. "Thank you for reaching out with this. I have been traveling too much and fallen behind on emails. I will do some homework on this and have some discussions with board members. Will be back in touch soon. Best regards, Neal Wilkins."

She heard nothing more from the foundation CEO on the issue.

Wilkins says that, after serious consideration, the board decided against foundation support for cancer research, "and I don't necessarily disagree with them. You have to make priorities, and you have to make trade-offs. One of the trade-offs that our board decided to make, and I don't disagree with it, was that we were to stay within our lane and stay within the bounds of the language that was given us for the purpose of the foundation, which did not explicitly include a cancer donation.

"It's kinda like the nation's Constitution, right? Either it's in the Constitution, or it's not. In this case, it is not in the purpose of the foundation, and we've made what I think is a wise choice to not wander from that."

The foundation board—all of whom declined to be interviewed for this book—still includes Dan Kinsel and Bryan Wagner, both hired by the original ruling group, plus Richard Evans, the former CEO and chairman of the Frost Bank, and the newest director, Tio Kleberg, a member of the King Ranch board of directors, as well as chair of the Caesar Kleberg Foundation. Kleberg arrived in 2014.

The fact that Tio Kleberg's older brother, Tres, had been disqualified by the ruling group from membership on the same East Foundation board on account of his kinship to Robert posed no problem in hiring Tio for the same position, according to Wilkins.

"We got a ruling from the attorney general's office," he says. "We actually had to draw a chart."

CHAPTER 64

F rank Yturria never gave up. Less than a year before his death in 2018, Yturria contacted FBI agent Tyler Kennedy of the Bureau's McAllen office in the hope of sparking a federal investigation of the East Foundation. He sent the agent a sheaf of documents, accompanied by a note.

"I have been a friend of the East family for many, many years," he wrote. "I only want to see that the men who conspired in Robert's early death, and stole his estate, be brought to justice."

Mike East hasn't backed down, either. In April of 2017, he spoke extemporaneously before a video camera, recording a CD that he sent to Neal Wilkins, as well as to the four East Foundation board members and dozens of others: friends, acquaintances, business associates, and community leaders, but no reporters.

In *Robert East: The Real Story*, as he called his recording, he speaks simply: "I want to tell some of the story of the East Foundation and who was responsible for getting it there and my dissatisfaction with them because of the way it is being operated. I feel the foundation is not portraying the values and the wishes of the family or my uncle, either one.

"My gripe," he closed nearly two hours later, "is Paul Price and the wildlife foundation. They have Paul Price there, who is responsible for all that was done to Robert. He was the main orchestrator and wasn't willing to spend any money for medical needs. He was a trustee for a while. We went complaining to the attorney general, and there were some changes made, and they got rid of Ron and Carlos, but he stayed on.

"He is still there, drawing salary. I have expressed that concern to Wilkins and that there should be money for cancer research. None of those things have been done. I feel like Paul Price should be fired and not be sucking money off the wildlife foundation."

"Mike," Wilkins wrote him after receiving the video, "I have watched your video several times over the last few weeks. I respect the courage that it takes to put that story together—and am glad you did it, as it is important history.

"I do hope we can find some time to talk through some of the issues. I realize not all can be remedied, but I do want to make sure we keep open communication between us."

Tio Kleberg also responded with a note. "Thank you for sending your video," he wrote. "Your recollections of the details of Robert and the San Antonio Viejo are helpful and will be recorded now and for the future. Thank you for sharing this important South Texas history. Sincerely, Tio."

Paul Price did finally leave the foundation, following years of useful service, according to Neal Wilkins.

"Paul," he says, "was effective at directing our investment managers, as well as providing legal services. In other words, he was qualified for the positions where we needed work done. He was a qualified attorney, and he had become adept at coordinating the foundation's investments."

According to the foundation's IRS form 990-PF for the period ending September 2018, Paul Price earned $248,450 as vice president in his last year of employment. He accrued another $31,603 in contributions to employee benefit plans and deferred compensation.

CHAPTER 65

Paul Price's departure from the foundation did not close either Mike or Letty East's issues with the lawyer. Although both recognized that Letty's late cousin, Oscar, had supervised Robert's cruel isolation, they regard him as Price's agent at the ranch and a convenient fall guy when the plot looked to be unraveling.

"Oscar was not smart," says Mike. "He was a small-time thief and con man to be used and then discarded."

Letty, who married Mike in 2014, has her own bill of particulars when it came to Paul Price. "You, Carilu, and Oscar had no right in telling a dying man I was trying to kill him," she once texted the lawyer. "That, Price, you always have to live with. I would say that is having hatred in your heart."

"Don't believe I said that," he replied, also by text.

"I beg to differ. Mean-spiritedness caused by greed. Now you hide with Christianity. This is Letty García, or as you refer to me, 'the girlfriend,' 'shocker.' 'She wants to shock you.' Letty the nurse."

"On what basis do you conclude I was motivated by greed?"

"Why would you let this elderly man get in such bad shape? As you know, he could afford the best medical help possible."

"I concur with one of our greatest presidents," Price responded, "who said at the end of the Civil War and tens of thousands of deaths: With charity for all and malice for none let us bind up our wounds.

"I know Mike cared for his uncle, and I cared for my client. My intent and Mike's intent were good. No human being is perfect. Not me. Not anyone. That's why we all need the Savior. I choose to forgive and move on in peace."

Mike braced Price as well in an October 30, 2020, cell phone call.

"I've been reminiscing about a lot of stuff lately," Mike says on the recording. "I know that you told me that all that bad stuff that happened to Robert was Oscar. I'd like for you to enlighten me on that, because I want to meet you halfway on this."

"Well, I appreciate that, Mike," Price answered affably. "I wish the very best for you and your family. I remember we had that mediation, and I know that you wanted Oscar off the ranch and his people off the ranch. And I know we visited. I have all respect for you, and I want nothing but the best for you."

East did not repay the compliment. "That still doesn't answer my question," he says. "How was Oscar the one responsible for all the bad stuff that happened to Robert?"

"I'm not here to hold grudges or anything, but the reality is that I was up in Corpus Christi. I wasn't down on the ranch," said Price. "I was a long ways away.

"And I knew Robert. The last thing Robert would have wanted was for any lawyer to come down there and run his life. Robert didn't want that. He didn't want me coming down there and running things."

"Yeah, what about all the documents, Paul? How did all that come about? All the legal documents?"

"Well, just so you know, I would love to sit down and tell the story from my perspective, but I have to maintain client confidentiality. Just like, when you pass on, your lawyers are not allowed to talk about their conversations with you. That's confidential."

"What did Oscar have to do with the legal documents?" East interrupted him.

"Well, I mean. I don't know what you're saying."

"I mean how they were drawn and who benefited from them and all that. What was Oscar's input on those documents?"

"Well, those decisions were made on those documents. Robert made those decisions."

"Robert was the one who made those decisions on the legal documents, as far as who got what and who was appointed to what and all that kind of stuff?" East asked.

"Yeah," Price replied, then changed the subject. "I mean, at the time when Charlie Hury was your lawyer, before Robert's death, and I met with him down in Kingsville. His position was that you were upset with Oscar. Oscar's the one [who] wouldn't let you on the ranch, and you were very upset with him, and you wanted him out. We had that big mediation. I know you contributed to it, got Oscar to enter into a settlement agreement."

"Hury talked me into it," says East. "I agreed with Hury to do it because it was taking too long, and I knew that Robert didn't have any time. I needed to go in and see how he really was. I couldn't get in there.

"So that's why I agreed to the mediation to get Oscar out. Had I known that Robert was on his last legs by the time I went in there, I wouldn't have agreed to any of it.

"In the process, I also had to agree that you and Carlos and Ron could appoint yourselves as trustees. And after all that was said and done, *then* I could go in and see how Robert was. That was the whole package right there."

"Hmmm."

"And I'm not through, Paul. I may still do that. This isn't over with."

"Hmm."

"It's not over with by any means."

"What does justice look like for you?"

"For you to make a full confession."

"Of what?"

"Of what you did wrong."

"What do you think I did wrong?"

"Paul, you can answer that a whole lot better than I can."

"So, I'm just trying to understand."

"You say it was Oscar. Oscar said it was you. It was both of you. You all used each other. You had Oscar because he was dispensable. You could dispense with him, easily. Which you did. That's what happened."

East then turns to the April 2005 power of attorney Price drew up. "When we got those medical records out of Dr. Falcón's office," he says, "there's a document there that names both of you with Robert's medical power of attorney. Both of you are on that document. So who drew up that document?"

"Mike, the person was—"

"I don't give a shit, Paul, who the person was. Who drew up the goddamn document?"

"Okay. But Mike. You [garble] medical power of attorney. And you said that—"

"That you and Oscar Ozuna are on there," Mike interrupted again. "If one's not there, the other takes his place. Was family ever notified about that medical document?"

"Okay. But Mike, Mike. You've probably seen the medical power of attorney. I'm asking you, who was named as Robert's medical—who had the power of attorney? Was it Oscar, or was it me?"

"Both of you. It's a joint medical power of attorney. If one's not there, the other one takes over."

"Okay. But who was in place until one of them . . ."

"My question is who drew up the document?"

"But Mike, if you've seen the medical power of attorney, you know who was in charge of Robert's medical care. Oscar never . . ."

"Oscar what? If Oscar wasn't there, who took his place?"

"But Oscar was there."

Many attorneys will refuse to serve as a client's health care power of attorney without a family member or close friend serving as co-power of attorney. Oscar was not a close friend. Price was not family.

Mike then moved on, wanting to discuss whose idea it was to encourage Robert to move his assets out of his estate into his management fund.

"You suggested it there. So, whose idea was that? . . ."

"You are now going into attorney-client conversations," Price replied.

"All I want from you is honesty. That's all. A straightforward answer. Not this bullshit with attorney-client privilege."

"You are entitled to your opinion. I believe deeply in justice, and I believe deeply in people being treated justly."

"But why, Paul?" East asked. "This is why I get so damn angry. I had to really jump through hoops to go out and see him at Thanksgiving of 2006. When I get out there, this man is crying. He's *crying*. Why? Why was he crying?

"And he says these people are treating him like he's crazy. Hell, I didn't know what he was talking about until later. And that, Paul, is why I am angry. This man had no reason to cry about how he was treated. A multimillionaire, who's old and isolated, had no business crying about how people were treating him."

"I agree. I agree, Mike," Price replied, then offered an oddly inappropriate afterthought: "Robert got upset at various people at various times."

"Yeah," Mike answered, ready to end the conversation. "But this wasn't just upset. Robert could get angry and all that. He wasn't just upset. This man was crying."

Six months later, Mike texted Price with a question. He wanted to know what became of a table lamp that his grandparents received from their vaqueros as a wedding gift more than a century before. Someone took it from the main house soon after Robert's death, and it wasn't a member of the East family.

Price texted back that Mike would have to ask Neal Wilkins about it.

East was having none of it. "You were initially responsible and only because we put you there," he texted back. "Once you appointed yourself as a trustee, you did whatever you wanted. Even had Robert's DNA done without even asking the family. You can blame Oscar. You can blame Neal. But the buck stops with you."

"Mike," came Price's reply, "I have responded to you out of respect to you. I'm concerned, however, that it results in stirring up further upset for you. For that reason, I'm going to limit my responses. As you know, I was one out of three cotrustees that you agreed would serve in lieu of a group you opposed. All of the decisions of the trustees were by majority vote. Independent directors were appointed who hired Neal Wilkins. My role has been limited all along.

"I am more than willing to take responsibility for my decisions but not the decisions of others. Carlos, Ron, and I were careful to preserve Robert's property. We did agree to turn over to you and your sisters certain items of great value to you that you requested. The post-death testing was done without my knowledge or consent. I'm sorry for the upsets you have experienced. Best, Paul."

"So why, after the meeting I had with you and Carlos and Ron [when I asked] that you leave the house as it was for the sake of memory—why was that completely disregarded? Also, with my grandmother's spurs, you said I could take them for the time being but might have to bring them back. Huff even insisted [on] a picture of me holding them in my hand with you present."

Price ignored the accusations.

"Although independent directors hired Dr. Wilkins, I had a different viewpoint than he did on some decisions," he wrote. "Neal is a man of integrity and an esteemed wildlife scientist who has sought to honor the East family and, on the whole, did a good job while I was there.

"He is the guy in charge today and for almost 10 years. He is in a far better position than I to address your concerns. I have no power today to do anything.

"Mike, I hope you and your family have a wonderful Easter. I have made many mistakes in life, just like every human being except one, Jesus. I am thankful that, despite my sins, I can have peace with God through the death and resurrection of Jesus to pay for my sins. Because He rose again, I believe that all those who place their trust in Him can look forward to eternal life with Him.

"I am 71 with grandchildren and realize that this life passes so quickly. I will soon die and stand before God. At that time, I will seek God's pardon and forgiveness based not on anything I did but solely on the blood of Christ shed for me.

"Is there anything more important than examining the amazing claims in the Bible that Jesus was resurrected? Is it possible those claims are true? And if they are true, isn't the key to having joy and peace a relationship with Jesus?

"I don't presume to know your faith. I simply wish and pray the best for you and your family. Paul."

"All I have to say, Paul, is that you better pray there are no East family members on the jury when you go."

CHAPTER 66

Over the years since the East Foundation was formally organized, its statements of mission and purpose have appeared in a number of formats at various lengths. Much of the material has been a reworking of cattleman Rob H. Welder's will, composed for him by M. Harvey Weil in the 1950s, and cribbed into drafts of Robert's management trust documents by Paul Pearson in the 1990s. In an interview, foundation CEO Neal Wilkins agreed to provide, verbally, a single, comprehensive and official East Foundation statement laying out its version of the foundation's history and a review of the principles that guide its operation:

"Robert left an incredible legacy," Wilkins said. "He left the legacy of land—220,000 acres of land. He left financial resources dedicated toward the management of that land and toward the activities of the foundation. Then he left a mission, and that didn't come about in five minutes under pressure by a bevy of slimy attorneys.

"I'm not saying there wasn't a bevy of slimy attorneys. There was definitely that. But there was premeditation over a 20-some-odd year period for the formation of the foundation. So that wasn't something that somebody pressured onto Robert East at the final moment of his life, regardless of how nefarious some of those characters actually are. The evidence is that there were bad guys all around.

"So, here it is, chapter and verse. Upon a documentary foundation, if you will, we feel comfortable saying what we say and doing what we're doing, okay?

"What came out post Robert East's death was the fact that there was a legitimate foundation established from his will and testament and his trust document. It did not result from something that was instantaneous on the deathbed, right there at the last minute. I'm confident that the legal process, as much as this thing was litigated, would have reversed that if that were the case.

"I'm not going to try to relitigate it. I'm a wildlife biologist. I can tell you what I read and what I know, and I do know that the East family both spoke of and wrote about and documented their desire for their land to be held in trust for the future and that no one else would own it.

"Therefore, it would be held by a foundation. And it had to be put to a charitable use. That charitable use that they chose was research into how live-stock production and wildlife conservation can coexist. Then they laid out some education objectives and then said, you know, 'Go forth.'

"I'm sure that every foundation does things and pushes the frontier for-ward beyond what the founder would have understood or recognized. I'm sure that the Kaiser Family Foundation has done that. I'm sure that the Rockefeller Foundation has done that. The Noble Foundation has done that. All these foundations are doing good things the founders didn't understand or conceive of what they're doing at present.

"We are carrying out the overall big picture vision of not only Robert East but the East family. That's borne out in the stuff that we write and publish. It's not written by historians. It's written by scientists and managers.

"We write and publish excerpts and vignettes from the East family that speak to that pretty heavily. Not only a written desire of the family, and then Robert East acting upon it in the end. If his sister had been the last one alive, I'm sure she would have established a foundation. His mother, who was almost the last one alive, would have established a foundation. That appears to be the situation.

"This is historical East stuff that we have from our archives. Just to clarify, even though I wish I could go back in time and would have met Robert East and known him, I did not meet him. I did not know him. I knew of him.

"I'm pretty plainspoken about this. I'm duty bound—and I take it seriously—to defend the legacy of the family, but not in a way that's ridiculous and against facts. That's within my job description.

"Whether the current family members view us as the defender of that legacy or not, nevertheless that's still in my job description, and that job description was written by people that aren't alive. So they don't get to change it. And making sure that our archives and the information that we have are put to a use that is appropriate and to the benefit of the purposes of the foundation."

Lica Elena Pinkston responds thus on behalf of her siblings and herself to Wilkins's statement. She asserts that the foundation owes its existence not to Robert's supposed vision of the future, encompassing his family's wishes, but only to a gas field, named after her father, that made her uncle a very rich and confused old man, and therefore a vulnerable target.

"I can tell you this," she writes, "if that money had not been there, Pearson and Price would not have wanted anything to do with those ranches. They would have found a way to sell them off. There would be no East Foundation today."

She quotes Jesus from John 8:32: "'You shall know the truth, and the truth shall make you free.'"

"We, Robert's nieces and nephew, know what happened to our uncle— not the false narrative but the truth—which has brought us some closure. Had the foundation chosen honesty and admitted there was wrongdoing, we would have accepted the outcome. But after we gave them the facts and named the people who played a role in the wrongdoing, they turned a blind eye and even kept some of them on the foundation payroll.

"Despite the board of directors and CEO's manufactured narrative, we can assure you that a foundation of any kind, much less a wildlife foundation, was not part of our grandparents' vision. They built their lives together on land that not only was hard on animals but on humans as well. They were just trying to survive hard times.

"After our grandfather died way too young, at age 54, his children and widow, Old Mama, built on what he and she had begun together. Tom East Jr., our father, led the family. Old Mama worked cattle into her 80s. Lica lovingly accepted her role as Old Mama's caretaker, and Robert, in his simple way, lived life on his own terms.

"By the year 2002, he was alone and overwhelmed, ripe for the manipulation and abuse he would suffer. Had either Paul Pearson or Paul Price and their associates acted according to their professional oaths, helping an elderly and confused client rather than helping themselves, this sad story might have ended very differently."

Alice East, Lica Elena and Mike's sister, adds a note of her own: "You know," she says, "Old Mama and Lica weren't going to do anything unless Daddy told them to."

EPILOG

The East family's San Antonio Viejo ranch, once a scruffy, sun-baked outpost on a wild frontier, overseen by a pair of brash American originals, has, in the wake of Robert East's death in 2007, flourished luxuriantly on a rich diet of mineral royalties—far beyond anything Tom Timmons East and Alice Kleberg East or their son, Robert, might have imagined.

At this writing, the foundation reports total net assets just north of $710 million. According to Neal Wilkins, foundation land holdings exceed those of all but a few other foundations anywhere in the United States. Wilkins earns $410,000 a year, as president and CEO, plus $43,762 in contributions to employee benefits plans and deferred compensation. The foundation's four-person board of directors—Richard W. Evans, Jr., Dan Kinsell III, Stephen J. ("Tio") Kleberg, and Bryan Wagner are paid $65,500 each per annum.

Wilkins and his board manage the foundation out of executive offices in San Antonio, Texas. There are 45 employees on the payroll stationed in San Antonio and at the ranches, as well as at facilities in Hebbronville, Kingsville, Harlingen, and Laredo. They keep busy at everything from herding cows to directing educational programs, conducting agricultural science, cultivating friends in high places, and tending to 217,000 acres of ranch land originally acquired by the East family—which no longer has any stake in the operation.

The foundation describes itself as at the forefront of efforts to advance responsible, private land stewardship. This means, in a general way, that they nurture both livestock and wildlife on shared acreage and educate ranchers, biologists, scientists, and various decision-makers in the ways of keeping the land and its animals healthy, diverse, and productive. This is a vision first articulated by M. Harvey Weil on behalf of the Welder Family, and then appropriated word-for-word in estate documents created by Paul Pearson for Robert.

The foundation reports annual "direct charitable activities" amounting to $6,669,329 (see Appendix B). Funding cancer research is not among them.

Robert and Lica East and their parents, in whose names the foundation operates, rest together in a tidy row at the San Antonio Viejo ranch cemetery. As Neal Wilkins says of the Kaisers, Rockefellers, Nobles, and others, these four Easts would be astonished to see what has become of their once-struggling South Texas cattle operation. They'd also be distressed to learn that no East among the three succeeding generations of the family takes any part—or pride—in what has become of their forebears' vision, and they likely never shall.

APPENDIX A

ROBERT'S SIGNATURES IN HIS LATER YEARS

In Testimony Whereof, I hereunto sign my name to this my Last Will and Testament, consisting of this page and sixteen (16) preceding pages, each of which I am initialing for the purpose of identification, all in the presence of _Martha AGilmore_, and _Linda Parchman_, each of whom signed this Will at my request, in my presence, and in the presence of each other, this the _16_ day of _October_, 1995.

Robert C. East

Robert C. East
Testator

In Witness Whereof, this **Robert C. East Management Trust - 1995** has been signed, executed, and delivered this _16_ day of _October_, 1995.

Grantor:

Robert C. East

Robert C. East

Trustee:

Robert East

Robert C. East

I agree that any third party who receives a copy of this document may act under it. Revocation of the durable power of attorney is not effective as to a third party until the third party receives actual notice of the revocation. I agree to indemnify the third party for any claims that arise against the third party because of reliance on this power of attorney.

Signed this _20th_ day of April, 1998.

Robert C. East

Robert C. East

Robert East
Robert C. East
Testator

Martha A. Gilmore
Witness Martha A. Gilmore

Deanne Pierce
Witness Deanne Pierce

Subscribed and Sworn to before me by the said **Robert C. East**, the Testator, and by the said _Martha A. Gilmore_ and _Deanne Pierce_ , witnesses, this the 26th day of _November_ , 2002.

HARRIET I GONZALEZ
Notary Public
STATE OF TEXAS
My Comm. Exp. 02-25-2006

Harriet L Gonzalez
Notary Public, State of Texas
My commission expires: _2/25/2006_

East, Robert C. Fourth Codicil.doc   -5-   _R.C.E._
Initials

I, **Robert C. East**, Trustee, hereby certify that the foregoing is a true and correct copy of the Sixth Amendment to the **Robert C. East** Management Trust - 1995 executed on the _26th_ day of _November_ , 2002, by and between **Robert C. East**, as Grantor, and **Robert C. East**, as Trustee.

Robert East
Robert C. East, Trustee

In Testimony Whereof, I sign, publish and declare this instrument to be the Fifth Codicil to my Last Will and Testament, in the presence of _Tina S. Grace_ and _Emilio A. Alberto_ , as subscribing witnesses, each of whom signed this Fifth Codicil to my Last Will and Testament at my request, in my presence and in the presence of each other, this _21st_ day of April, 2005.

Robert East
Robert C. East
Testator

I, Robert C. East, Trustee, hereby certify that the foregoing is a true and correct copy of the Seventh Amendment to the Robert C. East Management Trust - 1995, executed on the __21__ day of April, 2005, by and between **Robert C. East, as Grantor,** and **Robert C. East, as Trustee.**

Robert East
_____
Robert C. East, Trustee

I, **Robert C. East, Trustee,** hereby certify that the foregoing is a true and correct copy of the **Eighth Amendment to the Robert C. East Management Trust - 1995,** executed on the __21st__ day of December, 2005, by and between **Robert C. East, as Grantor,** and **Robert C. East, as Trustee.**

_____
Robert C. East, Trustee

_____
Robert C. East
Testator

Witness (print): _Carilu Cantu Leal_

Witness (print): _Ann Marquez_

_____ **Subscribed and Sworn to** before me by the said **Robert C. East,** Testator, and by the said _Carilu Cantu Leal_ and _Ann Marquez_, witnesses, this the __8th__ day of _September_, 2006.

In Testimony Whereof, I sign, publish and declare this instrument to be the Seventh Codicil to my Last Will and Testament, in the presence of _J. I. Ochoa_, _Gus Perez, Jr._, and _Fausto Salinas Jr_, as subscribing witnesses, each of whom signed this Seventh Codicil to my Last Will and Testament at my request, in my presence and in the presence of each other, this __16th__ day of November, 2006.

_____
Robert C. East
Testator

I, Robert C. East, Trustee, hereby certify that the foregoing is a true and correct copy of the Ninth Amendment to the Robert C. East Management Trust - 1995, executed on the _8th_ day of _September_, 2006, by and between Robert C. East, as Grantor, and Robert C. East, as Trustee.

Robert C. East, Trustee

I, Robert C. East, Trustee, hereby certify that the foregoing is a true and correct copy of the Tenth Amendment to the Robert C. East Management Trust – 1995, executed on the _10th_ day of November, 2006, by and between Robert C. East, as Grantor, and Robert C. East, as Trustee.

Robert C. East, Trustee

If any part of this document shall be invalid or unenforceable under applicable law, the remaining provisions of this document shall remain effective.

Signed this _10th_ day of November, 2006.

ROBERT C. EAST

APPENDIX B

EAST FOUNDATION'S FEDERAL TAX RETURN FOR 2018

2949100903603 1

Form **990-PF**	**Return of Private Foundation** or Section 4947(a)(1) Trust Treated as Private Foundation	OMB No 1545 0052
Department of the Treasury Internal Revenue Service	► Do not enter social security numbers on this form as it may be made public. ► Go to *www irs gov/Form990PF* for instructions and the latest information.	**2018** Open to Public Inspection

For calendar year 2018 or tax year beginning 10/01 , 2018, and ending 9/30 , 2019

Tom T East Sr and Alice K East and Alice
H East and Robert C East Wildlife Fnd
200 Concord Plaza Drive #410
San Antonio, TX 78216

A Employer identification number 26-1380672

B Telephone number (see instructions) 210-447-0126

C If exemption application is pending, check here ►

G Check all that apply:
- Initial return
- Final return
- Address change
- Initial return of a former public charity
- Amended return
- Name change

D 1 Foreign organizations, check here ►
2 Foreign organizations meeting the 85% test, check here and attach computation ►

H Check type of organization: [X] Section 501(c)(3) exempt private foundation
Section 4947(a)(1) nonexempt charitable trust [ ] Other taxable private foundation

E If private foundation status was terminated under section 507(b)(1)(A), check here ►

I Fair market value of all assets at end of year (from Part II, column (c), line 16) ► $ 602,067,032.

J Accounting method: [ ] Cash [X] Accrual [ ] Other (specify) (Part I, column (d) must be on cash basis)

F If the foundation is in a 60-month termination under section 507(b)(1)(B), check here ► [X]

Part I — Analysis of Revenue and Expenses (The total of amounts in columns (b), (c), and (d) may not necessarily equal the amounts in column (a) (see instructions))

		(a) Revenue and expenses per books	(b) Net investment income	(c) Adjusted net income	(d) Disbursements for charitable purposes (cash basis only)
1	Contributions, gifts, grants etc received (attach schedule)	44,800.			
2	Check ► [ ] if the foundation is not required to attach Sch B				
3	Interest on savings and temporary cash investments	7,016.	7,016.	7,016.	
4	Dividends and interest from securities	421,202.	421,202.	421,202.	
5a	Gross rents	139,912.	139,912.	139,912.	
b	Net rental income or (loss) 139,912.				
6a	Net gain or (loss) from sale of assets not on line 10	4,729,734.			
b	Gross sales price for all assets on line 6a 25,179,004.				
7	Capital gain net income (from Part IV, line 2)		3,973,452.		
8	Net short term capital gain			274,135.	
9	Income modifications				
10a	Gross sales less returns and allowances 6,828,175.				
b	Less Cost of goods sold 2,922,288.				
c	Gross profit or (loss) (attach schedule) See St 1	3,905,887.		3,905,887.	
11	Other income (attach schedule) See Statement 2	4,736,443.	4,412,723.	4,686,726.	
12	**Total** Add lines 1 through 11	13,984,994.	8,954,305.	9,434,878.	
13	Compensation of officers, directors, trustees, etc	1,037,000.	148,920.	214,305.	800,046.
14	Other employee salaries and wages	2,424,023.	199,664.	860,757.	1,472,299.
15	Pension plans, employee benefits	760,738.	67,734.	279,958.	451,194.
16a	Legal fees (attach schedule) See St 3	109,195.	54,598.	57,638.	45,466.
b	Accounting fees (attach sch) See St 4	75,390.	3,349.	17,357.	78,956.
c	Other professional fees (attach sch) See St 5	1,698,099.	1,304,244.	1,152,270.	329,784.
17	Interest	69,133.	34,567.	36,492.	28,785.
18	Taxes (attach schedule)(see instrs) See Stm 6	384,634.	200,595.	208,160.	154,476.
19	Depreciation (attach schedule) and depletion See Stmt 7	1,257,339.			
20	Occupancy	341,300.	23,162.	66,653.	268,579.
21	Travel, conferences, and meetings	229,890.	23,804.	55,962.	168,014.
22	Printing and publications	169,656.	1,084.	1,909.	165,037.
23	Other expenses (attach schedule) See Statement 8	8,337,527.	2,972,937.	6,483,417.	2,235,438.
24	Total operating and administrative expenses Add lines 13 through 23	16,893,924.	5,034,658.	9,434,878.	6,198,074.
25	Contributions, gifts, grants paid Part XV	266,450.			266,450.
26	Total expenses and disbursements Add lines 24 and 25	17,160,374.	5,034,658.	9,434,878.	6,464,524.
27	Subtract line 26 from line 12				
a	Excess of revenue over expenses and disbursements	-3,175,380.			
b	Net investment income (if negative, enter 0)		3,919,647.		
c	Adjusted net income (if negative, enter 0)			0.	

BAA For Paperwork Reduction Act Notice, see instructions. TEEA0301L 12/12/18 Form 990-PF (2018)

Form 990-PF (2018) Tom T East Sr and Alice K East and Alice   26-1380672   Page 2

Part II	Balance Sheets	Attached schedules and amounts in the description column should be for end of year amounts only (See instructions)	Beginning of year (a) Book Value	End of year (b) Book Value	End of year (c) Fair Market Value
	1 Cash – non-interest-bearing				
	2 Savings and temporary cash investments		181,243.	1,694,028.	1,694,028.
	3 Accounts receivable ▶ 48,389				
	Less allowance for doubtful accounts ▶		426,678.	48,389.	48,389.
	4 Pledges receivable ▶				
	Less allowance for doubtful accounts ▶				
	5 Grants receivable				
	6 Receivables due from officers, directors, trustees, and other disqualified persons (attach schedule) (see instructions)				
	7 Other notes and loans receivable (attach sch) ▶				
	Less allowance for doubtful accounts ▶				
Assets	8 Inventories for sale or use				
	9 Prepaid expenses and deferred charges		65,195.	284,672.	284,672.
	10a Investments – U S and state government obligations (attach schedule) Statement 9		6,047,338.	3,362,614.	3,362,614.
	b Investments – corporate stock (attach schedule) Statement 10		7,700,768.	13,929,287.	9,442,610.
	c Investments – corporate bonds (attach schedule)				
	11 Investments – land, buildings, and equipment basis ▶				
	Less accumulated depreciation (attach schedule) ▶				
	12 Investments – mortgage loans				
	13 Investments – other (attach schedule) Statement 11		200,907,809.	196,805,836.	204,655,127.
	14 Land, buildings, and equipment basis ▶ 504,928,391.				
	Less accumulated depreciation (attach schedule) See Stmt 12 ▶ 9,384,179.		496,212,890.	495,544,212.	380,146,688.
	15 Other assets (describe ▶ See Statement 13)		3,841,510.	2,432,904.	2,432,904.
	16 Total assets (to be completed by all filers – see the instructions Also, see page 1, item I)		715,383,431.	714,101,942.	602,067,032.
Liabilities	17 Accounts payable and accrued expenses		816,376.	949,339.	
	18 Grants payable				
	19 Deferred revenue		523,928.	447,585.	
	20 Loans from officers, directors, trustees, & other disqualified persons				
	21 Mortgages and other notes payable (attach schedule)		2,314,123.		
	22 Other liabilities (describe ▶)				
	23 Total liabilities (add lines 17 through 22)		3,654,427.	1,396,924.	
Net Assets or Fund Balances	Foundations that follow SFAS 117, check here ▶ [X] and complete lines 24 through 26, and lines 30 and 31.				
	24 Unrestricted		711,729,004.	712,705,018.	
	25 Temporarily restricted				
	26 Permanently restricted				
	Foundations that do not follow SFAS 117, check here ▶ [ ] and complete lines 27 through 31.				
	27 Capital stock, trust principal, or current funds				
	28 Paid-in or capital surplus, or land, bldg, and equipment fund				
	29 Retained earnings, accumulated income, endowment, or other funds				
	30 Total net assets or fund balances (see instructions)		711,729,004.	712,705,018.	
	31 Total liabilities and net assets/fund balances (see instructions)		715,383,431.	714,101,942.	

Part III	Analysis of Changes in Net Assets or Fund Balances		
1	Total net assets or fund balances at beginning of year – Part II, column (a), line 30 (must agree with end-of-year figure reported on prior year's return)	1	711,729,004.
2	Enter amount from Part I, line 27a	2	-3,175,380.
3	Other increases not included in line 2 (itemize) ▶ See Statement 14	3	4,151,394.
4	Add lines 1, 2, and 3	4	712,705,018.
5	Decreases not included in line 2 (itemize) ▶	5	
6	Total net assets or fund balances at end of year (line 4 minus line 5) – Part II, column (b), line 30	6	712,705,018.

BAA   TEEA0302L 05/10/19   Form 990-PF (2018)

Form 990-PF (2018) Tom T East Sr and Alice K East and Alice   26-1380672   Page 3

Part IV | Capital Gains and Losses for Tax on Investment Income

(a) List and describe the kind(s) of property sold (for example, real estate, 2-story brick warehouse, or common stock, 200 shs MLC Co)	(b) How acquired P — Purchase D — Donation	(c) Date acquired (mo., day, yr)	(d) Date sold (mo., day, yr)
1a See Statement 15			
b			
c			
d			
e			

(e) Gross sales price	(f) Depreciation allowed (or allowable)	(g) Cost or other basis plus expense of sale	(h) Gain or (loss) ((e) plus (f) minus (g))
a			
b			
c			
d			
e			

Complete only for assets showing gain in column (h) and owned by the foundation on 12/31/69

(i) FMV as of 12/31/69	(j) Adjusted basis as of 12/31/69	(k) Excess of col (i) over col (j), if any	(l) Gains (Col (h) gain minus col (k), but not less than -0-) or Losses (from col (h))
a			
b			
c			
d			
e			

2	Capital gain net income or (net capital loss). { If gain, also enter in Part I, line 7 / If (loss), enter -0- in Part I, line 7 }		2	3,973,452.
3	Net short-term capital gain or (loss) as defined in sections 1222(5) and (6) If gain, also enter in Part I, line 8, column (c) See instructions If (loss), enter -0- in Part I, line 8		3	274,135.

Part V | Qualification Under Section 4940(e) for Reduced Tax on Net Investment Income

(For optional use by domestic private foundations subject to the section 4940(a) tax on net investment income)

If section 4940(d)(2) applies, leave this part blank

Was the foundation liable for the section 4942 tax on the distributable amount of any year in the base period?   ☐ Yes   ☒ No
If 'Yes,' the foundation doesn't qualify under section 4940(e) Do not complete this part

1   Enter the appropriate amount in each column for each year, see the instructions before making any entries

(a) Base period years Calendar year (or tax year beginning in)	(b) Adjusted qualifying distributions	(c) Net value of noncharitable-use assets	(d) Distribution ratio (col (b) divided by col (c))
2017	6,984,655.	214,283,595.	0.032595
2016	5,797,188.	195,451,305.	0.029661
2015	5,947,067.	180,636,456.	0.032923
2014	9,523,357.	199,490,573.	0.047738
2013	5,645,257.	195,938,565.	0.028811

2	Total of line 1, column (d)	2	0.171728
3	Average distribution ratio for the 5-year base period — divide the total on line 2 by 5 0, or by the number of years the foundation has been in existence if less than 5 years	3	0.034346
4	Enter the net value of noncharitable-use assets for 2018 from Part X, line 5	4	218,955,004.
5	Multiply line 4 by line 3	5	7,520,229.
6	Enter 1% of net investment income (1% of Part I, line 27b)	6	39,196.
7	Add lines 5 and 6	7	7,559,425.
8	Enter qualifying distributions from Part XII, line 4	8	6,935,779.

If line 8 is equal to or greater than line 7, check the box in Part VI, line 1b, and complete that part using a 1% tax rate See the Part VI instructions

BAA   TEEA0303L 12/12/18   Form 990-PF (2018)

Form 990-PF (2018) Tom T East Sr and Alice K East and Alice   26-1380672   Page 4

Part VI — Excise Tax Based on Investment Income (Section 4940(a), 4940(b), 4940(e), or 4948 — see instructions)

1a Exempt operating foundations described in section 4940(d)(2), check here ► ☐ and enter 'N/A' on line 1		
Date of ruling or determination letter _____ (attach copy of letter if necessary — see instructions)		
b Domestic foundations that meet the section 4940(e) requirements in Part V, check here ► ☐ and enter 1% of Part I, line 27b	1	78,393.
c All other domestic foundations enter 2% of line 27b Exempt foreign organizations enter 4% of Part I, line 12, col (b)		
2 Tax under section 511 (domestic section 4947(a)(1) trusts and taxable foundations only, others, enter -0-)	2	0.
3 Add lines 1 and 2	3	78,393.
4 Subtitle A (income) tax (domestic section 4947(a)(1) trusts and taxable foundations only, others, enter -0-)	4	0.
5 **Tax based on investment income.** Subtract line 4 from line 3 If zero or less, enter -0- **No Tax Due**	5	78,393.
6 Credits/Payments **60-month termination applies**		
a 2018 estimated tax pmts and 2017 overpayment credited to 2018 6a		
b Exempt foreign organizations — tax withheld at source 6b		
c Tax paid with application for extension of time to file (Form 8868) 6c		
d Backup withholding erroneously withheld 6d		
7 Total credits and payments Add lines 6a through 6d	7	0.
8 Enter any **penalty** for underpayment of estimated tax Check here ☐ if Form 2220 is attached	8	
9 Tax due If the total of lines 5 and 8 is more than line 7, enter amount owed **872-B consent form attached** ►	9	78,393.
10 Overpayment If line 7 is more than the total of lines 5 and 8, enter the amount overpaid ►	10	
11 Enter the amount of line 10 to be Credited to 2019 estimated tax ► _____ Refunded ►	11	

Part VII-A — Statements Regarding Activities

	Yes	No
1a During the tax year, did the foundation attempt to influence any national, state, or local legislation or did it participate or intervene in any political campaign? 1a		X
b Did it spend more than $100 during the year (either directly or indirectly) for political purposes? See the instructions for the definition 1b		X
If the answer is 'Yes' to 1a or 1b, attach a detailed description of the activities and copies of any materials published or distributed by the foundation in connection with the activities		
c Did the foundation file Form 1120-POL for this year? 1c		X
d Enter the amount (if any) of tax on political expenditures (section 4955) imposed during the year		
(1) On the foundation ► $ 0. (2) On foundation managers ► $ 0.		
e Enter the reimbursement (if any) paid by the foundation during the year for political expenditure tax imposed on foundation managers ► $ 0.		
2 Has the foundation engaged in any activities that have not previously been reported to the IRS? 2		X
If 'Yes,' attach a detailed description of the activities		
3 Has the foundation made any changes, not previously reported to the IRS, in its governing instrument, articles of incorporation, or bylaws, or other similar instruments? If 'Yes,' attach a conformed copy of the changes 3		X
4a Did the foundation have unrelated business gross income of $1,000 or more during the year? 4a	X	
b If 'Yes,' has it filed a tax return on Form 990-T for this year? 4b	X	
5 Was there a liquidation, termination, dissolution, or substantial contraction during the year? 5		X
If 'Yes,' attach the statement required by General Instruction T		
6 Are the requirements of section 508(e) (relating to sections 4941 through 4945) satisfied either		
• By language in the governing instrument, or		
• By state legislation that effectively amends the governing instrument so that no mandatory directions that conflict with the state law remain in the governing instrument? 6	X	
7 Did the foundation have at least $5,000 in assets at any time during the year? If 'Yes,' complete Part II, col (c), and Part XV 7	X	
8a Enter the states to which the foundation reports or with which it is registered See instructions ► TX		
b If the answer is 'Yes' to line 7, has the foundation furnished a copy of Form 990-PF to the Attorney General (or designate) of each state as required by General Instruction G? If 'No,' attach explanation 8b	X	
9 Is the foundation claiming status as a private operating foundation within the meaning of section 4942(j)(3) or 4942(j)(5) for calendar year 2018 or the tax year beginning in 2018? See the instructions for Part XIV If 'Yes,' complete Part XIV 9		X
10 Did any persons become substantial contributors during the tax year? If 'Yes,' attach a schedule listing their names and addresses 10		X

BAA   Form 990-PF (2018)

TEEA0304L 12/12/18

Form 990-PF (2018) Tom T East Sr and Alice K East and Alice   26-1380672   Page 5

Part VII-A Statements Regarding Activities (continued)

		Yes	No
11	At any time during the year, did the foundation, directly or indirectly, own a controlled entity within the meaning of section 512(b)(13)? If 'Yes,' attach schedule See instructions	11	X
12	Did the foundation make a distribution to a donor advised fund over which the foundation or a disqualified person had advisory privileges? If 'Yes,' attach statement See instructions	12	X
13	Did the foundation comply with the public inspection requirements for its annual returns and exemption application?	13	X	

Website address   ▶ www.eastfoundation.net

14 The books are in care of ▶ Nicolas Rangel   Telephone no ▶ 210-447-0126

Located at ▶ 200 Concord Plaza, Suite 410 San Antonio TX   ZIP + 4 ▶ 78216

15 Section 4947(a)(1) nonexempt charitable trusts filing Form 990-PF in lieu of **Form 1041** — check here   N/A ▶ ☐

and enter the amount of tax-exempt interest received or accrued during the year   ▶ | 15 | N/A

		Yes	No
16	At any time during calendar year 2018, did the foundation have an interest in or a signature or other authority over a bank, securities, or other financial account in a foreign country?	16	X

See the instructions for exceptions and filing requirements for FinCEN Form 114 If 'Yes,' enter the name of the foreign country   ▶

Part VII-B Statements Regarding Activities for Which Form 4720 May Be Required

File Form 4720 if any item is checked in the 'Yes' column, unless an exception applies.

		Yes	No
1 a During the year, did the foundation (either directly or indirectly)			
(1) Engage in the sale or exchange, or leasing of property with a disqualified person? ☐ Yes ☒ No			
(2) Borrow money from, lend money to, or otherwise extend credit to (or accept it from) a disqualified person? ☐ Yes ☒ No			
(3) Furnish goods, services, or facilities to (or accept them from) a disqualified person? ☐ Yes ☒ No			
(4) Pay compensation to, or pay or reimburse the expenses of, a disqualified person? ☒ Yes ☐ No			
(5) Transfer any income or assets to a disqualified person (or make any of either available for the benefit or use of a disqualified person)? ☐ Yes ☒ No			
(6) Agree to pay money or property to a government official? (**Exception.** Check 'No' if the foundation agreed to make a grant to or to employ the official for a period after termination of government service, if terminating within 90 days) ☐ Yes ☒ No			
b If any answer is 'Yes' to 1a(1)–(6), did any of the acts fail to qualify under the exceptions described in Regulations section 53 4941(d)-3 or in a current notice regarding disaster assistance? See instructions	1b		X
Organizations relying on a current notice regarding disaster assistance, check here ▶ ☐			
c Did the foundation engage in a prior year in any of the acts described in 1a, other than excepted acts, that were not corrected before the first day of the tax year beginning in 2018?	1c		X
2 Taxes on failure to distribute income (section 4942) (does not apply for years the foundation was a private operating foundation defined in section 4942(j)(3) or 4942(j)(5))			
a At the end of tax year 2018, did the foundation have any undistributed income (lines 6d and 6e, Part XIII) for tax year(s) beginning before 2018? ☐ Yes ☒ No			
If 'Yes,' list the years ▶ 20 _ _ , 20 _ _ , 20 _ _ , 20 _ _			
b Are there any years listed in 2a for which the foundation is not applying the provisions of section 4942(a)(2) (relating to incorrect valuation of assets) to the year's undistributed income? (If applying section 4942(a)(2) to all years listed, answer 'No' and attach statement — see instructions)	2b	N/A	
c If the provisions of section 4942(a)(2) are being applied to any of the years listed in 2a, list the years here			
▶ 20 _ _ , 20 _ _ , 20 _ _ , 20 _ _			
3 a Did the foundation hold more than a 2% direct or indirect interest in any business enterprise at any time during the year? ☐ Yes ☒ No			
b If 'Yes,' did it have excess business holdings in 2018 as a result of (1) any purchase by the foundation or disqualified persons after May 26, 1969, (2) the lapse of the 5-year period (or longer period approved by the Commissioner under section 4943(c)(7)) to dispose of holdings acquired by gift or bequest, or (3) the lapse of the 10-, 15-, or 20-year first phase holding period? (Use Schedule C, Form 4720, to determine if the foundation had excess business holdings in 2018)	3b	N/A	
4 a Did the foundation invest during the year any amount in a manner that would jeopardize its charitable purposes?	4a		X
b Did the foundation make any investment in a prior year (but after December 31, 1969) that could jeopardize its charitable purpose that had not been removed from jeopardy before the first day of the tax year beginning in 2018?	4b		X

BAA   Form **990-PF** (2018)

TEEA0305L 12/12/18

Form 990-PF (2018) Tom T East Sr and Alice K East and Alice 26-1380672 Page 6

Part VII-B Statements Regarding Activities for Which Form 4720 May Be Required (continued)

5a During the year, did the foundation pay or incur any amount to

		Yes	No

(1) Carry on propaganda, or otherwise attempt to influence legislation (section 4945(e))? — ☐ Yes ☒ No

(2) Influence the outcome of any specific public election (see section 4955), or to carry on, directly or indirectly, any voter registration drive? — ☐ Yes ☒ No

(3) Provide a grant to an individual for travel, study, or other similar purposes? — ☐ Yes ☒ No

(4) Provide a grant to an organization other than a charitable, etc, organization described in section 4945(d)(4)(A)? See instructions — ☐ Yes ☒ No

(5) Provide for any purpose other than religious, charitable, scientific, literary, or educational purposes, or for the prevention of cruelty to children or animals? — ☐ Yes ☒ No

b If any answer is 'Yes' to 5a(1)–(5), did any of the transactions fail to qualify under the exceptions described in Regulations section 53 4945 or in a current notice regarding disaster assistance? See instructions — **5b** N/A

Organizations relying on a current notice regarding disaster assistance, check here ▶ ☐

c If the answer is 'Yes' to question 5a(4), does the foundation claim exemption from the tax because it maintained expenditure responsibility for the grant? N/A ☐ Yes ☐ No

If 'Yes,' attach the statement required by Regulations section 53 4945–5(d)

6a Did the foundation, during the year, receive any funds, directly or indirectly, to pay premiums on a personal benefit contract? — ☐ Yes ☒ No

b Did the foundation, during the year, pay premiums, directly or indirectly, on a personal benefit contract? — **6b** X

If 'Yes' to 6b, file Form 8870

7a At any time during the tax year, was the foundation a party to a prohibited tax shelter transaction? — ☐ Yes ☒ No

b If 'Yes,' did the foundation receive any proceeds or have any net income attributable to the transaction? N/A **7b**

8 Is the foundation subject to the section 4960 tax on payment(s) of more than $1,000,000 in remuneration or excess parachute payment(s) during the year? — ☐ Yes ☒ No

Part VIII Information About Officers, Directors, Trustees, Foundation Managers, Highly Paid Employees, and Contractors

1 List all officers, directors, trustees, and foundation managers and their compensation. See instructions.

(a) Name and address	(b) Title, and average hours per week devoted to position	(c) Compensation (If not paid, enter -0-)	(d) Contributions to employee benefit plans and deferred compensation	(e) Expense account, other allowances
See Statement 16				
		1,037,000.	85,184.	0.

2 Compensation of five highest-paid employees (other than those included on line 1 – see instructions). If none, enter 'NONE.'

(a) Name and address of each employee paid more than $50,000	(b) Title, and average hours per week devoted to position	(c) Compensation	(d) Contributions to employee benefit plans and deferred compensation	(e) Expense account, other allowances
Trey R. Dyer 200 Concord Plaza, Ste 410 San Antonio, TX 78216	Land/F.A. Dir 40	175,000.	21,363.	0.
Vincent F. Linney 200 Concord Plaza, Ste 410 San Antonio, TX 78216	Ranch Ops Dir 40	163,000.	20,493.	0.
Robert T. Snelgrove 200 Concord Plaza, Ste 410 San Antonio, TX 78216	Ops Supp Dir 40	150,000.	19,446.	0.
Gilbert J. Riojas 200 Concord Plaza, Ste 410 San Antonio, TX 78216	Ranch Manager 40	125,000.	17,552.	0.
Christopher H. Huff 200 Concord Plaza, Ste 410 San Antonio, TX 78216	Field Ops/Sec 40	132,000.	10,410.	0.

Total number of other employees paid over $50,000 ▶ 22

BAA TEEA0306L 12/12/18 Form 990-PF (2018)

Form 990-PF (2018) Tom T East Sr and Alice K East and Alice   26-1380672   Page 7

Part VIII Information About Officers, Directors, Trustees, Foundation Managers, Highly Paid Employees, and Contractors *(continued)*

3 Five highest-paid independent contractors for professional services. See instructions. If none, enter 'NONE.'

(a) Name and address of each person paid more than $50,000	(b) Type of service	(c) Compensation
Makena Capital 2755 Sand Hill Road, Suite 200 Menlo Park, CA 94025	Investment mgmt	1,012,420.
Texas A&M University-Kingsville 700 University Blbd., MSC 201 Kingsville, TX 78363	Research services	409,342.
Texas A&M AgriLife Research 400 Harvey Mitchell Pkwy South, Ste College Station, TX 77845	Research services	289,886.
DeWitt Industries LLC 10805 Red I Ranch CR Raymondville, TX 78580	Construction	189,975.
Texas A&M AgriLife Extension 400 Harvey Mitchell Pkwy South, Ste College Station, TX 77845	·Extension services	143,201.

Total number of others receiving over $50,000 for professional services ▶ 9

Part IX-A Summary of Direct Charitable Activities

List the foundation's four largest direct charitable activities during the tax year. Include relevant statistical information such as the number of organizations and other beneficiaries served, conferences convened, research papers produced, etc	Expenses
1 See Statement 17	
	6,669,329.
2	
3	
4	

Part IX-B Summary of Program-Related Investments (see instructions)

Describe the two largest program-related investments made by the foundation during the tax year on lines 1 and 2	Amount
1 N/A	
2	
All other program-related investments. See instructions	
3	
Total. Add lines 1 through 3 ▶	0.

BAA   Form **990-PF** (2018)

TEEA0307L 12/12/18

Form 990-PF (2018) Tom T East Sr and Alice K East and Alice   26-1380672   Page 8

Part X Minimum Investment Return (All domestic foundations must complete this part. Foreign foundations, see instructions.)

1 Fair market value of assets not used (or held for use) directly in carrying out charitable, etc, purposes		
a Average monthly fair market value of securities	1a	23,232,757.
b Average of monthly cash balances	1b	693,385.
c Fair market value of all other assets (see instructions)	1c	198,363,202.
d Total (add lines 1a, b, and c)	1d	222,289,344.
e Reduction claimed for blockage or other factors reported on lines 1a and 1c (attach detailed explanation) 1e 0.		
2 Acquisition indebtedness applicable to line 1 assets	2	0.
3 Subtract line 2 from line 1d	3	222,289,344.
4 Cash deemed held for charitable activities Enter 1-1/2% of line 3 (for greater amount, see instructions)	4	3,334,340.
5 Net value of noncharitable-use assets. Subtract line 4 from line 3 Enter here and on Part V, line 4	5	218,955,004.
6 Minimum investment return. Enter 5% of line 5	6	10,947,750.

Part XI Distributable Amount (see instructions) (Section 4942(j)(3) and (j)(5) private operating foundations and certain foreign organizations, check here ► [X] and do not complete this part.)

1 Minimum investment return from Part X, line 6 N/A	1	
2a Tax on investment income for 2018 from Part VI, line 5 2a		
b Income tax for 2018 (This does not include the tax from Part VI) 2b		
c Add lines 2a and 2b	2c	
3 Distributable amount before adjustments Subtract line 2c from line 1	3	
4 Recoveries of amounts treated as qualifying distributions	4	
5 Add lines 3 and 4	5	
6 Deduction from distributable amount (see instructions)	6	
7 Distributable amount as adjusted Subtract line 6 from line 5 Enter here and on Part XIII, line 1	7	

Part XII Qualifying Distributions (see instructions)

1 Amounts paid (including administrative expenses) to accomplish charitable, etc, purposes		
a Expenses, contributions, gifts, etc — total from Part I, column (d), line 26	1a	6,464,524.
b Program-related investments — total from Part IX-B	1b	
2 Amounts paid to acquire assets used (or held for use) directly in carrying out charitable, etc, purposes	2	471,255.
3 Amounts set aside for specific charitable projects that satisfy the		
a Suitability test (prior IRS approval required)	3a	
b Cash distribution test (attach the required schedule)	3b	
4 Qualifying distributions. Add lines 1a through 3b Enter here and on Part V, line 8, and Part XIII, line 4	4	6,935,779.
5 Foundations that qualify under section 4940(e) for the reduced rate of tax on net investment income Enter 1% of Part I, line 27b See instructions	5	
6 Adjusted qualifying distributions. Subtract line 5 from line 4	6	6,935,779.

Note: The amount on line 6 will be used in Part V, column (b), in subsequent years when calculating whether the foundation qualifies for the section 4940(e) reduction of tax in those years

BAA   Form 990-PF (2018)

TEEA0308L 12/12/18

Form 990-PF (2018) Tom T East Sr and Alice K East and Alice   26-1380672   Page **9**

Part XIII   Undistributed Income (see instructions)

N/A

	(a) Corpus	(b) Years prior to 2017	(c) 2017	(d) 2018
1 Distributable amount for 2018 from Part XI, line 7				
2 Undistributed income, if any, as of the end of 2018				
a Enter amount for 2017 only				
b Total for prior years: 20___, 20___, 20___				
3 Excess distributions carryover, if any, to 2018				
a From 2013				
b From 2014				
c From 2015				
d From 2016				
e From 2017				
f Total of lines 3a through e				
4 Qualifying distributions for 2018 from Part XII, line 4: ► $				
a Applied to 2017, but not more than line 2a				
b Applied to undistributed income of prior years (Election required — see instructions)				
c Treated as distributions out of corpus (Election required — see instructions)				
d Applied to 2018 distributable amount				
e Remaining amount distributed out of corpus				
5 Excess distributions carryover applied to 2018 (If an amount appears in column (d), the same amount must be shown in column (a).)				
6 Enter the net total of each column as indicated below:				
a Corpus Add lines 3f, 4c, and 4e Subtract line 5				
b Prior years' undistributed income Subtract line 4b from line 2b				
c Enter the amount of prior years' undistributed income for which a notice of deficiency has been issued, or on which the section 4942(a) tax has been previously assessed				
d Subtract line 6c from line 6b Taxable amount — see instructions				
e Undistributed income for 2017 Subtract line 4a from line 2a Taxable amount — see instructions				
f Undistributed income for 2018 Subtract lines 4d and 5 from line 1 This amount must be distributed in 2019				
7 Amounts treated as distributions out of corpus to satisfy requirements imposed by section 170(b)(1)(F) or 4942(g)(3) (Election may be required — see instructions)				
8 Excess distributions carryover from 2013 not applied on line 5 or line 7 (see instructions)				
9 Excess distributions carryover to 2019. Subtract lines 7 and 8 from line 6a				
10 Analysis of line 9				
a Excess from 2014				
b Excess from 2015				
c Excess from 2016				
d Excess from 2017				
e Excess from 2018				

BAA   Form **990-PF** (2018)

TEEA0309L 12/12/18

Form 990-PF (2018) Tom T East Sr and Alice K East and Alice   26-1380672   Page 10

Part XIV | Private Operating Foundations (see instructions and Part VII-A, question 9)

1 a If the foundation has received a ruling or determination letter that it is a private operating foundation, and the ruling is effective for 2018, enter the date of the ruling ► 4/21/08

b Check box to indicate whether the foundation is a private operating foundation described in section [X] 4942(j)(3) or [ ] 4942(j)(5)

	Tax year		Prior 3 years		(e) Total
	(a) 2018	(b) 2017	(c) 2016	(d) 2015	
2 a Enter the lesser of the adjusted net income from Part I or the minimum investment return from Part X for each year listed	0.		241,031.	411,017.	652,048.
b 85% of line 2a			204,876.	349,364.	554,240.
c Qualifying distributions from Part XII, line 4 for each year listed	6,935,779.	6,984,655.	5,797,188.	5,947,067.	25,664,689.
d Amounts included in line 2c not used directly for active conduct of exempt activities	266,450.	214,985.			481,435.
e Qualifying distributions made directly for active conduct of exempt activities. Subtract line 2d from line 2c	6,669,329.	6,769,670.	5,797,188.	5,947,067.	25,183,254.
3 Complete 3a, b, or c for the alternative test relied upon					
a 'Assets' alternative test — enter					
(1) Value of all assets	605139406.	602359433.	600433520.	569542420.	2377474779.
(2) Value of assets qualifying under section 4942(j)(3)(B)(i)	382850062.	384812636.	402005798.	387941690.	1557610186.
b 'Endowment' alternative test — enter 2/3 of minimum investment return shown in Part X, line 6 for each year listed					
c 'Support' alternative test — enter					
(1) Total support other than gross investment income (interest, dividends, rents, payments on securities loans (section 512(a)(5)), or royalties)					
(2) Support from general public and 5 or more exempt organizations as provided in section 4942(j)(3)(B)(iii).					
(3) Largest amount of support from an exempt organization					
(4) Gross investment income					

Part XV | Supplementary Information (Complete this part only if the foundation had $5,000 or more in assets at any time during the year — see instructions.)

1 Information Regarding Foundation Managers:

a List any managers of the foundation who have contributed more than 2% of the total contributions received by the foundation before the close of any tax year (but only if they have contributed more than $5,000) (See section 507(d)(2))

None

b List any managers of the foundation who own 10% or more of the stock of a corporation (or an equally large portion of the ownership of a partnership or other entity) of which the foundation has a 10% or greater interest

None

2 Information Regarding Contribution, Grant, Gift, Loan, Scholarship, etc., Programs:

Check here ► [ ] if the foundation only makes contributions to preselected charitable organizations and does not accept unsolicited requests for funds If the foundation makes gifts, grants, etc , to individuals or organizations under other conditions, complete items 2a, b, c, and d See instructions

a The name, address, and telephone number or email address of the person to whom applications should be addressed

See Statement 18

b The form in which applications should be submitted and information and materials they should include

See Statement for Line 2a

c Any submission deadlines

See Statement for Line 2a

d Any restrictions or limitations on awards, such as by geographical areas, charitable fields, kinds of institutions, or other factors

See Statement for Line 2a

BAA   TEEA0310L 12/12/18   Form **990-PF** (2018)

Form 990-PF (2018) Tom T East Sr and Alice K East and Alice   26-1380672   Page 11

Part XV. Supplementary Information (continued)

3   Grants and Contributions Paid During the Year or Approved for Future Payment

Recipient — Name and address (home or business)	If recipient is an individual, show any relationship to any foundation manager or substantial contributor	Foundation status of recipient	Purpose of grant or contribution	Amount
a *Paid during the year*				
IDEA Public Schools 2115 W Pike Blvd Weslaco TX 78596	N/A	PC	General support	50,000.
Texas Wildlife Association Foundation 3660 Thousand Oaks Drive, Suite 126 San Antonio TX 78247	N/A	PC	Discovery Trunks program, general support	116,450.
Witte Museum 3801 Broadway St San Antonio TX 78209	N/A	PC	General support	100,000.
Total			► 3a	266,450.
b *Approved for future payment*				
Total			► 3b	

BAA   TEEA0501L 12/12/18   Form 990-PF (2018)

Form 990-PF (2018)   Tom T East Sr and Alice K East and Alice   26-1380672   Page 12

Part XVI-A Analysis of Income-Producing Activities

Enter gross amounts unless otherwise indicated

		Unrelated business income		Excluded by section 512, 513, or 514		(e)
		(a) Business code	(b) Amount	(c) Exclusion code	(d) Amount	Related or exempt function income (See instructions.)
1	Program service revenue					
a	Books					4,834.
b	Drought insurance					204,130.
c						
d						
e						
f						
g	Fees and contracts from government agencies					
2	Membership dues and assessments					
3	Interest on savings and temporary cash investments			14	7,016.	
4	Dividends and interest from securities			14	421,202.	
5	Net rental income or (loss) from real estate					
a	Debt-financed property					
b	Not debt-financed property			16	139,912.	
6	Net rental income or (loss) from personal property					
7	Other investment income					
8	Gain or (loss) from sales of assets other than inventory	523000	386,288.	18	4,343,446.	
9	Net income or (loss) from special events					
10	Gross profit or (loss) from sales of inventory					3,905,887.
11	Other revenue					
a	From Sch K-1 (Form 1065)	523000	54,379.	14	4,064,158.	
b	Other Revenue			1	30,436.	
c	Royalties			15	378,506.	
d						
e						
12	Subtotal Add columns (b), (d), and (e)		440,667.		9,384,676.	4,114,851.
13	Total. Add line 12, columns (b), (d), and (e)				13	13,940,194.

(See worksheet in line 13 instructions to verify calculations.)

Part XVI-B Relationship of Activities to the Accomplishment of Exempt Purposes

Line No. ▼ Explain below how each activity for which income is reported in column (e) of Part XVI-A contributed importantly to the accomplishment of the foundation's exempt purposes (other than by providing funds for such purposes) (See instructions.)

12(e) The East Foundation's principal function is the direct conduct of agricultural research in conjunction with the Texas A&M University System, a land grant university system, on its primary asset, a working laboratory and unique natural resource, i.e., over 215,000 acres of native rangeland in the South Texas Brush Country and Coastal Sand Plain lying between the Nueces River and Rio Grande River of Texas. The Foundation's purposes encompass 1) using scientific research to understand and improve the productivity of native rangelands for both wildlife conservation and livestock production, 2) managing ranch lands as a working laboratory that includes cattle ranching and native wildlife as an integral part of the research program, and 3) educating the general public on wildlife conservation, and the relationship of wildlife existing alongside a cattle operation. In short, the Foundation seeks through its agricultural research to identify and encourage wise land stewardship practices by private landowners across native rangelands that will be beneficial to the public. It follows that the Foundation's exempt purposes can only be achieved through the active management of a livestock ranch that is representative of the 14.1 million acres of native rangeland in the South Texas Brush Country and Coastal Sand Plain region. This ranch serves as a laboratory for agricultural research that will facilitate wildlife conservation and livestock production throughout these 14.1 million acres of native rangeland and encourage wildlife conservation and livestock production in similar habitats across the United States and around the world.

BAA   TEEA0502L 12/12/18   Form 990-PF (2018)

Form 990-PF (2018)   Tom T East Sr and Alice K East and Alice   26-1380672   Page **13**

Part XVII | Information Regarding Transfers to and Transactions and Relationships With Noncharitable Exempt Organizations

		Yes	No
1 Did the organization directly or indirectly engage in any of the following with any other organization described in section 501(c) (other than section 501(c)(3) organizations) or in section 527, relating to political organizations?			
a Transfers from the reporting foundation to a noncharitable exempt organization of			
(1) Cash	1 a (1)		X
(2) Other assets	1 a (2)		X
b Other transactions			
(1) Sales of assets to a noncharitable exempt organization	1 b (1)		X
(2) Purchases of assets from a noncharitable exempt organization	1 b (2)		X
(3) Rental of facilities, equipment, or other assets	1 b (3)		X
(4) Reimbursement arrangements	1 b (4)		X
(5) Loans or loan guarantees	1 b (5)		X
(6) Performance of services or membership or fundraising solicitations	1 b (6)		X
c Sharing of facilities, equipment, mailing lists, other assets, or paid employees	1 c		X

d If the answer to any of the above is 'Yes,' complete the following schedule Column **(b)** should always show the fair market value of the goods, other assets, or services given by the reporting foundation If the foundation received less than fair market value in any transaction or sharing arrangement, show in column (d) the value of the goods, other assets, or services received

(a) Line no	(b) Amount involved	(c) Name of noncharitable exempt organization	(d) Description of transfers, transactions, and sharing arrangements
N/A			

2 a Is the foundation directly or indirectly affiliated with, or related to, one or more tax-exempt organizations described in section 501(c) (other than section 501(c)(3)) or in section 527?   ☐ Yes ☒ No

b If 'Yes,' complete the following schedule

(a) Name of organization	(b) Type of organization	(c) Description of relationship
N/A		

Under penalties of perjury, I declare that I have examined this return, including accompanying schedules and statements, and to the best of my knowledge and belief, it is true, correct, and complete Declaration of preparer (other than taxpayer) is based on all information of which preparer has any knowledge

Sign Here

Signature of officer or trustee   Date 6·22·2020   Title President & CEO

May the IRS discuss this return with the preparer shown below? See instructions ☒ Yes ☐ No

Paid Preparer Use Only	Print/Type preparer's name	Preparer's signature	Date	Check ☐ self employed	PTIN
	Jody Blazek		6·18·20		P00072674
	Firm's name ► Blazek & Vettertling			Firm's EIN ► 76-0269860	
	Firm's address ► 2900 Weslayan, Suite 200 Houston, TX 77027-5132			Phone no (713) 439-5739	

BAA   Form **990-PF** (2018)

TEEA0503L 12/12/18

Schedule B
(Form 990, 990-EZ, or 990-PF)

Department of the Treasury
Internal Revenue Service

OMB No 1545 0047

Schedule of Contributors

► Attach to Form 990, Form 990-EZ, or Form 990-PF.
► Go to *www.irs.gov/Form990* for the latest information.

2018

Name of the organization: Tom T East Sr and Alice K East and Alice H East and Robert C East Wildlife Fnd

Employer identification number: 26-1380672

Organization type (check one)

Filers of:

Section:

Form 990 or 990-EZ

☐ 501(c)( ) (enter number) organization

☐ 4947(a)(1) nonexempt charitable trust **not** treated as a private foundation

☐ 527 political organization

Form 990-PF

☒ 501(c)(3) exempt private foundation

☐ 4947(a)(1) nonexempt charitable trust treated as a private foundation

☐ 501(c)(3) taxable private foundation

Check if your organization is covered by the **General Rule** or a **Special Rule.**

Note: Only a section 501(c)(7), (8), or (10) organization can check boxes for both the General Rule and a Special Rule See instructions

General Rule

☒ For an organization filing Form 990, 990-EZ, or 990-PF that received, during the year, contributions totaling $5,000 or more (in money or property) from any one contributor Complete Parts I and II See instructions for determining a contributor's total contributions

Special Rules

☐ For an organization described in section 501(c)(3) filing Form 990 or 990-EZ that met the 33-1/3% support test of the regulations under sections 509(a)(1) and 170(b)(1)(A)(vi), that checked Schedule A (Form 990 or 990-EZ), Part II, line 13, 16a, or 16b, and that received from any one contributor, during the year, total contributions of the greater of (1) $5,000, or (2) 2% of the amount on (i) Form 990, Part VIII, line 1h, or (ii) Form 990-EZ, line 1 Complete Parts I and II

☐ For an organization described in section 501(c)(7), (8), or (10) filing Form 990 or 990-EZ that received from any one contributor, during the year, total contributions of more than $1,000 *exclusively* for religious, charitable, scientific, literary, or educational purposes, or for the prevention of cruelty to children or animals Complete Parts I (entering 'N/A' in column (b) instead of the contributor name and address), II, and III

☐ For an organization described in section 501(c)(7), (8), or (10) filing Form 990 or 990-EZ that received from any one contributor, during the year, contributions *exclusively* for religious, charitable, etc , purposes, but no such contributions totaled more than $1,000 If this box is checked, enter here the total contributions that were received during the year for an *exclusively* religious, charitable, etc , purpose Don't complete any of the parts unless the **General Rule** applies to this organization because it received *nonexclusively* religious, charitable, etc , contributions totaling $5,000 or more during the year ► $ _____

Caution: An organization that isn't covered by the General Rule and/or the Special Rules doesn't file Schedule B (Form 990, 990-EZ, or 990-PF), but it **must** answer 'No' on Part IV, line 2, of its Form 990, or check the box on line H of its Form 990-EZ or on its Form 990-PF, Part I, line 2, to certify that it doesn't meet the filing requirements of Schedule B (Form 990, 990-EZ, or 990-PF)

BAA For Paperwork Reduction Act Notice, see the instructions for Form 990, 990-EZ, or 990-PF

Schedule B (Form 990, 990-EZ, or 990-PF) (2018)

TEEA0701L 09/20/18

Schedule B (Form 990, 990-EZ, or 990-PF) (2018)   1   1   Page **2**

Name of organization	Employer identification number
Tom T East Sr and Alice K East and Alice	26-1380672

Part I Contributors (see instructions) Use duplicate copies of Part I if additional space is needed

(a) Number	(b) Name, address, and ZIP + 4	(c) Total contributions	(d) Type of contribution
1	Las Huellas Inc 134 E Price Rd Brownsville, TX 78521	$ 15,000.	Person ☒ Payroll ☐ Noncash ☐ (Complete Part II for noncash contributions)
2	Capital Farm Credit, FLCA 1708 Ave M, P.O. Box 488 Hondo, TX 78861	$ 25,000.	Person ☒ Payroll ☐ Noncash ☐ (Complete Part II for noncash contributions)
		$	Person ☐ Payroll ☐ Noncash ☐ (Complete Part II for noncash contributions)
		$	Person ☐ Payroll ☐ Noncash ☐ (Complete Part II for noncash contributions)
		$	Person ☐ Payroll ☐ Noncash ☐ (Complete Part II for noncash contributions)
		$	Person ☐ Payroll ☐ Noncash ☐ (Complete Part II for noncash contributions)

BAA   TEEA0702L 09/20/18   Schedule B (Form 990, 990-EZ, or 990-PF) (2018)

Schedule B (Form 990, 990-EZ, or 990-PF) (2018)   1   1   Page **3**

Name of organization	Employer identification number
Tom T East Sr and Alice K East and Alice	26-1380672

Part II Noncash Property (see instructions) Use duplicate copies of Part II if additional space is needed

(a) No. from Part I	(b) Description of noncash property given	(c) FMV (or estimate) (See instructions.)	(d) Date received
	N/A	$	
	(b) Description of noncash property given	(c) FMV (or estimate) (See instructions.)	(d) Date received
		$	
(a) No. from Part I	(b) Description of noncash property given	(c) FMV (or estimate) (See instructions.)	(d) Date received
		$	
(a) No. from Part I	(b) Description of noncash property given	(c) FMV (or estimate) (See instructions.)	(d) Date received
		$	
(a) No. from Part I	(b) Description of noncash property given	(c) FMV (or estimate) (See instructions.)	(d) Date received
		$	
(a) No. from Part I	(b) Description of noncash property given	(c) FMV (or estimate) (See instructions.)	(d) Date received
		$	

BAA   Schedule B (Form 990, 990-EZ, or 990-PF) (2018)

TEEA0703L 09/20/18

Schedule B (Form 990, 990-EZ, or 990-PF) (2018)

| | | 1 | 1 | Page **4** |

Name of organization

Tom T East Sr and Alice K East and Alice

Employer identification number

26-1380672

Part III *Exclusively* religious, charitable, etc., contributions to organizations described in section 501(c)(7), (8), or (10) that total more than $1,000 for the year from any one contributor. Complete columns (a) through (e) and the following line entry For organizations completing Part III, enter the total of *exclusively* religious, charitable, etc , contributions of $1,000 or less for the year (Enter this information once See instructions)   ▶ $_____ N/A

Use duplicate copies of Part III if additional space is needed

(a) No. from Part I	(b) Purpose of gift	(c) Use of gift	(d) Description of how gift is held
N/A			

	(e) Transfer of gift	
Transferee's name, address, and ZIP + 4		Relationship of transferor to transferee

(a) No. from Part I	(b) Purpose of gift	(c) Use of gift	(d) Description of how gift is held

	(e) Transfer of gift	
Transferee's name, address, and ZIP + 4		Relationship of transferor to transferee

(a) No. from Part I	(b) Purpose of gift	(c) Use of gift	(d) Description of how gift is held

	(e) Transfer of gift	
Transferee's name, address, and ZIP + 4		Relationship of transferor to transferee

(a) No. from Part I	(b) Purpose of gift	(c) Use of gift	(d) Description of how gift is held

	(e) Transfer of gift	
Transferee's name, address, and ZIP + 4		Relationship of transferor to transferee

BAA

Schedule B (Form 990, 990-EZ, or 990-PF) (2018)

TEEA0704L 09/20/18

Tom T East Sr and Alice K East and Alice H East and Robert C East Wildlife Fnd   26-1380672
2018 Form 990-PF

Part I, Line 6 - Net Capital Gain/Loss

	Proceeds	Cost	Gain/Loss
Amounts reported in Part IV	$ 24,775,933	20,802,481 $	3,973,452
Charitable Asset Like-Kind Exchange (Cattle)	403,071	33,077	369,994
UBTI - Passthrough K-1 Capital Gain	54,187		54,187
UBTI - Passthrough K-1 Sec 1231 Gain	147,861		147,861
UBTI - Section 751 Gain	184,240		184,240
Total Gain/Loss per Part I, Line 6	$ 25,565,292	20,835,558 $	4,729,734

2018	**Federal Statements**	Page 1
	Tom T East Sr and Alice K East and Alice H East and Robert C East Wildlife Fnd	26-1380672

Statement 1
Form 990-PF, Part I, Line 10c
Gross Profit (Loss) From Sales Of Inventory

Items Sold	Amount
Livestock sales	$ 6,828,175.
Gross Sales	$ 6,828,175.
Less Returns & Allowances	0.
Net Sales	$ 6,828,175.
Less Cost Of Goods Sold	2,922,288.
Gross Profit From Sales Of Inventory	$ 3,905,887.

Statement 2
Form 990-PF, Part I, Line 11
Other Income

	(a) Revenue per Books	(b) Net Investment Income	(c) Adjusted Net Income
Books	$ 4,834.		$ 4,834.
Drought insurance	204,130.		204,130.
From Sch K-1 (Form 1065)	4,118,537.	$ 4,014,441.	4,068,820.
Other Revenue	30,436.	19,776.	30,436.
Royalties	378,506.	378,506.	378,506.
Total	$ 4,736,443.	$ 4,412,723.	$ 4,686,726.

Statement 3
Form 990-PF, Part I, Line 16a
Legal Fees

	(a) Expenses Per Books	(b) Net Investment Income	(c) Adjusted Net Income	(d) Charitable Purposes
Legal fees	$ 109,195.	$ 54,598.	$ 57,638.	$ 45,466.
Total	$ 109,195.	$ 54,598.	$ 57,638.	$ 45,466.

Statement 4
Form 990-PF, Part I, Line 16b
Accounting Fees

	(a) Expenses per Books	(b) Net Investment Income	(c) Adjusted Net Income	(d) Charitable Purposes
Audit services	$ 52,483.	$ 829.	$ 12,083.	$ 54,965.
Tax compliance	22,907.	2,520.	5,274.	23,991.
Total	$ 75,390.	$ 3,349.	$ 17,357.	$ 78,956.

2018   **Federal Statements**   **Page 2**

Tom T East Sr and Alice K East and Alice
H East and Robert C East Wildlife Fnd   26-1380672

Statement 5
Form 990-PF, Part I, Line 16c
Other Professional Fees

	(a) Expenses per Books	(b) Net Investment Income	(c) Adjusted Net Income	(d) Charitable Purposes
Advisor fees	$ 78,746.	$ 8,662.	$ 15,835.	$ 65,567.
Committee consultants	50,920.	5,601.	10,239.	39,599.
Executive coaching	17,747.	1,952.	3,569.	14,777.
HR services	51,530.	5,668.	10,362.	42,906.
Investment fees	1,270,842.	1,262,916.	1,059,103.	
Janitorial, grounds, contract svcs	48,951.	1,526.	6,610.	41,250.
Livestock services	16,464.		13,795.	
Recruiting fees	104,835.	11,532.	21,081.	81,527.
Software development	58,064.	6,387.	11,676.	44,158.
Total	$ 1,698,099.	$ 1,304,244.	$ 1,152,270.	$ 329,784.

Statement 6
Form 990-PF, Part I, Line 18
Taxes

	(a) Expenses per Books	(b) Net Investment Income	(c) Adjusted Net Income	(d) Charitable Purposes
Foreign tax	$ 16,555.	$ 16,555.	$ 13,871.	$ 1,219.
Property tax	364,821.	182,411.	192,569.	151,901.
Royalty tax	3,258.	1,629.	1,720.	1,356.
Total	$ 384,634.	$ 200,595.	$ 208,160.	$ 154,476.

Statement 7
Form 990-PF, Part I, Line 19
Allocated Depreciation

Date Acquired	Cost Basis	Prior Yr Depr	Method	Rate	Life	Current Yr Depr	Net Invest Income	Adjusted Net Income
Vehicles								
Various	2,025,592	1,689,782	S/L		5	136,440	0	0
Buildings								
Various	5,202,940	791,109	S/L		27.5	177,532	0	0
Improvements/fences								
Various	8,034,166	3,123,141	S/L		20	516,131	0	0
Furniture and fixtures								
Various	618,739	407,634	S/L		5	76,858	0	0
Livestock								
Various	4,876,829	2,228,889	S/L		5	350,378	0	0

2018	**Federal Statements**	**Page 3**

Tom T East Sr and Alice K East and Alice
H East and Robert C East Wildlife Fnd   26-1380672

Statement 8
Form 990-PF, Part I, Line 23
Other Expenses

	(a) Expenses per Books	(b) Net Investment Income	(c) Adjusted Net Income	(d) Charitable Purposes
Bank fees	$ 44,452.	$ 17,267.	$ 22,050.	$ 20,072.
Community outreach	54,300.	5,643.	10,316.	42,894.
Dues and subscriptions	14,705.	1,476.	8,448.	5,364.
Education programs	47,808.			47,808.
Equipment rental	16,573.	86.	1,715.	14,677.
From Sch K-1 (Form 1065)	4,143,040.	2,870,836.	3,471,248.	
Insurance	162,369.	43,045.	109,352.	41,460.
Licenses, fees, and permits	6,031.	4,986.	4,296.	1,281.
Office supplies	107,989.	4,619.	24,049.	81,429.
Payroll expenses	8,755.	516.	4,351.	3,944.
Postage and mailing services	4,238.	520.	914.	3,464.
Ranch program - feed	1,764,775.		1,478,618.	527,724.
Ranch program other expenses	547,295.	6,431.	1,204,049.	228,171.
Repairs and maintenance	222,188.	8,911.	36,977.	179,467.
Research and monitoring	965,212.			928,239.
Royalty expenses	15,750.	7,875.	8,314.	6,558.
Storage	6,596.	726.	1,326.	5,129.
Transportation	205,451.		97,394.	97,757.
Total	$ 8,337,527.	$ 2,972,937.	$ 6,483,417.	$ 2,235,438.

Statement 9
Form 990-PF, Part II, Line 10a
Investments - U.S. and State Government Obligations

U.S. Government Obligations	Valuation Method	Book Value	Fair Market Value
U.S. government obligations	Mkt Val	$ 3,362,614.	$ 3,362,614.
Total		$ 3,362,614.	$ 3,362,614.

Statement 10
Form 990-PF, Part II, Line 10b
Investments - Corporate Stocks

Corporate Stocks	Valuation Method	Book Value	Fair Market Value
Artisan Global Value Inst	Mkt Val	$ 7,849,291.	$ 7,849,291.
iShares Short Treasury Bond ETF	Mkt Val	3,628,653.	3,628,653.
Touchstone Sands Capital Emrg Mkts Gwth	Mkt Val	2,451,343.	2,451,343.
Total		$ 13,929,287.	$ 13,929,287.

2018	**Federal Statements**	Page 4

Tom T East Sr and Alice K East and Alice
H East and Robert C East Wildlife Fnd   26-1380672

Statement 11
Form 990-PF, Part II, Line 13
Investments - Other

Other Investments	Valuation Method	Book Value	Fair Market Value
Carlyle International Energy Partners	Mkt Val	$ 4,143,127.	$ 4,143,127.
Carlyle Partners VI	Mkt Val	4,638,962.	4,638,962.
Carlyle Power Partners II	Mkt Val	1,855,430.	1,855,430.
CCAP Fund 6 - 2015, L.P.	Mkt Val	2,559,203.	2,559,203.
CCAP Fund 8 - 2015, L.P.	Mkt Val	2,215,097.	2,215,097.
CCAP Fund 8 - 2016, L.P.	Mkt Val	1,094,946.	1,094,946.
Makena Capital Blocker Y (Cayman) LP	Mkt Val	51,042,308.	51,042,308.
Makena Capital Splitter X LP	Mkt Val	117769583.	117,769,583.
Mineral rights	Mkt Val	4,424,242.	4,424,242.
Natural Resources Partners IX	Mkt Val	6,241,793.	6,241,793.
OHA European Strategic Credit Fund Offsh	Mkt Val	784,161.	784,161.
Reservoir Resource Partners LP	Mkt Val	36,984.	36,984.
	Total	$ 196805836.	$196,805,836.

Statement 12
Form 990-PF, Part II, Line 14
Land, Buildings, and Equipment

Category	Basis	Accum. Deprec.	Book Value	Fair Market Value
Auto./Transportation Equip.	$ 2,025,592.	$ 1,826,222.	$ 199,370.	$ 199,745.
Furniture and Fixtures	618,739.	484,492.	134,247.	134,247.
Machinery and Equipment	69,343.	9,244.	60,099.	60,099.
Buildings	5,202,940.	968,641.	4,234,299.	4,234,299.
Improvements	8,034,166.	3,639,272.	4,394,894.	4,394,519.
Land	484100782.		484100782.	368,703,258.
Miscellaneous	4,876,829.	2,456,308.	2,420,521.	2,420,521.
Total	$ 504928391.	$ 9,384,179.	$ 495544212.	$ 380,146,688.

Statement 13
Form 990-PF, Part II, Line 15
Other Assets

	Book Value	Fair Market Value
Archives/books	$ 208,337.	$ 208,337.
Livestock	2,215,997.	2,215,997.
Security deposits	8,570.	8,570.
Total	$ 2,432,904.	$ 2,432,904.

2018	**Federal Statements**	**Page 5**

Tom T East Sr and Alice K East and Alice
H East and Robert C East Wildlife Fnd

26-1380672

Statement 14
Form 990-PF, Part III, Line 3
Other Increases

Unrealized appreciation in value of investments $ 4,151,394.

Total $ 4,151,394.

Statement 15
Form 990-PF, Part IV, Line 1
Capital Gains and Losses for Tax on Investment Income

Item	(a) Description	(b) How Acquired	(c) Date Acquired	(d) Date Sold
1	Publicly traded securities			
2	From Sch K-1 (Form 1065)			
3	Artisan Global Value Ins	Purchased	1/01/2017	Various
4	Cevian Capital II Ltd USD Class A	Purchased	11/01/2014	11/30/2018
5	Children's Investment Fund	Purchased	Various	Various
6	OHA European Strategic Credit Fd (Offsh)	Purchased	7/07/2005	3/31/2019
7	Stelliam Offshore Long Fund Ltd Series A	Purchased	8/01/2016	10/31/2018
8	Tourbillon Global Equities, Ltd	Purchased	11/01/2015	12/31/2018
9	ValueAct Capital International I, LP	Purchased	1/01/2016	12/31/2018

Item	(e) Gross Sales	(f) Deprec. Allowed	(g) Cost Basis	(h) Gain (Loss)	(i) FMV 12/31/69	(j) Adj. Bas. 12/31/69	(k) Excess (i)-(j)	(l) Gain (Loss)
1	11452439.		14002620.	-2550181.				$-2550181.
2	5459449.	0.		5459449.				5459449.
3	1600000.		1405354.	194,646.				194,646.
4	2802034.		2381003.	421,031.				421,031.
5	1464340.		1037958.	426,382.				426,382.
6	183,867.		135,235.	48,632.				48,632.
7	893,570.		725,000.	168,570.				168,570.
8	467,698.		565,311.	-97,613.				-97,613.
9	452,536.		550,000.	-97,464.				-97,464.

Total $ 3973452.

Statement 16
Form 990-PF, Part VIII, Line 1
List of Officers, Directors, Trustees, and Key Employees

Name and Address	Title and Average Hours Per Week Devoted	Compensation	Contribution to EBP & DC	Expense Account/ Other
Robert N Wilkins 200 Concord Plaza Ste 410 San Antonio, TX 78216	President & CEO 40.00	$ 410,000.	$ 43,762.	$ 0.
Nicolas Rangel 200 Concord Plaza, Ste 410 San Antonio, TX 78216	CFO 40.00	150,000.	17,159.	0.

2018	Federal Statements	Page 6
	Tom T East Sr and Alice K East and Alice	
	H East and Robert C East Wildlife Fnd	26-1380672

Statement 16 (continued)
Form 990-PF, Part VIII, Line 1
List of Officers, Directors, Trustees, and Key Employees

Name and Address	Title and Average Hours Per Week Devoted	Compen- sation	Contri- bution to EBP & DC	Expense Account/ Other
Tyler Campbell 200 Concord Plaza, Ste 410 San Antonio, TX 78216	Chief Prog Off 40.00	$ 215,000.	$ 24,263.	$ 0.
Richard W. Evans Jr 200 Concord Plaza, Ste 410 San Antonio, TX 78216	Director 4.00	65,500.	0.	0.
Dan Kinsel III 200 Concord Plaza, Ste 410 San Antonio, TX 78216	Director 4.00	65,500.	0.	0.
Stephen J Kleberg 200 Concord Plaza, Ste 410 San Antonio, TX 78216	Director 4.00	65,500.	0.	0.
Bryan Wagner 200 Concord Plaza, Ste 410 San Antonio, TX 78216	Director 4.00	65,500.	0.	0.
Total		$ 1,037,000.	$ 85,184.	$ 0.

Statement 17
Form 990-PF, Part IX-A, Line 1
Summary of Direct Charitable Activities

Direct Charitable Activities	Expenses
The East Foundation's principal mission is the continuous and direct conduct of agricultural research in conjunction with the Texas A&M University System, a land grant university system. Our primary asset is a unique resource, a working laboratory for our research, comprising over 215,000 acres of native rangeland in the South Texas Brush Country and Coastal Sand Plain lying between the Nueces River and Rio Grande River of Texas.	$ 6,669,329.

The Foundation's mission is to promote the advancement of land stewardship through ranching, science, and education. In our working laboratory, scientists and managers work together to address issues important to wildlife management, rangeland health, and ranch productivity. We ensure that ranching and wildlife management work together to conserve healthy rangelands.

The purpose of our research program is to understand and improve the productivity of native rangelands for both wildlife conservation and livestock production. Our approach is to generate science-based solutions to help ranchers conserve wildlife habitats while sustaining livestock production.

Using state-of-the-art tools, we track over 625 wildlife species that are found across our rangelands and monitor response to drought, grazing, and other factors that influence native rangelands, such as

2018   **Federal Statements**   **Page 7**

Tom T East Sr and Alice K East and Alice
H East and Robert C East Wildlife Fnd   26-1380672

Statement 17 (continued)
Form 990-PF, Part IX-A, Line 1
Summary of Direct Charitable Activities

Direct Charitable Activities	Expenses

fire. We maintain biological collections of all vertebrate species
to serve as a long-term reference for scientific study. Additionally,
we use innovative methods to understand the competition among cattle,
native wildlife, and exotic animals. We also document the population
changes and structure on one of the largest un-hunted and un-managed
white-tailed deer herds in the state. Furthermore, we have developed
one of the nation's largest grazing demonstration studies to test the
influence of cattle stocking rates and grazing systems on rangeland,
wildlife, and cattle productivity.

The Foundation's purposes are further characterized in its Program
Priorities. In fulfilling our Program Priorities we 1) develop
research programs that intentionally focus on those factors that most
threaten the productivity of native rangelands (e.g., drought,
disease, invasive plants, and exotic animals), 2) engage with
universities to develop changes in undergraduate experiences,
graduate curricula, and faculty focus to train future leaders, land
managers, scientists, and policy-makers, 3) deliver programming,
knowledge, and leadership skills to the youth of South Texas
benefiting the region now and in the future, and 4) deliberately
engage partners at the local, state and national levels, allowing us
to leverage existing resources, while sharing our research and
successful education strategies, enhancing conservation around the
state and across the nation.

During 2019, Foundation scientists put 8 publications into
peer-reviewed scientific journals and made 65 scientific
presentations at state and national conferences. Since 2015,
Foundation scientists have authored and co-authored 33 publications
in peer-reviewed scientific journals. At present there are another 24
publications in process - either in review or in press.

The Foundation averaged 16 university researchers working on the
ranches per day (or 5,681 researcher-days), with peak activity months
from March-July 2019. Our field research involved 18 graduate students
and one post-doctoral fellows from two universities, along with 80
student volunteers and field technicians from 9 different states. One
of our wildlife monitoring projects provided hands-on experience to
over 30 students from four Texas universities. We had three students
receive graduate degrees. We partnered with IDEA Public Schools to
deliver adventure-based, natural resource programming. Over 150
program-days, we impacted 16,446 K-12 students. In partnership with
the Texas Wildlife Association, our Stewarding Texas Resource Guide
reached 13,148 students.

Additionally, 250 teachers received access to the Guide online, with
a potential reach of more than 100,000 students. In partnership with
the Texas Wildlife Association, our Educators stationed in South
Texas delivered Wildlife by Design lessons to 17,443 students and our
teacher workshops presented 300 teachers with curriculum on natural
resources and land stewardship. We held field lessons on our ranches
reaching 5,417 students and more than 325 adults. Through a day of
hands-on activities with our partners, students learned first-hand
about the many public benefits of ranching and private land
stewardship.

In partnership with San Antonio's Witte Museum, we launched the Land

2018	Federal Statements	Page 8
	Tom T East Sr and Alice K East and Alice H East and Robert C East Wildlife Fnd	26-1380672

Statement 17 (continued)
Form 990-PF, Part IX-A, Line 1
Summary of Direct Charitable Activities

Direct Charitable Activities	Expenses
Stewardship Ambassador Program, an intensive 10-week program designed to increase awareness of land stewardship principles, promote student engagement, and inspire students to seek careers supporting land stewardship. In 2019, the inaugural class of 26 students received their Ambassador certification.	

Statement 18
Form 990-PF, Part XV, Line 2a-d
Application Submission Information

Name of Grant Program:	East Foundation Three Minute Thesis
Name:	Tyler Campbell
Care Of:	East Foundation
Street Address:	200 Concord Plaza, Ste 410
City, State, Zip Code:	San Antonio, TX 78216
Telephone:	210-447-0126
E-Mail Address:	tcampbell@eastfoundation.net
Form and Content:	See attachment to Part XV, Line 2
Submission Deadlines:	See attachment to Part XV, Line 2
Restrictions on Awards:	See attachment to Part XV, Line 2

Tom T East Sr and Alice K East and Alice H East and Robert C East Wildlife Fdn   26-1380672
2018 Form 990-PF

Attachment to Part XV, Line 2

The Annual East Foundation Three Minute Thesis (3MT®) competition is a research communication competition developed by the University of Queensland in Australia It challenges graduate students to make a compelling presentation on their research topic and its significance in just three minutes. The competition helps students develop academic, presentation and research communication skills and the capacity to explain their research to a non-academic audience.

The mission of the East Foundation is to promote the advancement of land stewardship through ranching, science, and education. We engage with university programs to strengthen the pipeline of talented scientists and well-informed decision makers. We conduct programs such as 3MT® because we need more management-minded scientists and more science-minded managers. Through this, we are developing future leaders that will be well-grounded in applied science, able to communicate to decision-makers.

Why Compete?

- improve your ability to communicate science to people who are not scientists
- hone your "elevator speech"
- promote your research to decision makers
- significant cash awards
- because it is the right thing to do

Eligibility

The competition is open to all graduate students working on the East Foundation's lands – both MS and PhD. All 3MT® presentations will be professionally videoed.

Contact Information

For general information concerning the competition, please contact Tyler Campbell, Ph.D at tcampbell@eastfoundation.net

Submit all presentation information and slide content to Maria Hernandez at mhernandez@eastfoundation.net

Competition Information

There will be two categories of competition—general research and proposed research. You are encouraged to compete in both and eligible to win all three prizes – there is no limit to the number of presentations that each student can present. Also, "in progress" research efforts are encouraged.

- **General Research Category**

  o Directors Award
    - This category will be judged by the East Foundation Board of Directors and will awarded to the single presentation that best meets the judging criteria and captures the essence of our mission at the East Foundation. Our Directors are senior-level leaders; investment bankers, oil & gas developers, cattlemen, and businessmen, that hold a deep understanding of ranching, land management, and wildlife conservation.

Tom T East Sr and Alice K East and Alice H East and Robert C East Wildlife Fdn   26-1380672
2018 Form 990-PF

Attachment to Part XV, Line 2
> - Prize: **$3000***

> o Peoples's Choice Award
>> - This category will be judged by the audience in the room—peers, colleagues, university faculty, the East Foundation Professional Advisors Group, East Foundation professional staff, and other invited guests from a cross section of south Texas.
>> - Prize: **$2,000***

- **Proposed Research Category**—the best research often generates more questions than answers. This category will focus on proposals building on research or lessons learned while working on East Foundation ranches

> o Best Research Proposal Award
>> - This category will be judged by the East Foundation Professional Advisors Group. The East Foundation's Professional Advisors are among the nation's top experts in wildlife management, rangeland ecology, ranch management, livestock management, and veterinary science. They are responsible for advising the Foundation on the content and direction of research, education, and outreach efforts.
>> - Prize: **$1,000***

*The East Foundation reserves the right to make no awards if presentations do not meet minimum judging criteria

Rules

- A single static PowerPoint slide is permitted (no slide transitions, animations or movement of any kind, the slide is to be presented from the beginning of the oration).
- No additional electronic media (e.g., sound and video files) are permitted.
- No additional props (e.g, costumes, musical instruments, laboratory equipment) are permitted.
- Presentations are limited to 3 minutes. Presentations exceeding 3 minutes are subject to disqualification at the discretion of the judges.
- Presentations are to be spoken word (e g., no poems, raps or songs).
- Presentations are to commence from the stage.
- Presentations are considered to have commenced when a presenter starts their presentation through movement or speech.
- The decision of the adjudicating panel is final.

Judging Criteria

Each of the below three judging criteria have equal weight. Note what each criterion has in common: an emphasis on the audience--peers, colleagues, university faculty, the East Foundation Professional Advisors Group, East Foundation professional staff, and other invited guests from a cross section of south Texas.

- *Communication style:* Was the thesis topic and its significance communicated in language appropriate to an intelligent but non-specialist audience?
- *Comprehension:* Did the presentation help the audience understand the research?
- *Engagement:* Did the presentation make the audience want to know more?

INDEX